Second Sunrise Over New Mombasa
Brett Lewis and Moebius

Published by Marvel Publishing, Inc., a subsidiary of Marvel Entertainment, Inc. Office of Publication: 417 Fifth Avenue, New York, NY 10016.
ISBN #: 0-7851-2372-5
$24.99 per copy in the U.S. and $40.00 in Canada
(GST # R127032852); Canadian Agreement #40668537.
© 2008 Microsoft Corporation. Microsoft, Halo, the Halo logo, the Microsoft Game Studios logo, Xbox, Xbox 360, Xbox LIVE, and the Xbox logos are trademarks of the Microsoft group of companies. Bungie and the Bungie logo are trademarks or registered trademarks of Bungie, LLC.

FOREWORD

I remember looking at comics before I could read. I could pretty much figure out what was going on, but once I figured out how the letter combinations formed words, it got even more interesting.

My older brothers would just leave their comics lying around, but they were careful to make sure that the scary (and naughty) ones were tucked away where their baby sister couldn't get at them. They probably figured there was no harm in letting me get a hold of their issues of *G.I. Combat, Sgt. Rock, Tarzan, Detective Comics, Kamandi, X-Men, Superman*, what have you. No harm indeed. In fact, if I hadn't developed an appreciation for comics from such an early age, I would not be here. And quite possibly, the book you hold in your hands may not have existed. At least not in the form you see...

Following the success of Halo on the Xbox in 2001, there was natural pressure to expand the franchise by way of licensing. There was an entire team dedicated to it and they searched high and low for any and all opportunities. Now, I've seen a game concept or two turned into some awful comics; pages hacked together with hardly a story, barely a nod made to what makes sequential art great, drawn by whoever was available, cranked out to the printer in time to release with the game. And then promptly forgotten.

That scenario was something nobody at Bungie wanted to see happen to a Halo comic. But since the game had already come out, there was no artificial rush to get a Halo comic done. So there was still hope.

In January 2004, during one of the many meetings with a former licensing partner, a submission packet for a Halo graphic novel was presented. I was beside myself with excitement. I felt like a kid opening a Christmas present, thinking that Santa got my letter... but what I found was a lump of coal.

I asked the group if we could work with those guys and see about making changes, get rid of some continuity errors, fix some panel-to-panel flow, make Halo's central hero less like a robot and more a man in armor... basically see if we could get them to capture the spirit of the story, and be a little more spot on - things any art director would ask for. I think at that point Bungie's studio manager noticed the steam coming out of my ears. So that first attempt languished.

Why weren't we looking at multiple submission packets? If people wanted our business, shouldn't they be trying to wow us with their best stuff? Why couldn't we pick the artists and writers who we want to work on a Halo comic? Why couldn't we work with the writers on the story concepts? Why couldn't we have a say in who colored and lettered this thing?

Apparently, that was just not how things worked. The Xbox division was new, Microsoft Game Studios did things according to its established principles and in somewhat regimented ways. So the project was put on ice and my hopes were dashed.

I couldn't quite let the idea die without exploring other options, though. The first option being, "why not do the entire thing ourselves and then *pitch* it to publishers?" To begin I needed to know what it was that the rest of the guys at Bungie wanted in a comic book, or at least, what the comics fans at Bungie would love to see. And it boiled down to one statement.

"We want to see something cool."

In the same manner that Bungie makes *games* that they themselves want to play, we wanted a comic we wanted to look at and read. Something that would inspire us; a book that would be a great example of sequential art, not unlike those old comics we all loved, the comics that had driven me to pursue a career in art.

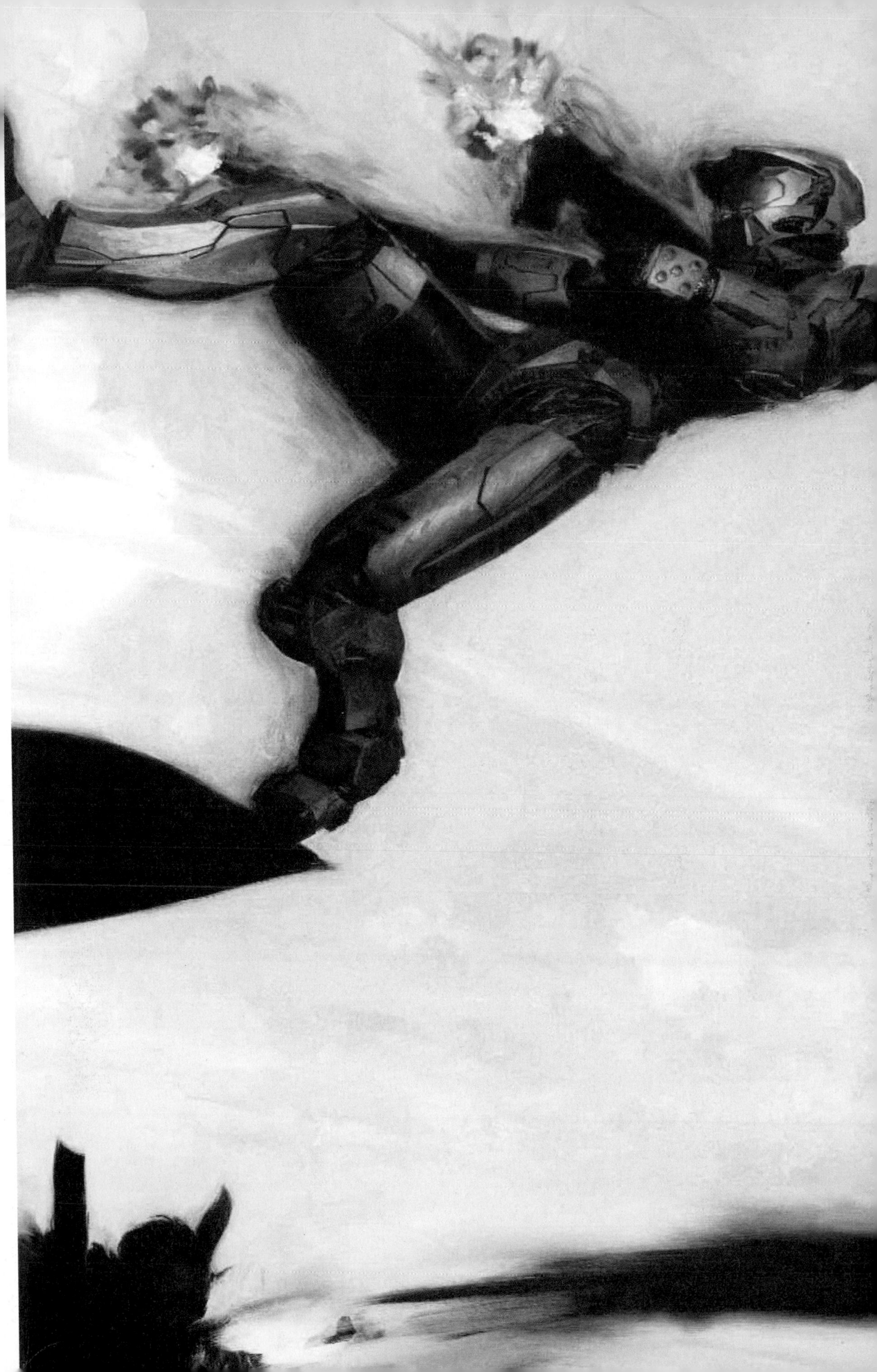

CREATIVE PRODUCER Maria Paz Cabardo
CREATIVE DIRECTOR Lorraine McLees
EDITORS Robert McLees, Frank O'Connor
EXECUTIVE PRODUCER Brian Jarrard
PRODUCER Allen Murray
PRODUCTION STAFF Chad Armstrong & Andrew Davis
ADMINISTRATIVE ASSISTANT Alta Hartmann
FRANCHISE DEVELOPMENT MANAGER Alicia Hatch
GRAND POOBAH Pete Parsons
MARVEL PROJECT MANAGER Ruwan Jayatilleke
MARVEL SENIOR EDITOR, SPECIAL PROJECTS Jeff Youngquist
MARVEL CHIEF CREATIVE OFFICER Avi Arad
PRESIDENT & CEO OF MARVEL TOYS & MARVEL PUBLISHING, INC. Alan Fine
MARVEL PUBLISHER Dan Buckley
MARVEL CCO & EDITOR IN CHIEF Joe Quesada
MARVEL VP OF PUBLISHING OPERATIONS David Bogart
MARVEL VP OF MARKETING & BUSINESS DEVELOPMENT John Dokes
MARVEL VP OF SALES David Gabriel
MARVEL EXECUTIVE DIRECTOR OF PUBLISHING TECHNOLOGY Dan Carr
MARVEL PRODUCTION Jerry Kalinowski

Halo Graphic Novel

GALLERY PAGES Doug Alexander, Rick Berry, Geof Darrow, Scott Fischer, Sterling Hundley, Craig Mullins, Tsutomu Nihei, George Pratt, Juan Ramirez, Greg Staples, Justin Sweet, John Van Fleet, Kent Williams

BUNGIE GALLERY PAGES Chris Barrett, Frank Capezzuto, Tom Doyle, Isaac Hannaford, Lorraine McLees, Robert McLees, Frank O'Connor, Eddie Smith, Shi Kai Wang

CONTRIBUTING ARTISTS Marty O'Donnell, Paul Russel, Lee Wilson

HGN COMMITTEE Chris Barrett, Chris Carney, Justin Hayward, Paul Russel, Nathan Walpole, Shi Kai Wang

GRAPHIC DESIGN John Pinsky & Smolhaus Design
STORIES LETTERED BY Studio 1137
COVER ART BY Phil Hale

This book was typeset in Ritafurey & Outlander Nova
All fonts in this book were created by Rian Hughes @ Device Fonts UK

The Last Voyage of the Infinite Succor
Lee Hammock and Simon Bisley

Armor Testing
Joy Foerber, Ed Lee, & Andrew Robinson

Breaking Quarantine
Tsutomu Nihei

Based on the Halo universe created by Jason Jones and Bungie Studios. Special thanks to: James Alsup III, Amanda Anderson, Carolyne Bastien, Michel Bastien, Vic Cabardo, Glenn Fabry, Christina Graf, Mutsumi Masada, Eagan Matalino Reyes McLees, Ben Nuñez, Simon Reed, Steve Schreck, Liam Sharp, Yo' Mom. Published by the awesome Marvel dudes. Printed by the folks at R.R. Donnelley. No animals were injured during the making of this publication, not even Ling Ling. Skip Weasel is not an animal. The characters in this book bear no resemblance to anyone living or dead, but if it so happens one of 'em looks like someone you know or saw, it's all coincidence and they should consider themselves lucky.

Produced by Bungie Studios (a subsidiary of Microsoft Corporation) in association with Maria P. Cabardo.
www.bungie.net
www.marvel.com
www.smolhaus.com

The key was to ask the right person the right question. "What would it take to make a cool comic?" It would be a comic that was more about "what we want" than something designed specifically to turn a profit. It would in some ways be a vanity piece; but still a prime example of good sequential art and art in general that would also serve to expand a universe already rich in detail.

In an amazing stroke of luck, we found that person in Maria Cabardo. My husband and colleague, Robt McLees, had worked with her nearly a decade ago and had maintained correspondence over the years. Having been involved in the game and comic book industries for nearly all those years, as well as producing a number of books, Maria had worked with people we never even dreamed we would be able to approach for this project. In a fateful phone call some time in March 2004, I spoke with Maria while sitting at Robt's desk and the conversation went something like this:

Maria: *I think we can do it in four months. It's going to be reeeeally tight though. But I know some really fast guys who can turn it around if you want to hit San Diego this year.*

Me: *Well, forget about San Diego then. I'd rather be sure we do it right than force everybody to hit Comic Con.*

Maria: *Serious?*

Me: *Yeah.*

Maria: *Are you for real?*

Me: *Huh? What do you mean?*

Maria: *But you're Microsoft. You're part of a monolithic corporation.*

Me: *So? We just want to make something cool.*

Maria: *You're really not kidding, are you? Well, why don't we shoot for the moon?*

We didn't have a budget, we had no release date, but we started getting commitments – based purely on Maria's background and contacts. Once we realized that Maria was able to get some of our all time comic *heroes* interested in the project, Pete, our studio manager, and Brian, our team lead, put a budget together based on Maria's projection for production costs. What really blew our minds was how the intent behind the project intrigued a lot of "A list" people. Everyone was interested in "making something cool." Maria aimed really high and won us round after round of victories.

Once the project got underway, we knew that we were going to have a book that would knock people's socks off. We started talking with the franchise people about the project again to get some support. But dropping names wasn't enough. Once we actually had finalized scripts, penciled pages, and a few colored pieces, everyone got pretty excited. It was just a matter of time until we'd find a publisher who would support our vision and treat the project with the same care as those who created it.

Marvel sent the most enthusiastic proposal and with it a robust release plan. It also helped that the folks who came to present the deal were also fans of Halo and, at the same time, deeply rooted in comics. And they completely shared our commitment to doing "what is right" for the book and for the franchise.

That brings us *here.*

And I hope that you agree that we have indeed made something cool.

Lorraine McLees
Bungie Studios

THE LAST VOYAGE OF THE INFINITE SUCCOR

Lee Hammock and Simon Bisley

You could say that this story parallels "Breaking Quarantine" at its most fundamental level. The idea was sparked by one of the interstitial scenes from *Halo 2*. This piece was conceived primarily as a vehicle to educate the fans about the real danger of the Flood: that they are a rapacious, intelligent, goal-oriented life-form with internal structure/proto-culture (and hopefully euthanize the idea that *they are just space zombies*). It was also made to show a bit about the inner workings of the Covenant. That they don't just stand around waiting for the Chief to blast them out of existence.

This story also gave us a chance to do a bit of an origin story for the SpecOps Commander: *Rtas 'Vadumee*. Showing why he knows what the Flood *smell* like, how he received his distinctive injury, and perhaps even why he felt he was able to speak in such a familiar tone with the Arbiter.

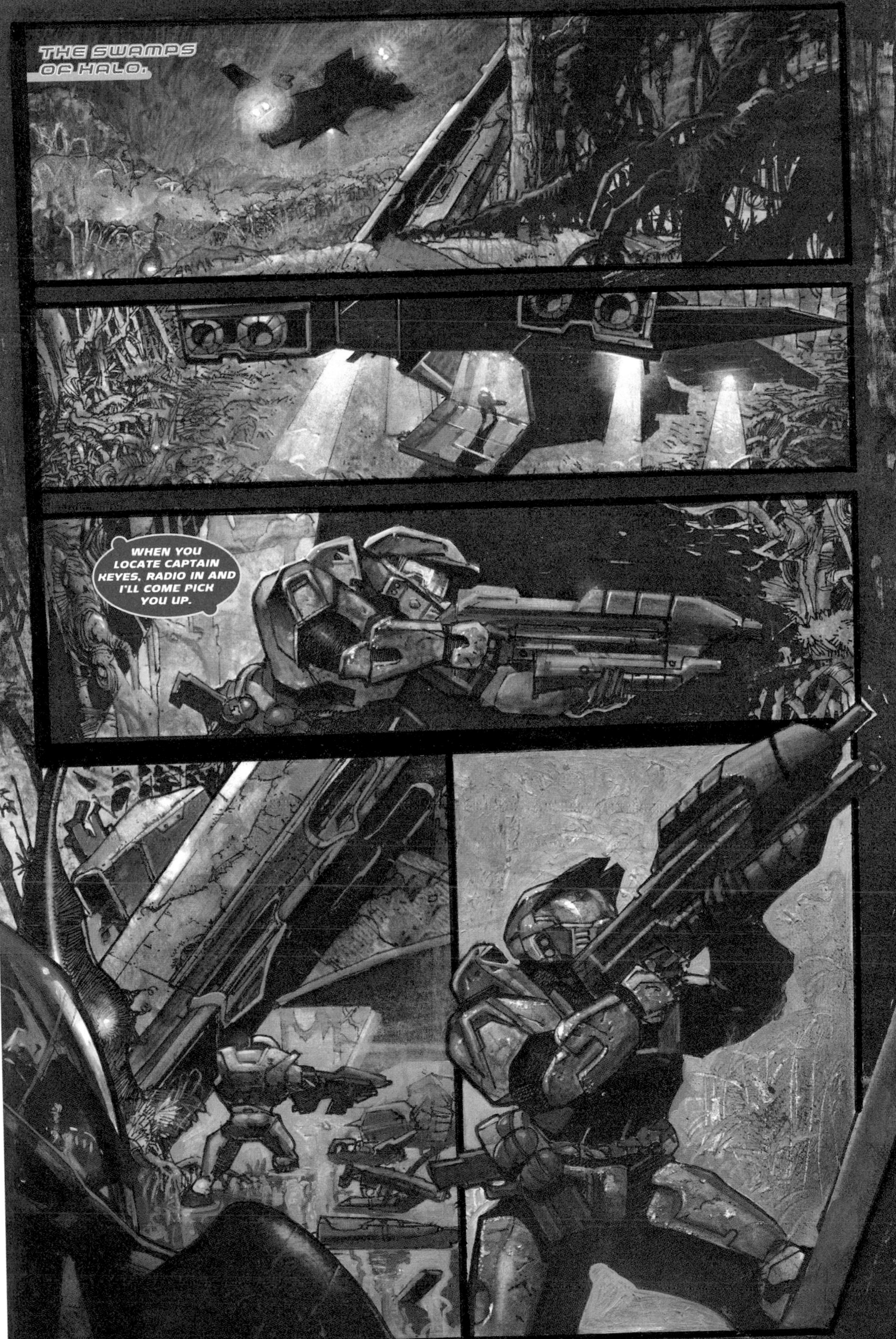
THE SWAMPS OF HALO.
WHEN YOU LOCATE CAPTAIN KEYES, RADIO IN AND I'LL COME PICK YOU UP.

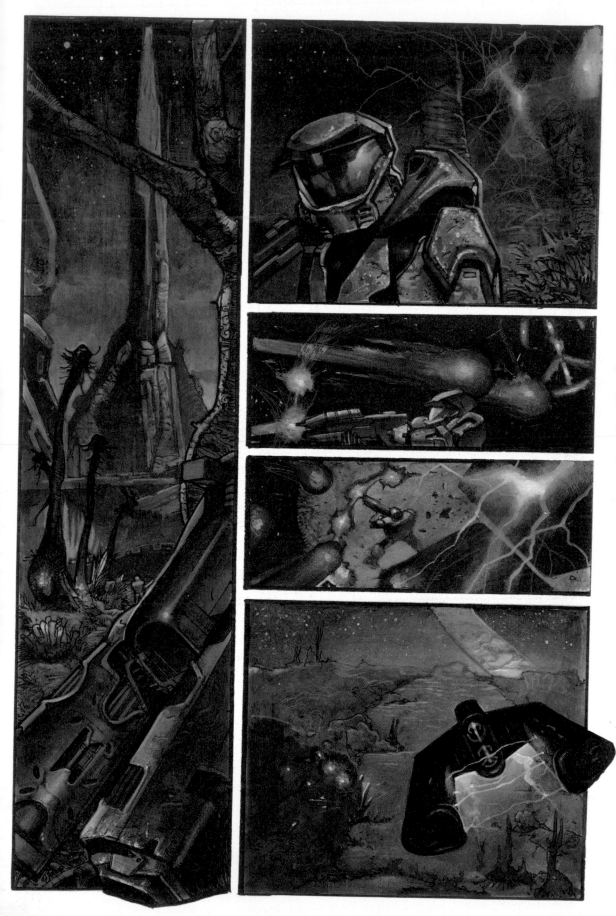

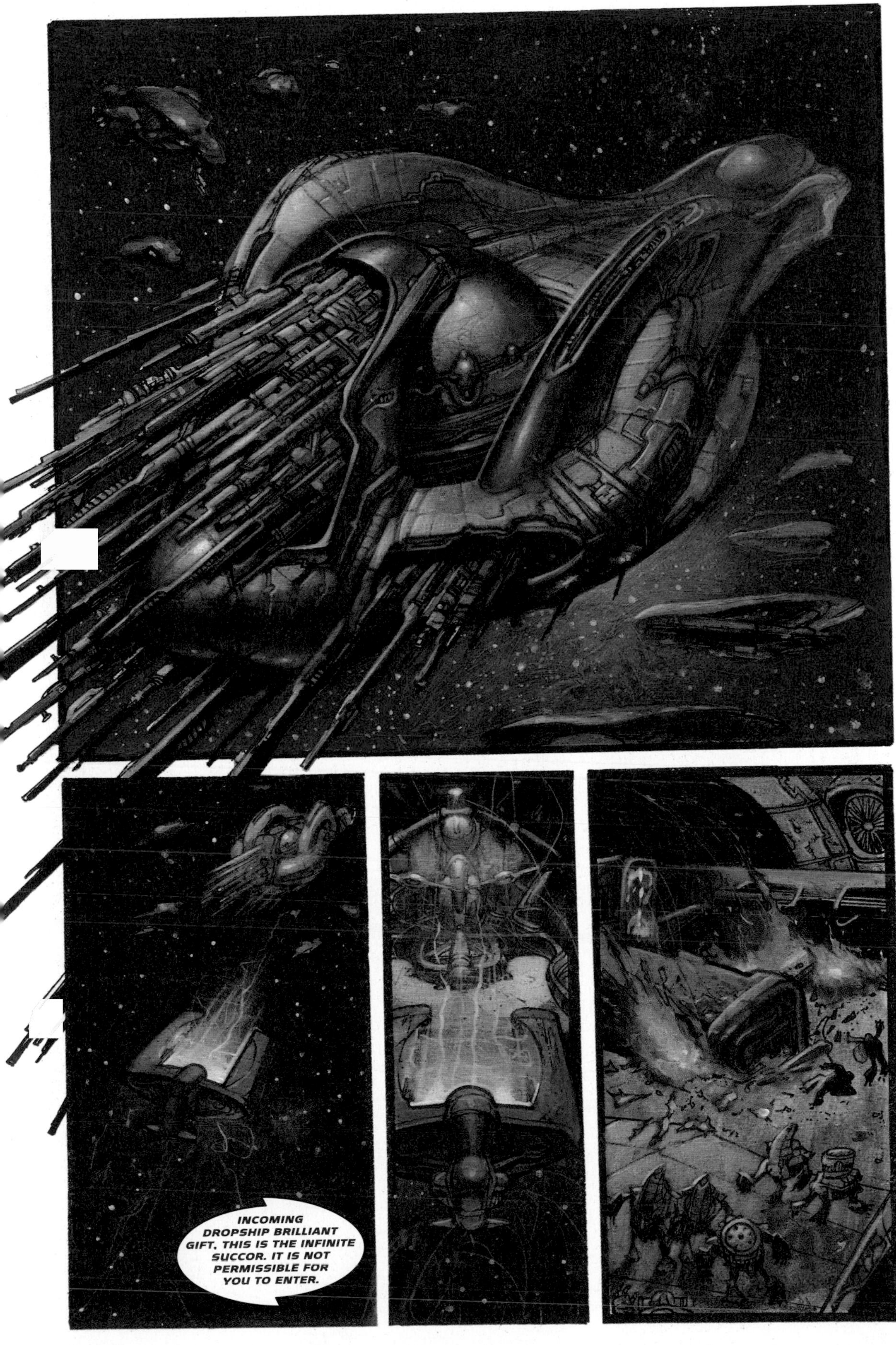
INCOMING DROPSHIP BRILLIANT GIFT, THIS IS THE INFINITE SUCCOR. IT IS NOT PERMISSIBLE FOR YOU TO ENTER.

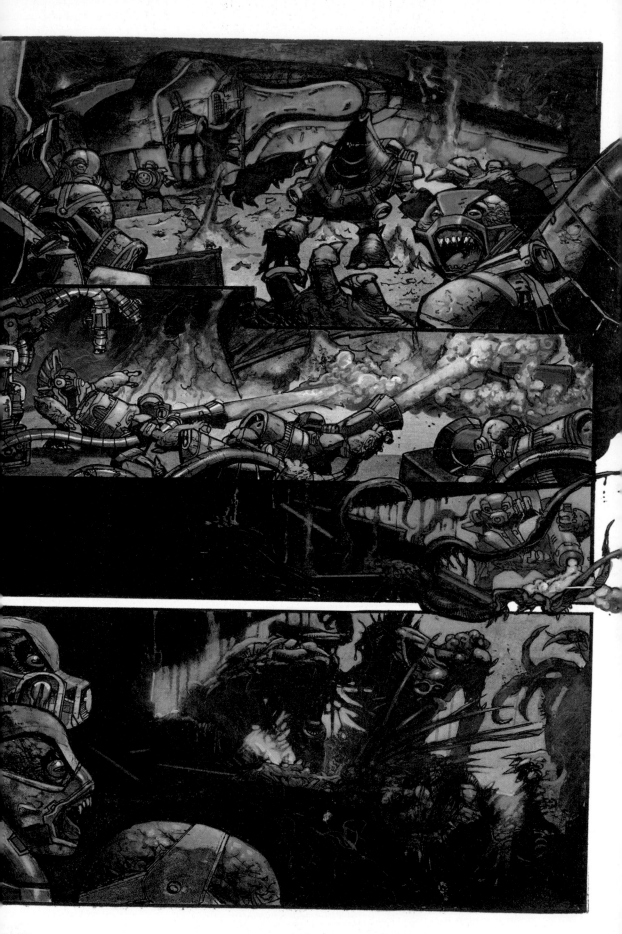

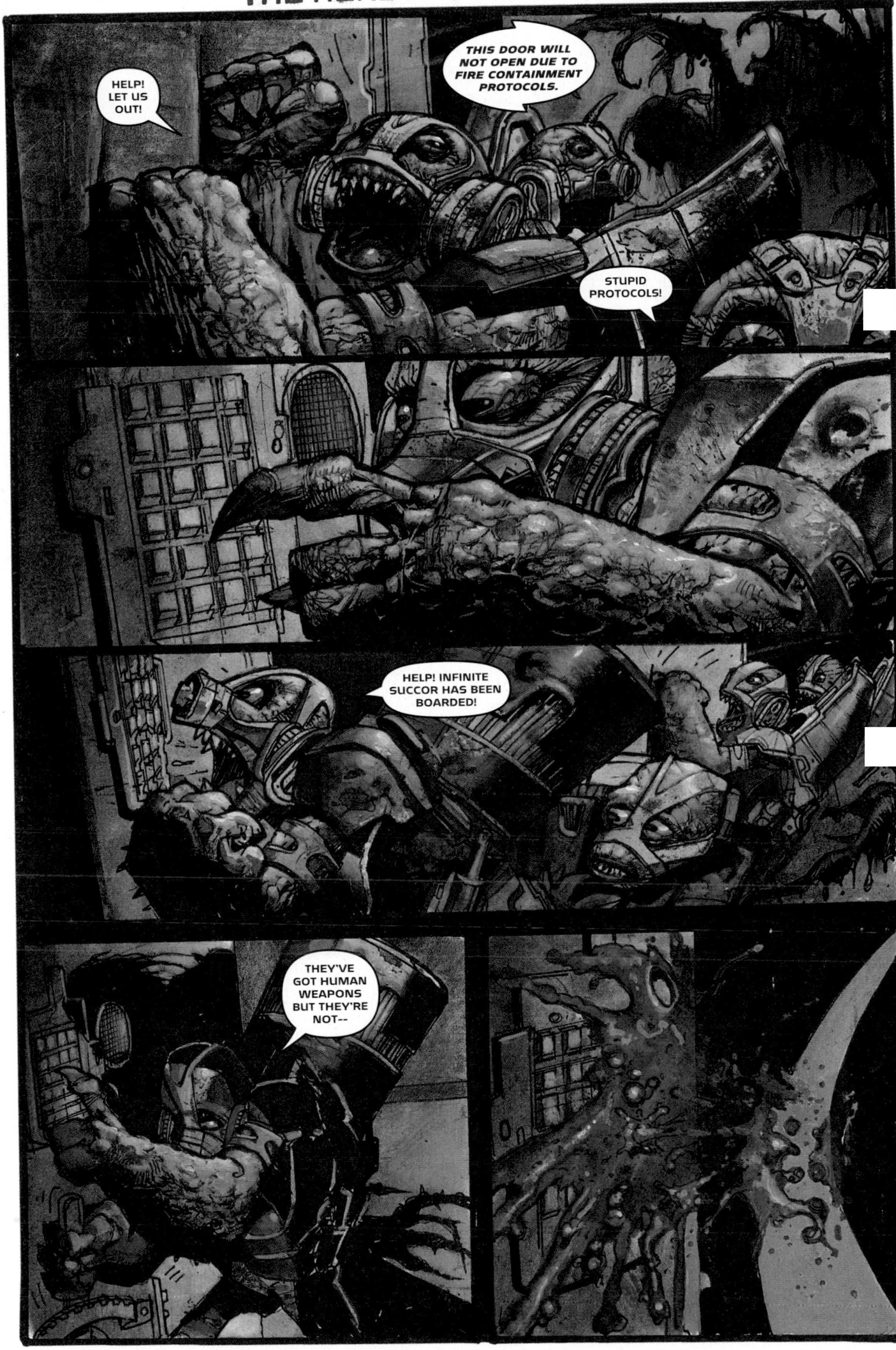
HELP! LET US OUT!
THIS DOOR WILL NOT OPEN DUE TO FIRE CONTAINMENT PROTOCOLS.
STUPID PROTOCOLS!
HELP! INFINITE SUCCOR HAS BEEN BOARDED!
THEY'VE GOT HUMAN WEAPONS BUT THEY'RE NOT--

SEEKER OF TRUTH, FLAGSHIP OF THE COVENANT FLEET OF PARTICULAR JUSTICE.

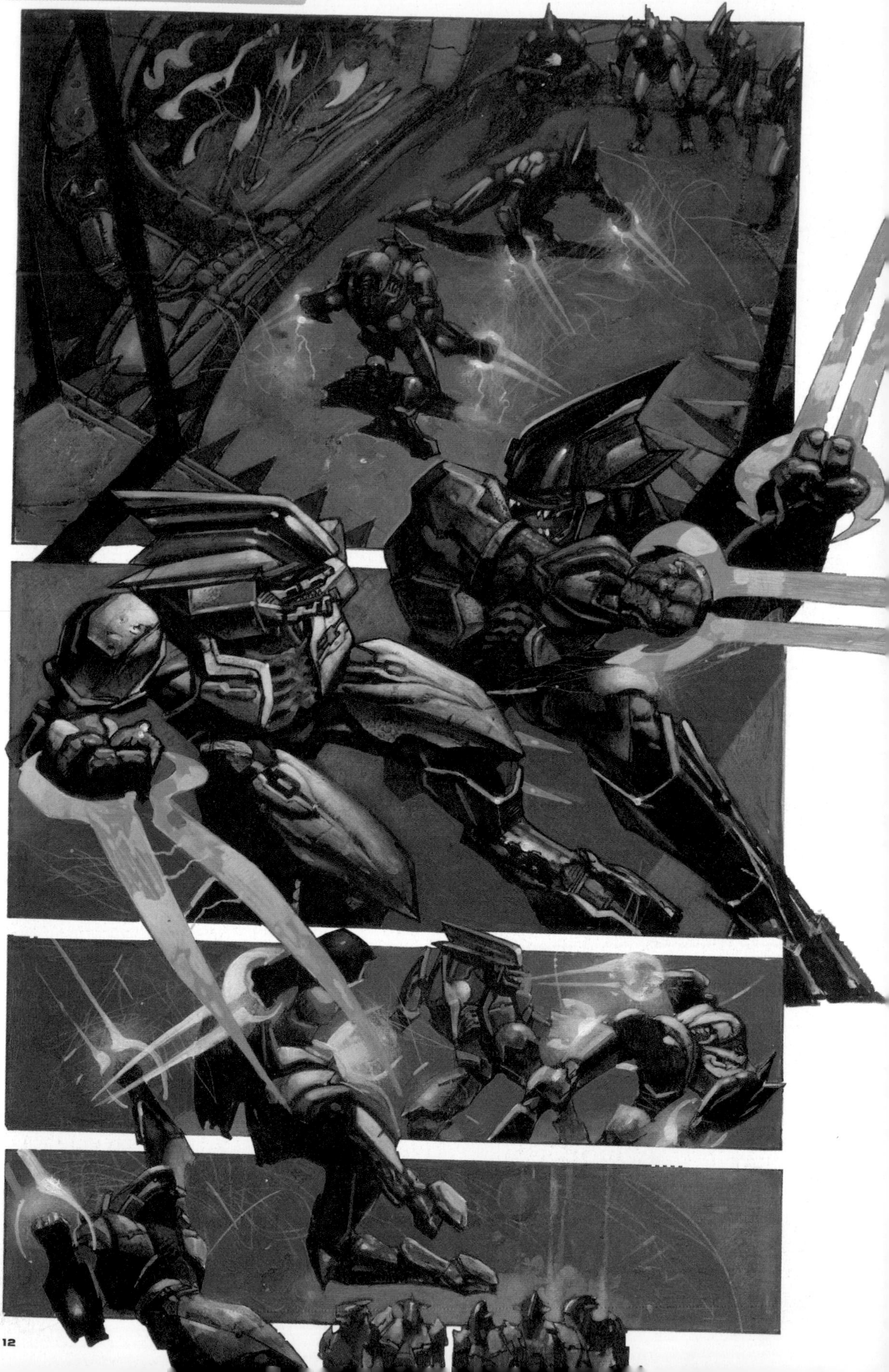

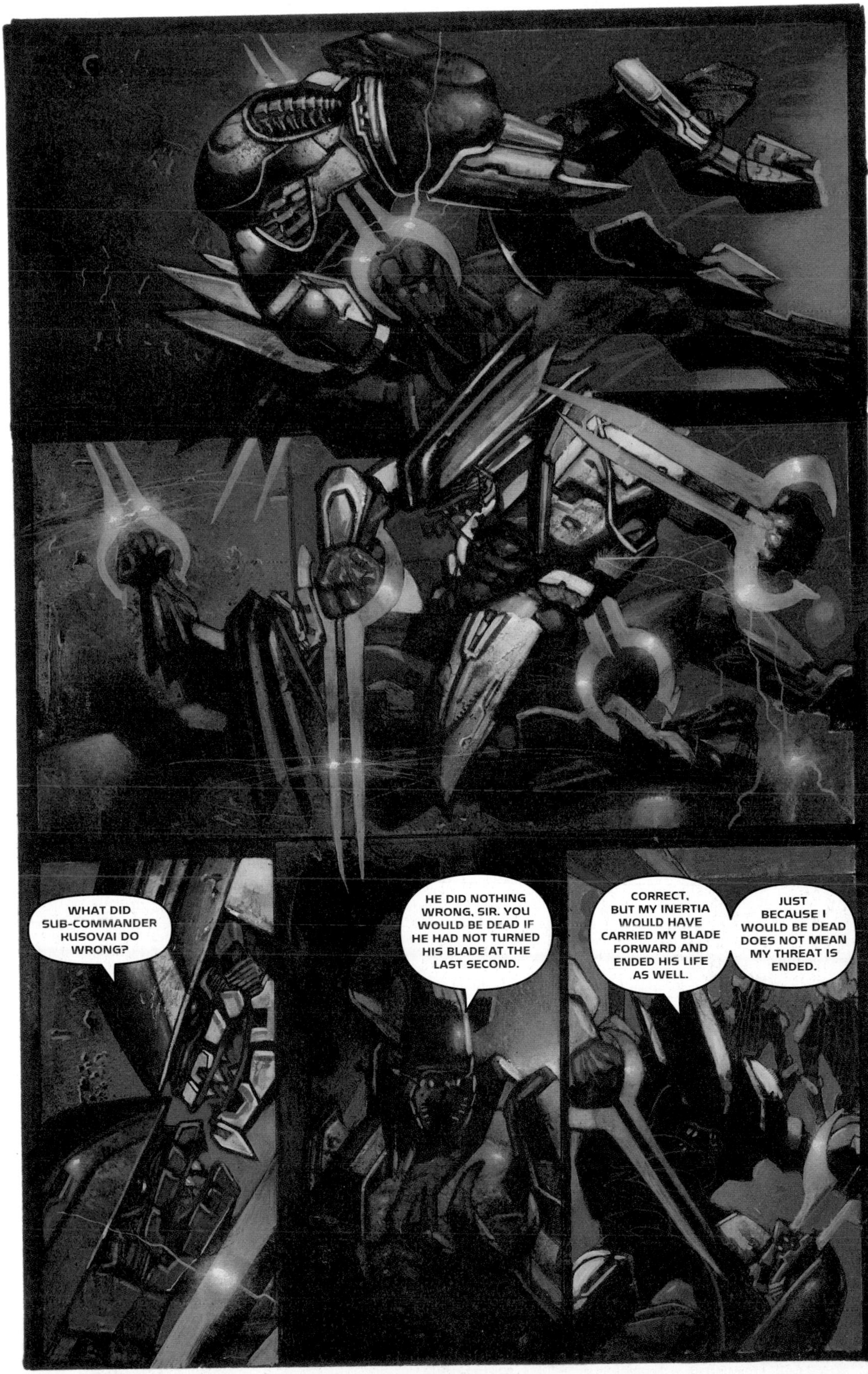
WHAT DID SUB-COMMANDER KUSOVAI DO WRONG?
HE DID NOTHING WRONG, SIR. YOU WOULD BE DEAD IF HE HAD NOT TURNED HIS BLADE AT THE LAST SECOND.
CORRECT, BUT MY INERTIA WOULD HAVE CARRIED MY BLADE FORWARD AND ENDED HIS LIFE AS WELL.
JUST BECAUSE I WOULD BE DEAD DOES NOT MEAN MY THREAT IS ENDED.

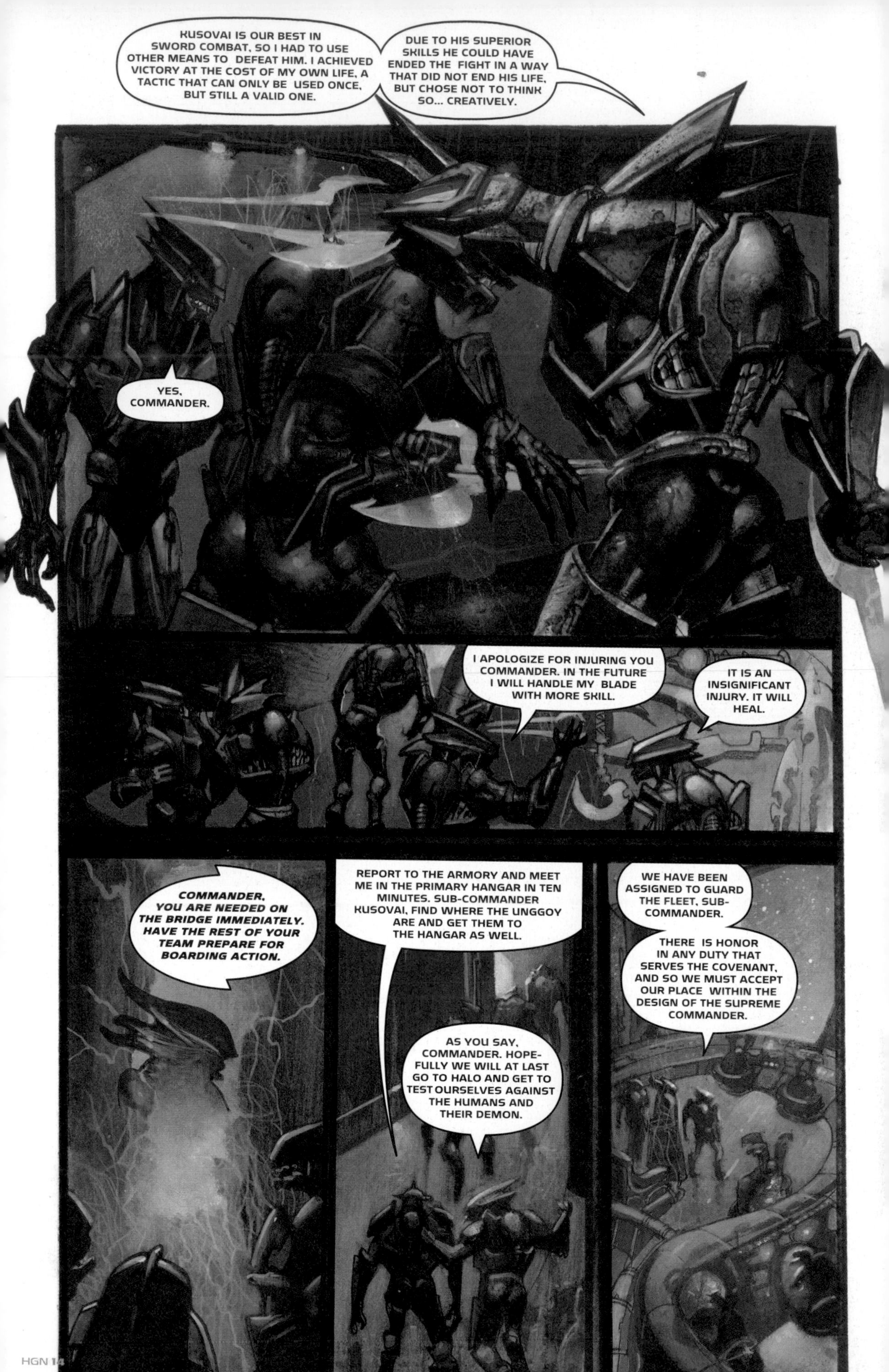
KUSOVAI IS OUR BEST IN SWORD COMBAT, SO I HAD TO USE OTHER MEANS TO DEFEAT HIM. I ACHIEVED VICTORY AT THE COST OF MY OWN LIFE, A TACTIC THAT CAN ONLY BE USED ONCE, BUT STILL A VALID ONE.
DUE TO HIS SUPERIOR SKILLS HE COULD HAVE ENDED THE FIGHT IN A WAY THAT DID NOT END HIS LIFE, BUT CHOSE NOT TO THINK SO... CREATIVELY.
YES, COMMANDER.
I APOLOGIZE FOR INJURING YOU COMMANDER. IN THE FUTURE I WILL HANDLE MY BLADE WITH MORE SKILL.
IT IS AN INSIGNIFICANT INJURY. IT WILL HEAL.
COMMANDER, YOU ARE NEEDED ON THE BRIDGE IMMEDIATELY. HAVE THE REST OF YOUR TEAM PREPARE FOR BOARDING ACTION.
REPORT TO THE ARMORY AND MEET ME IN THE PRIMARY HANGAR IN TEN MINUTES. SUB-COMMANDER KUSOVAI, FIND WHERE THE UNGGOY ARE AND GET THEM TO THE HANGAR AS WELL.
AS YOU SAY, COMMANDER. HOPE-FULLY WE WILL AT LAST GO TO HALO AND GET TO TEST OURSELVES AGAINST THE HUMANS AND THEIR DEMON.
WE HAVE BEEN ASSIGNED TO GUARD THE FLEET, SUB-COMMANDER.
THERE IS HONOR IN ANY DUTY THAT SERVES THE COVENANT, AND SO WE MUST ACCEPT OUR PLACE WITHIN THE DESIGN OF THE SUPREME COMMANDER.

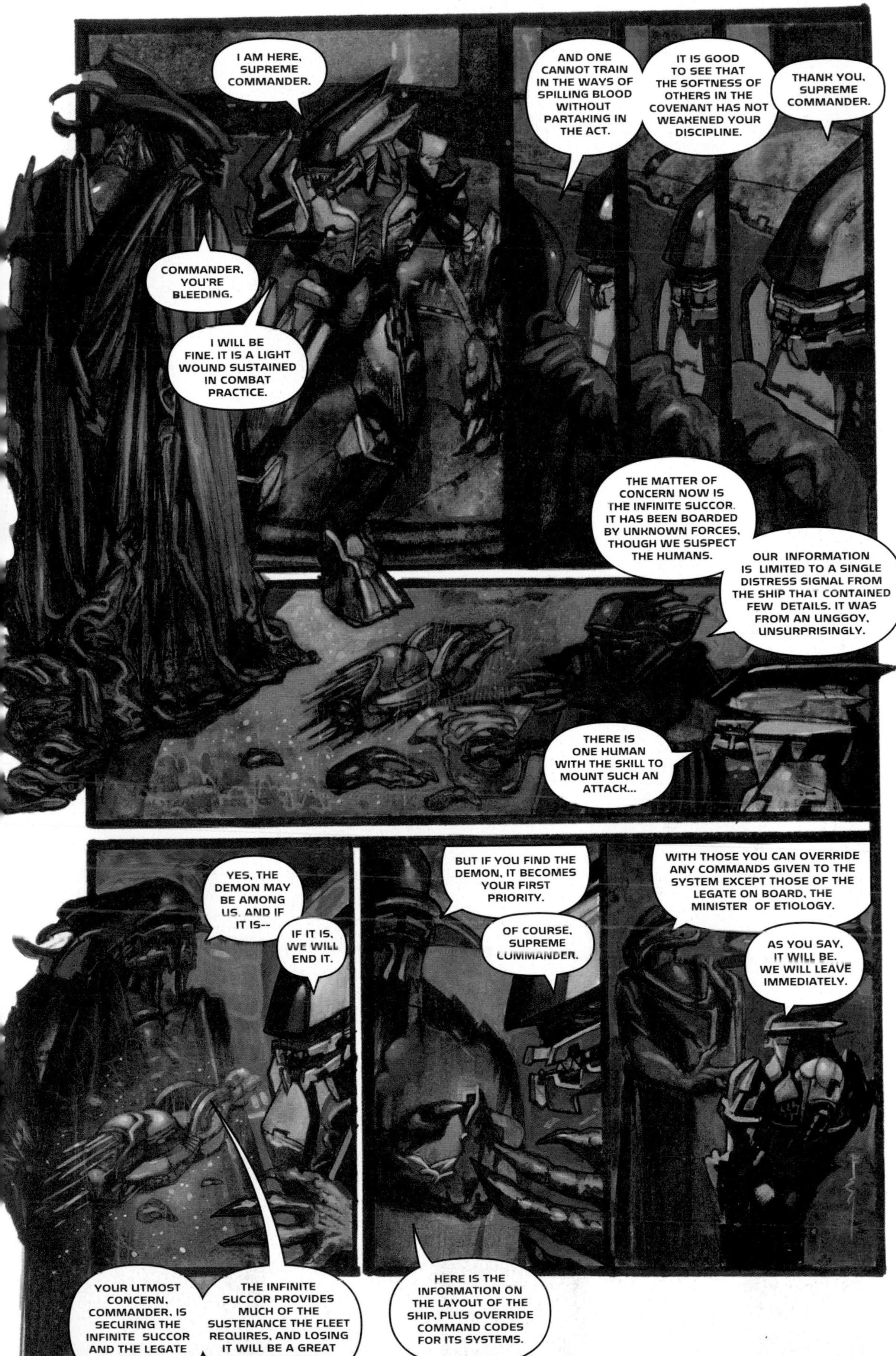

I AM HERE, SUPREME COMMANDER.
AND ONE CANNOT TRAIN IN THE WAYS OF SPILLING BLOOD WITHOUT PARTAKING IN THE ACT.
IT IS GOOD TO SEE THAT THE SOFTNESS OF OTHERS IN THE COVENANT HAS NOT WEAKENED YOUR DISCIPLINE.
THANK YOU, SUPREME COMMANDER.
COMMANDER, YOU'RE BLEEDING.
I WILL BE FINE. IT IS A LIGHT WOUND SUSTAINED IN COMBAT PRACTICE.
THE MATTER OF CONCERN NOW IS THE INFINITE SUCCOR. IT HAS BEEN BOARDED BY UNKNOWN FORCES, THOUGH WE SUSPECT THE HUMANS.
OUR INFORMATION IS LIMITED TO A SINGLE DISTRESS SIGNAL FROM THE SHIP THAT CONTAINED FEW DETAILS. IT WAS FROM AN UNGGOY, UNSURPRISINGLY.
THERE IS ONE HUMAN WITH THE SKILL TO MOUNT SUCH AN ATTACK...
YES, THE DEMON MAY BE AMONG US. AND IF IT IS--
IF IT IS, WE WILL END IT.
YOUR UTMOST CONCERN, COMMANDER, IS SECURING THE INFINITE SUCCOR AND THE LEGATE ONBOARD.
THE INFINITE SUCCOR PROVIDES MUCH OF THE SUSTENANCE THE FLEET REQUIRES, AND LOSING IT WILL BE A GREAT INCONVENIENCE.
BUT IF YOU FIND THE DEMON, IT BECOMES YOUR FIRST PRIORITY.
OF COURSE, SUPREME COMMANDER.
HERE IS THE INFORMATION ON THE LAYOUT OF THE SHIP, PLUS OVERRIDE COMMAND CODES FOR ITS SYSTEMS.
WITH THOSE YOU CAN OVERRIDE ANY COMMANDS GIVEN TO THE SYSTEM EXCEPT THOSE OF THE LEGATE ON BOARD, THE MINISTER OF ETIOLOGY.
AS YOU SAY, IT WILL BE. WE WILL LEAVE IMMEDIATELY.

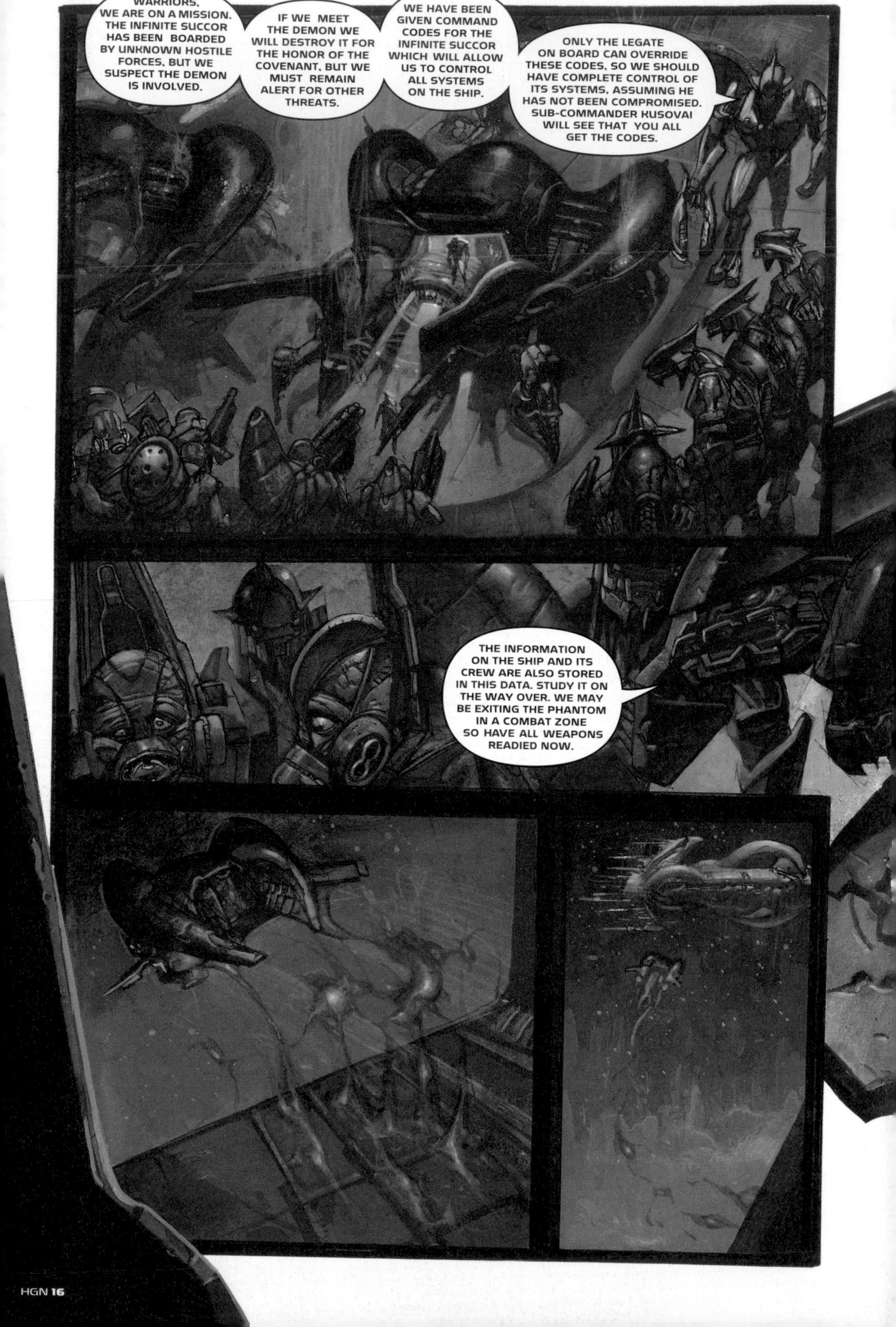
WARRIORS, WE ARE ON A MISSION. THE INFINITE SUCCOR HAS BEEN BOARDED BY UNKNOWN HOSTILE FORCES, BUT WE SUSPECT THE DEMON IS INVOLVED.
IF WE MEET THE DEMON WE WILL DESTROY IT FOR THE HONOR OF THE COVENANT, BUT WE MUST REMAIN ALERT FOR OTHER THREATS.
WE HAVE BEEN GIVEN COMMAND CODES FOR THE INFINITE SUCCOR WHICH WILL ALLOW US TO CONTROL ALL SYSTEMS ON THE SHIP.
ONLY THE LEGATE ON BOARD CAN OVERRIDE THESE CODES, SO WE SHOULD HAVE COMPLETE CONTROL OF ITS SYSTEMS, ASSUMING HE HAS NOT BEEN COMPROMISED. SUB-COMMANDER KUSOVAI WILL SEE THAT YOU ALL GET THE CODES.
THE INFORMATION ON THE SHIP AND ITS CREW ARE ALSO STORED IN THIS DATA. STUDY IT ON THE WAY OVER. WE MAY BE EXITING THE PHANTOM IN A COMBAT ZONE SO HAVE ALL WEAPONS READIED NOW.

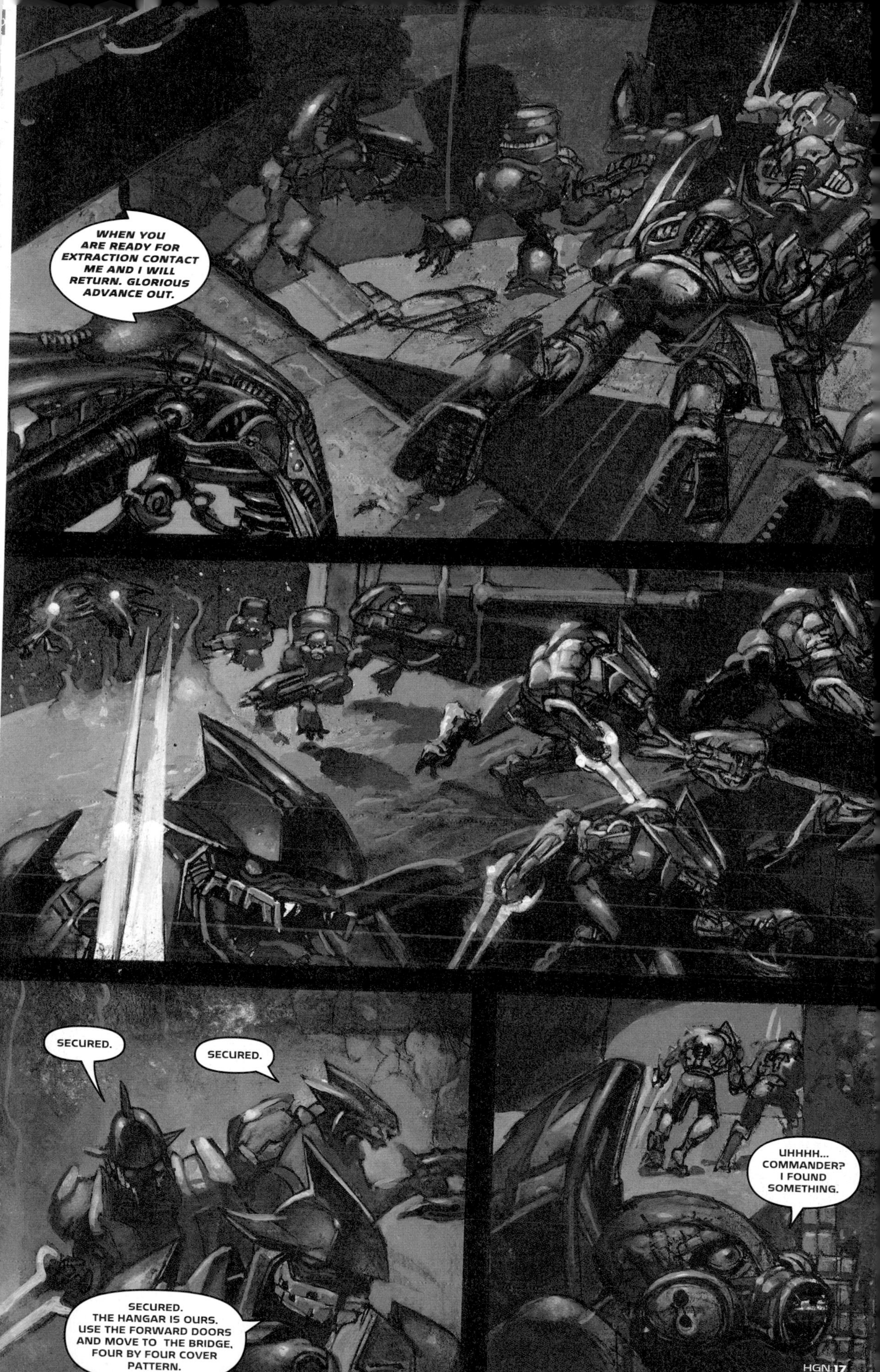
WHEN YOU ARE READY FOR EXTRACTION CONTACT ME AND I WILL RETURN. GLORIOUS ADVANCE OUT.
SECURED.
SECURED.
SECURED. THE HANGAR IS OURS. USE THE FORWARD DOORS AND MOVE TO THE BRIDGE, FOUR BY FOUR COVER PATTERN.
UHHHH... COMMANDER? I FOUND SOMETHING.

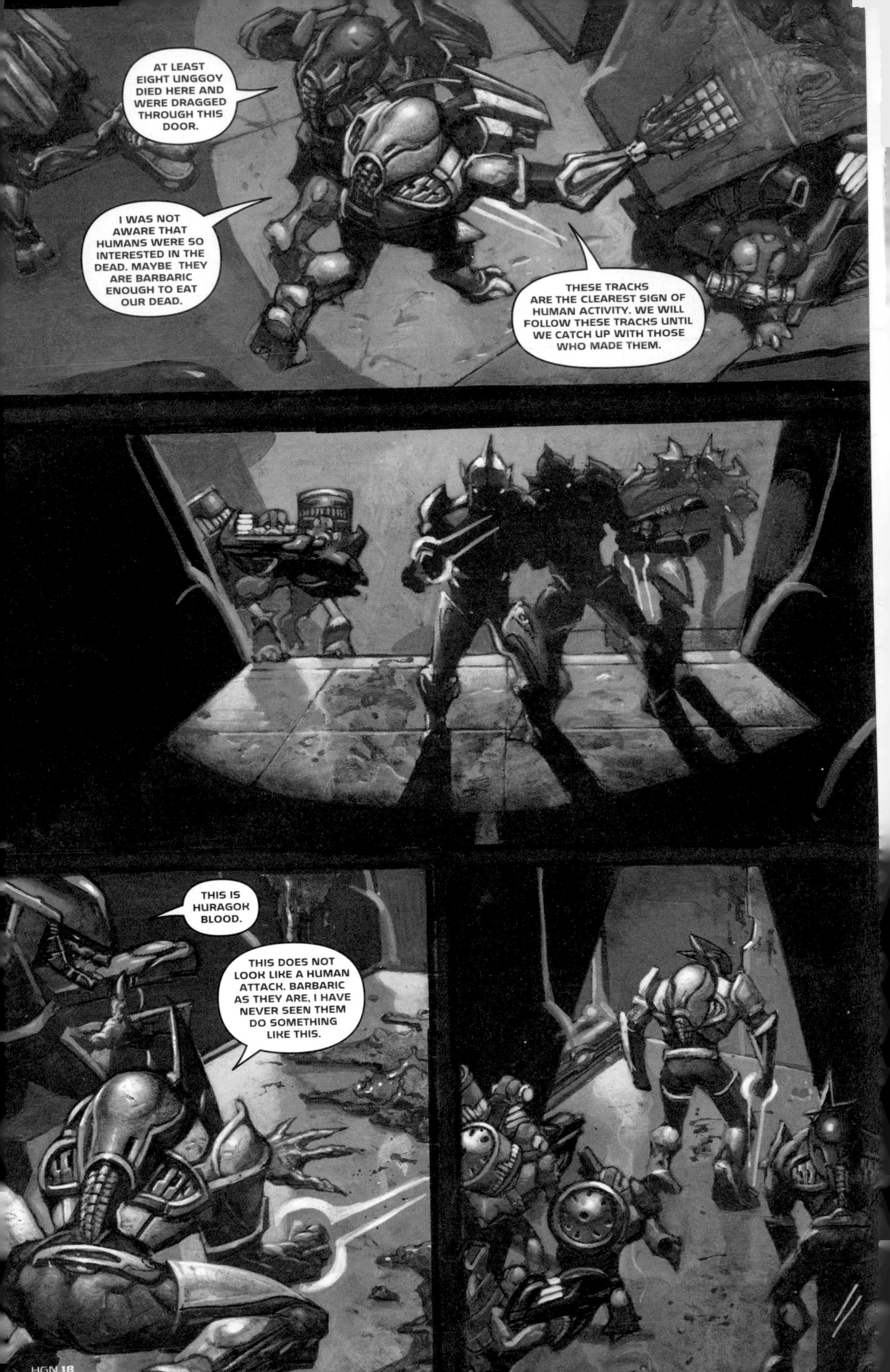
AT LEAST EIGHT UNGGOY DIED HERE AND WERE DRAGGED THROUGH THIS DOOR.
I WAS NOT AWARE THAT HUMANS WERE SO INTERESTED IN THE DEAD. MAYBE THEY ARE BARBARIC ENOUGH TO EAT OUR DEAD.
THESE TRACKS ARE THE CLEAREST SIGN OF HUMAN ACTIVITY. WE WILL FOLLOW THESE TRACKS UNTIL WE CATCH UP WITH THOSE WHO MADE THEM.
THIS IS HURAGOK BLOOD.
THIS DOES NOT LOOK LIKE A HUMAN ATTACK. BARBARIC AS THEY ARE, I HAVE NEVER SEEN THEM DO SOMETHING LIKE THIS.

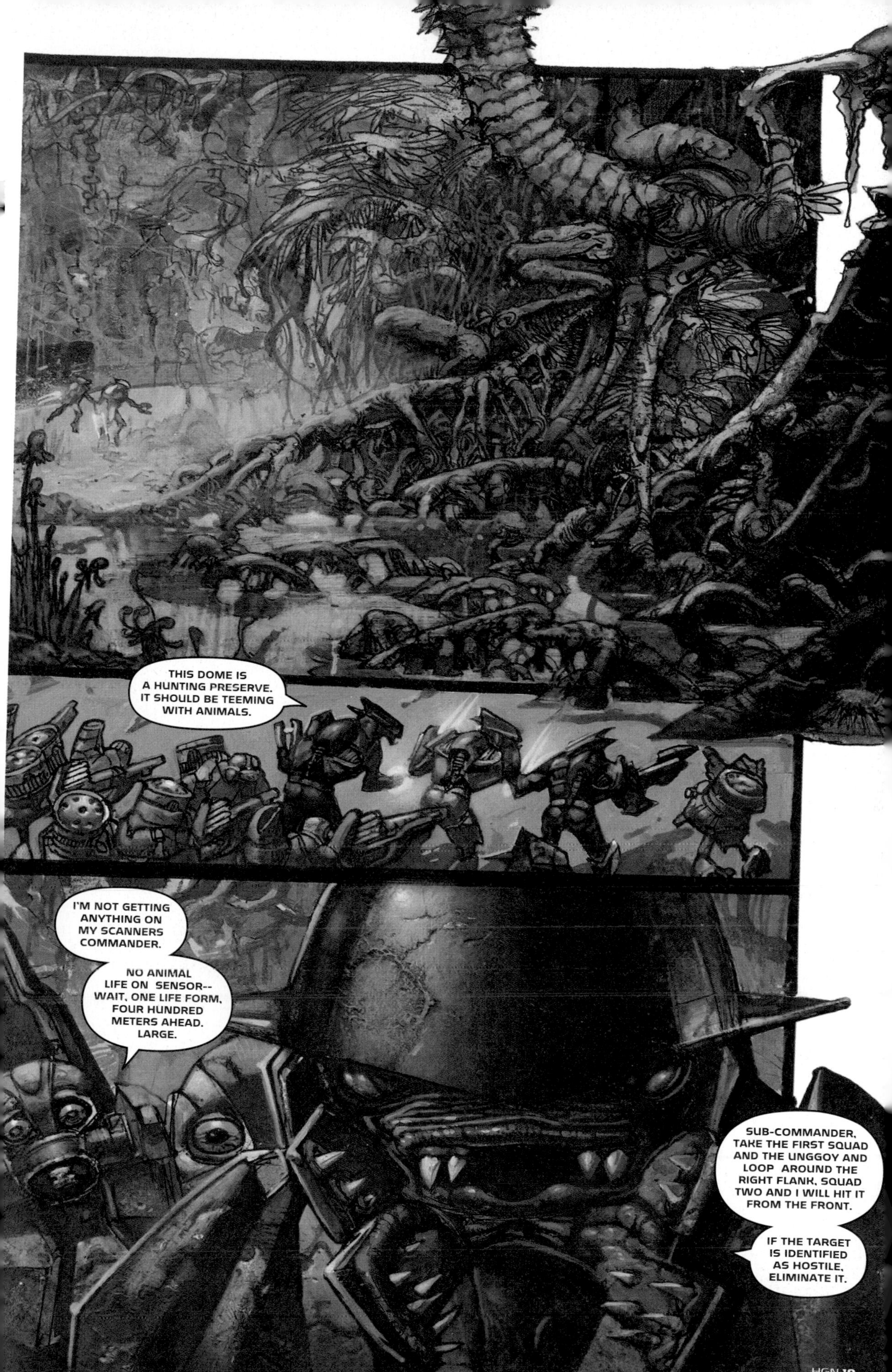
THIS DOME IS A HUNTING PRESERVE. IT SHOULD BE TEEMING WITH ANIMALS.
I'M NOT GETTING ANYTHING ON MY SCANNERS COMMANDER.
NO ANIMAL LIFE ON SENSOR-- WAIT, ONE LIFE FORM, FOUR HUNDRED METERS AHEAD. LARGE.
SUB-COMMANDER, TAKE THE FIRST SQUAD AND THE UNGGOY AND LOOP AROUND THE RIGHT FLANK, SQUAD TWO AND I WILL HIT IT FROM THE FRONT.
IF THE TARGET IS IDENTIFIED AS HOSTILE, ELIMINATE IT.

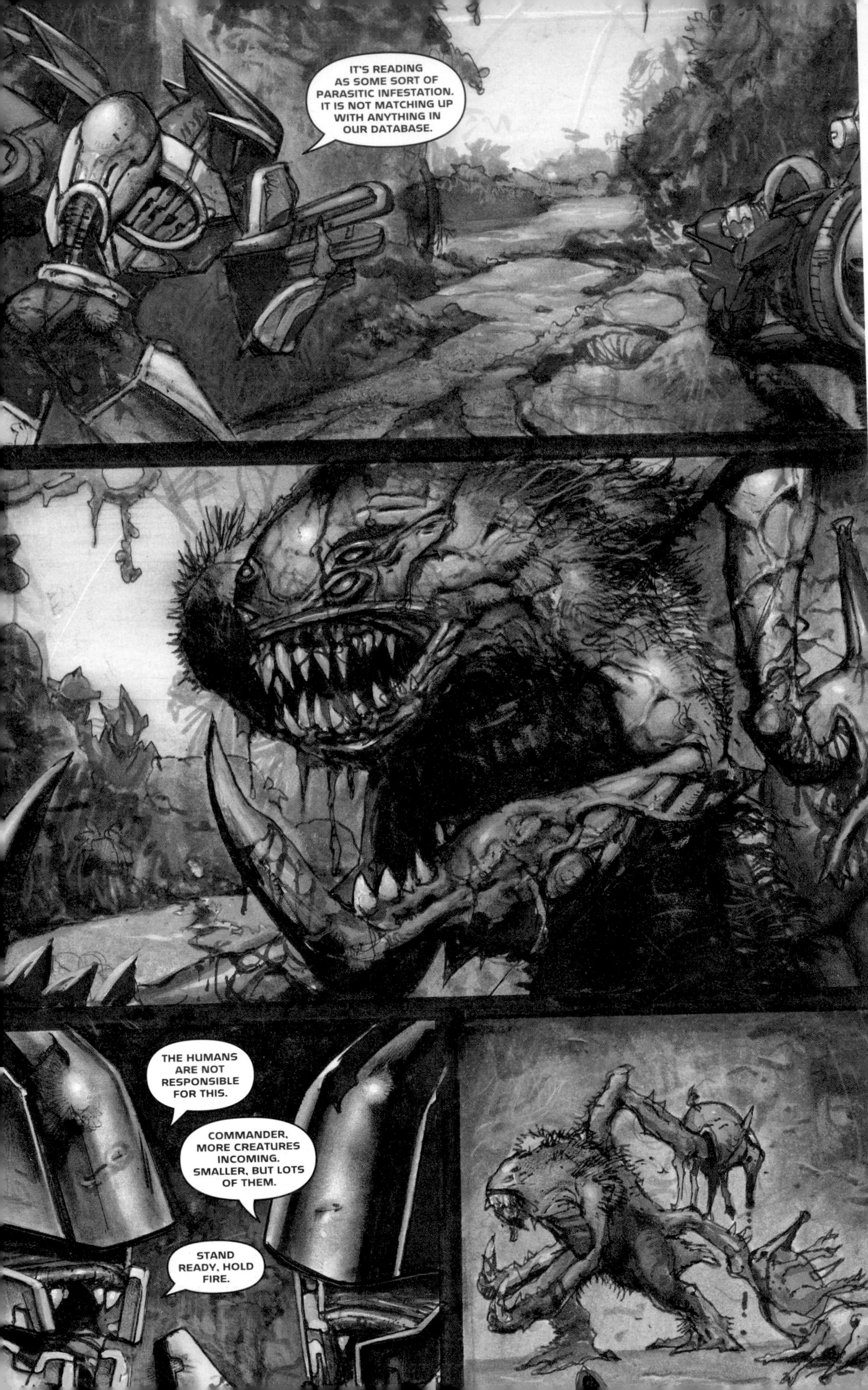
IT'S READING AS SOME SORT OF PARASITIC INFESTATION. IT IS NOT MATCHING UP WITH ANYTHING IN OUR DATABASE.
THE HUMANS ARE NOT RESPONSIBLE FOR THIS.
COMMANDER, MORE CREATURES INCOMING. SMALLER, BUT LOTS OF THEM.
STAND READY, HOLD FIRE.

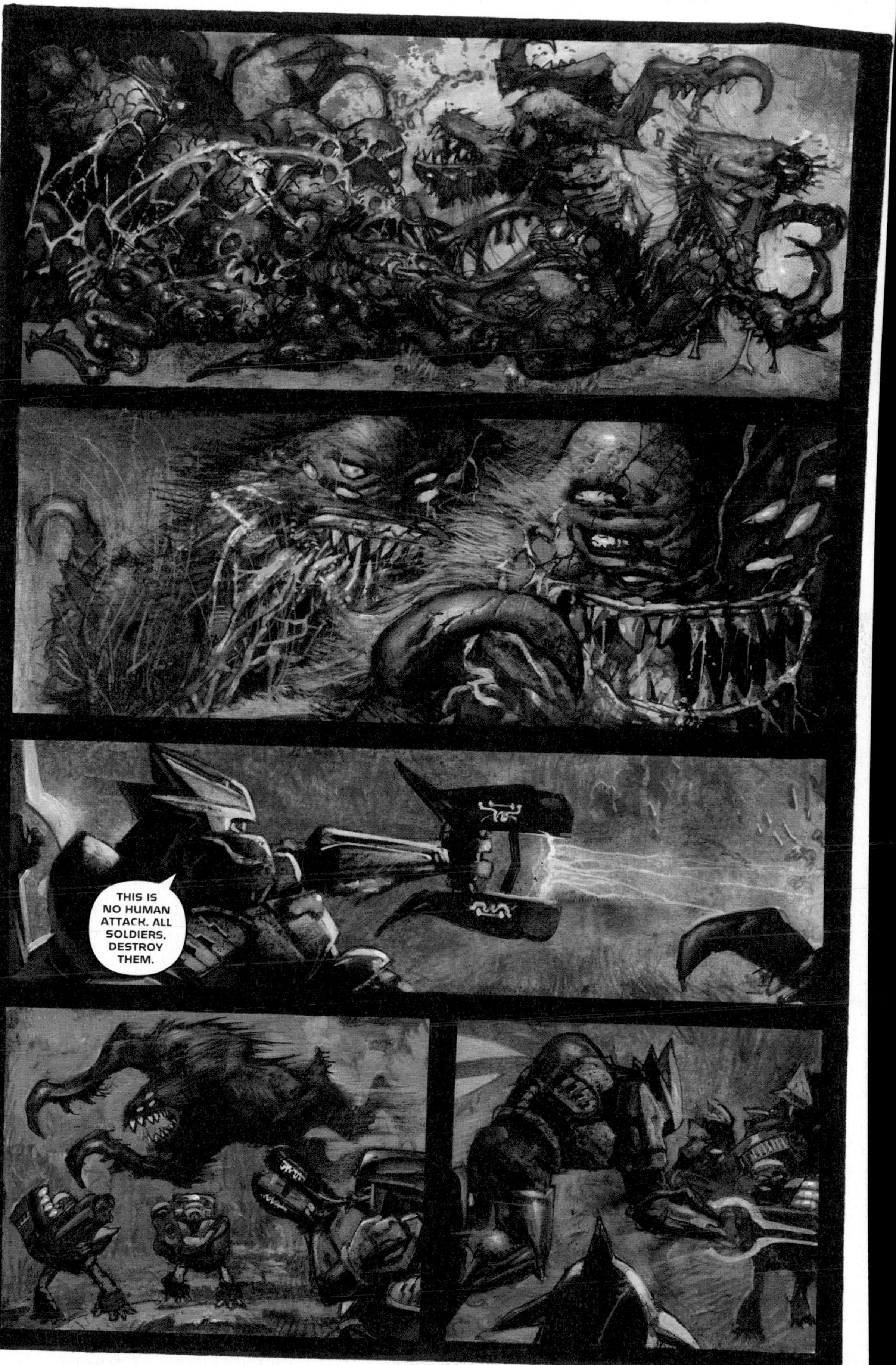
THIS IS NO HUMAN ATTACK. ALL SOLDIERS, DESTROY THEM.

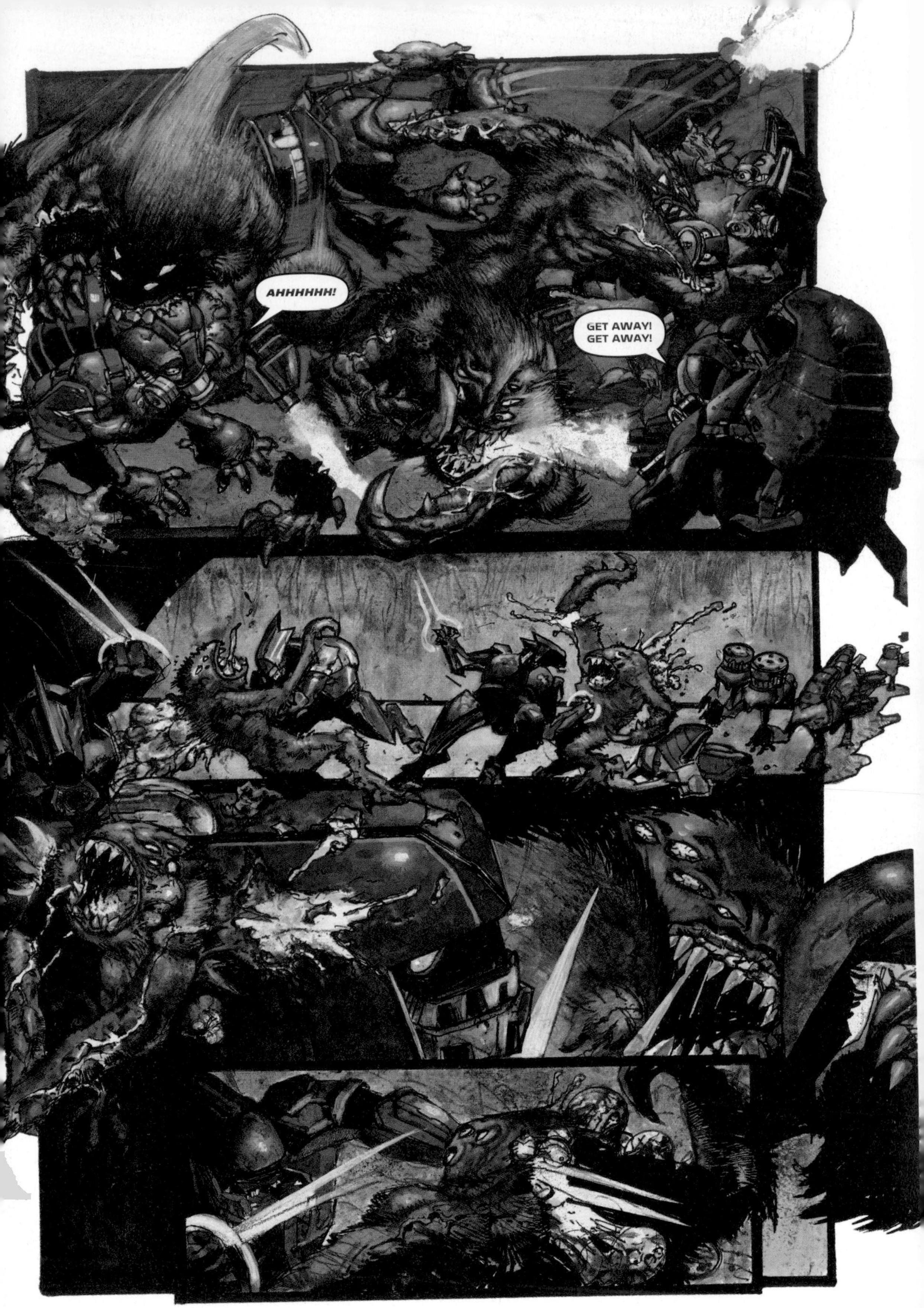
AHHHHHH!
GET AWAY! GET AWAY!

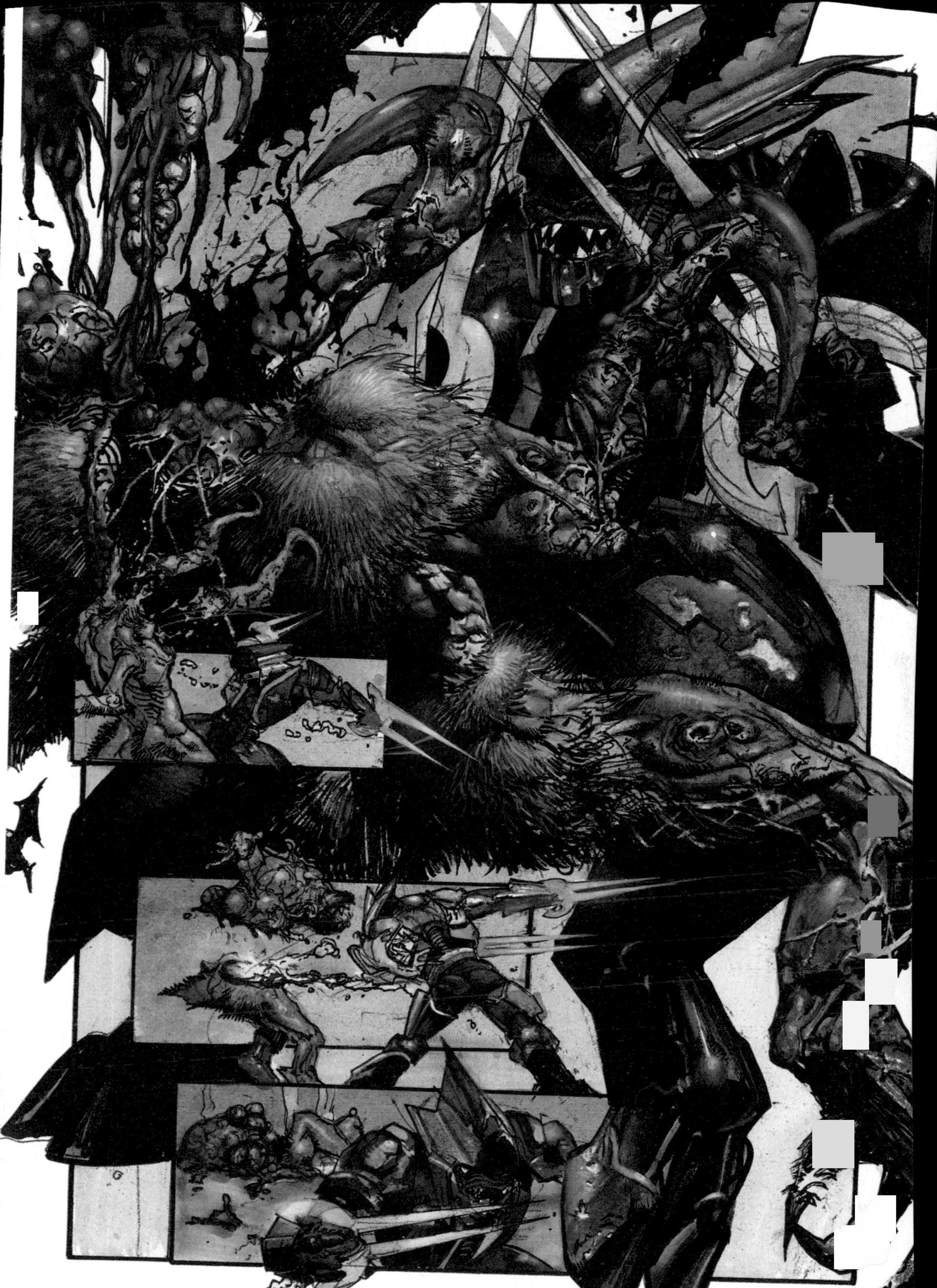

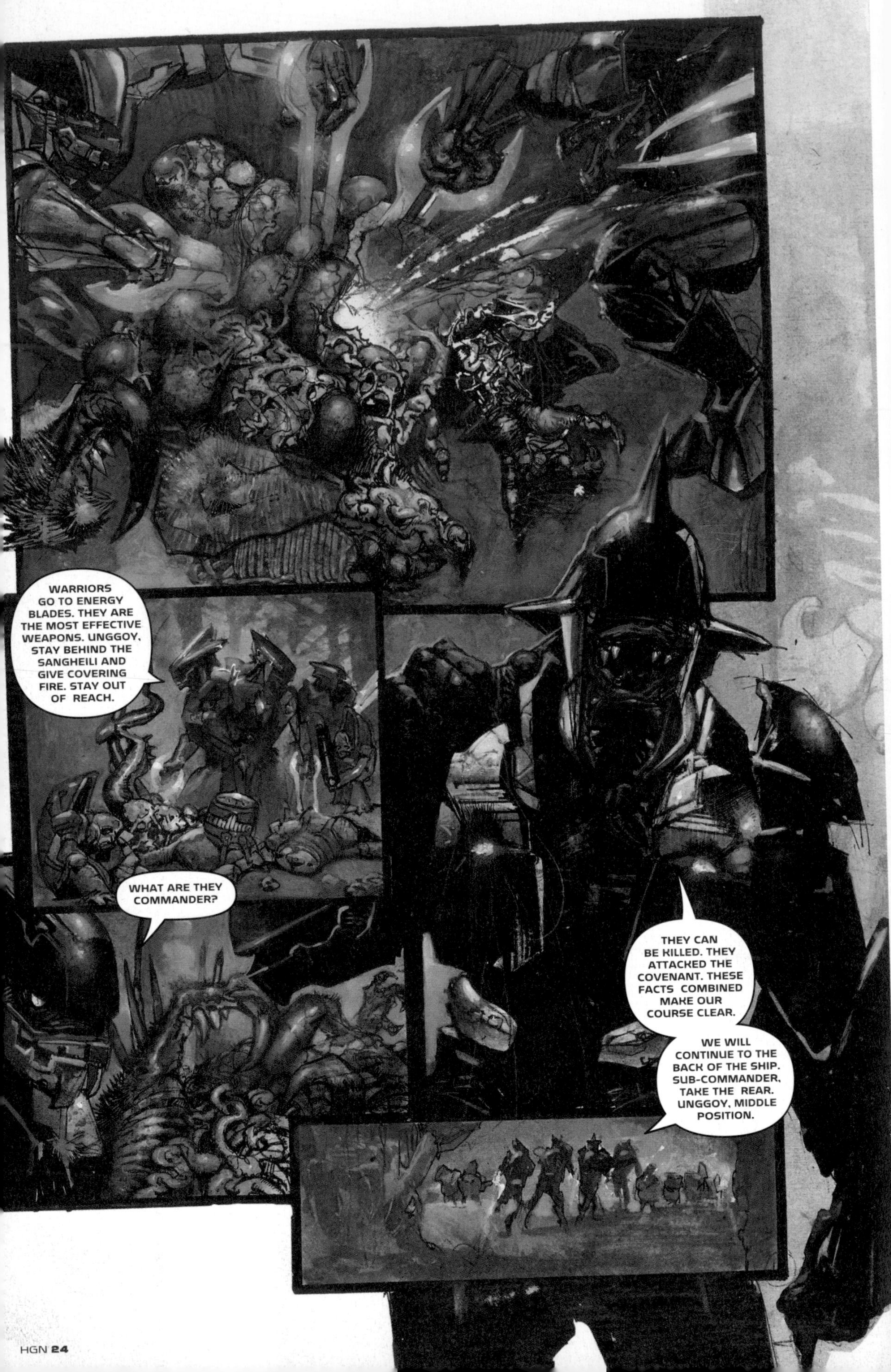
WARRIORS GO TO ENERGY BLADES. THEY ARE THE MOST EFFECTIVE WEAPONS. UNGGOY, STAY BEHIND THE SANGHEILI AND GIVE COVERING FIRE. STAY OUT OF REACH.
WHAT ARE THEY COMMANDER?
THEY CAN BE KILLED. THEY ATTACKED THE COVENANT. THESE FACTS COMBINED MAKE OUR COURSE CLEAR.
WE WILL CONTINUE TO THE BACK OF THE SHIP. SUB-COMMANDER, TAKE THE REAR. UNGGOY, MIDDLE POSITION.

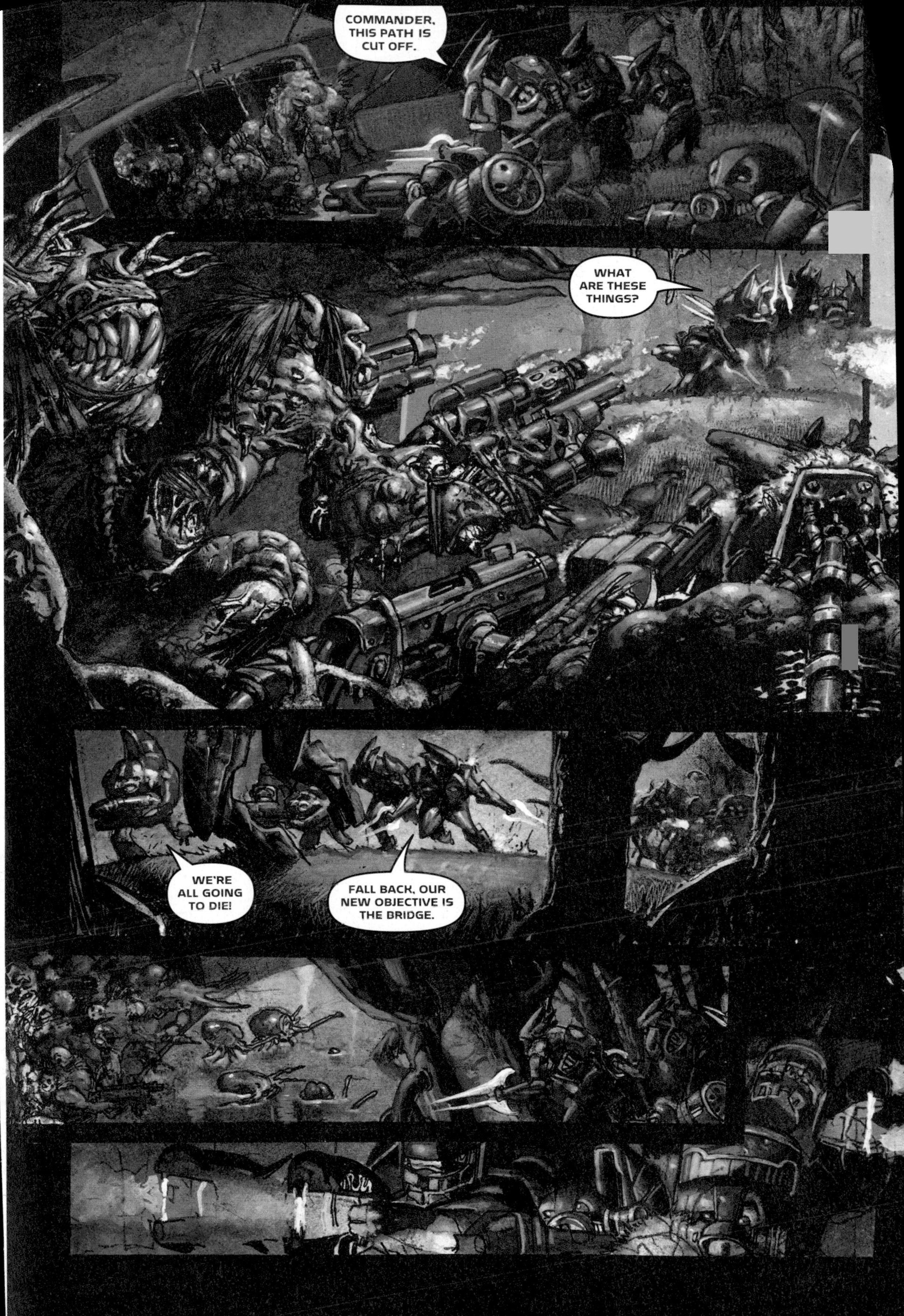
COMMANDER, THIS PATH IS CUT OFF.
WHAT ARE THESE THINGS?
WE'RE ALL GOING TO DIE!
FALL BACK, OUR NEW OBJECTIVE IS THE BRIDGE.

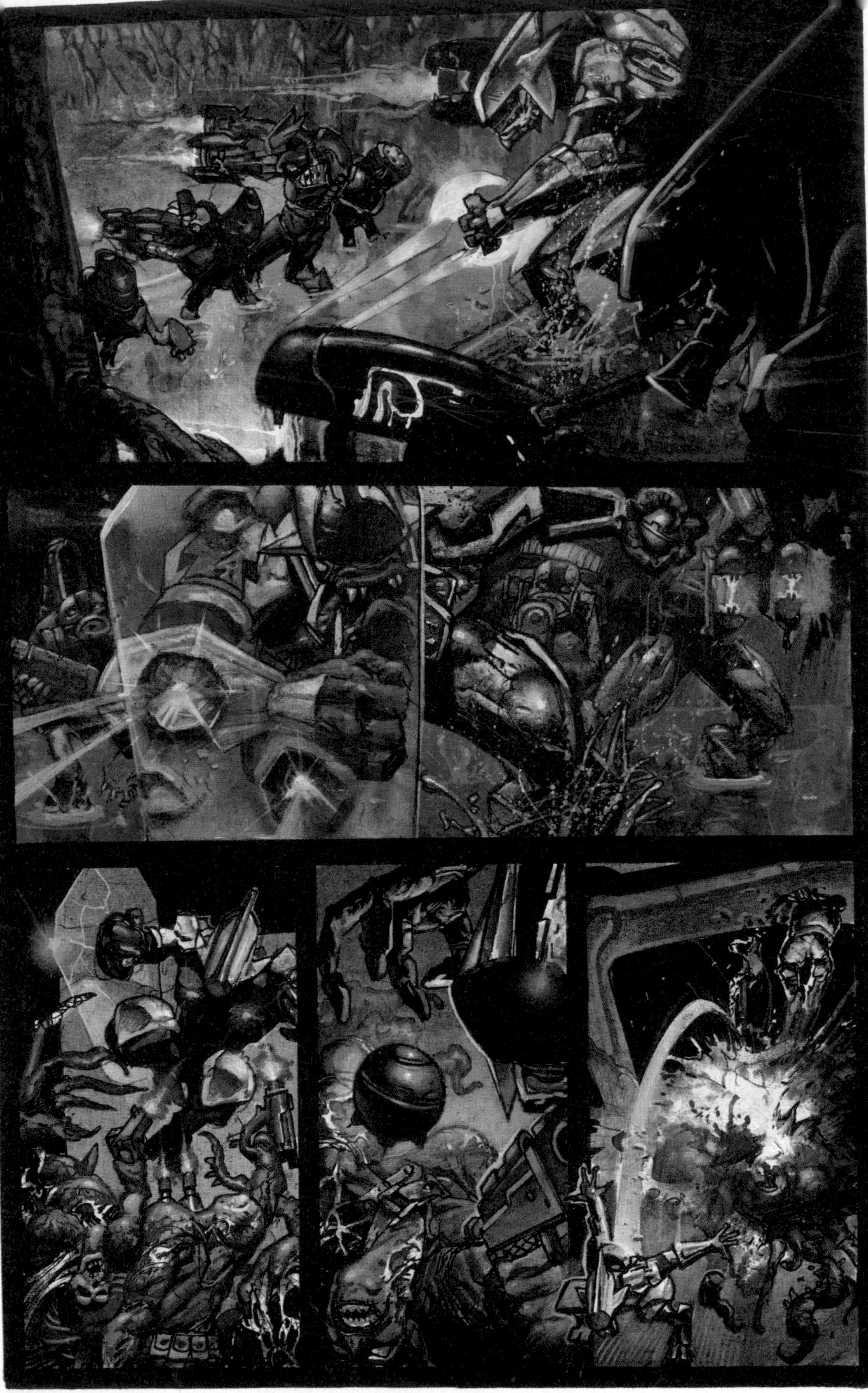

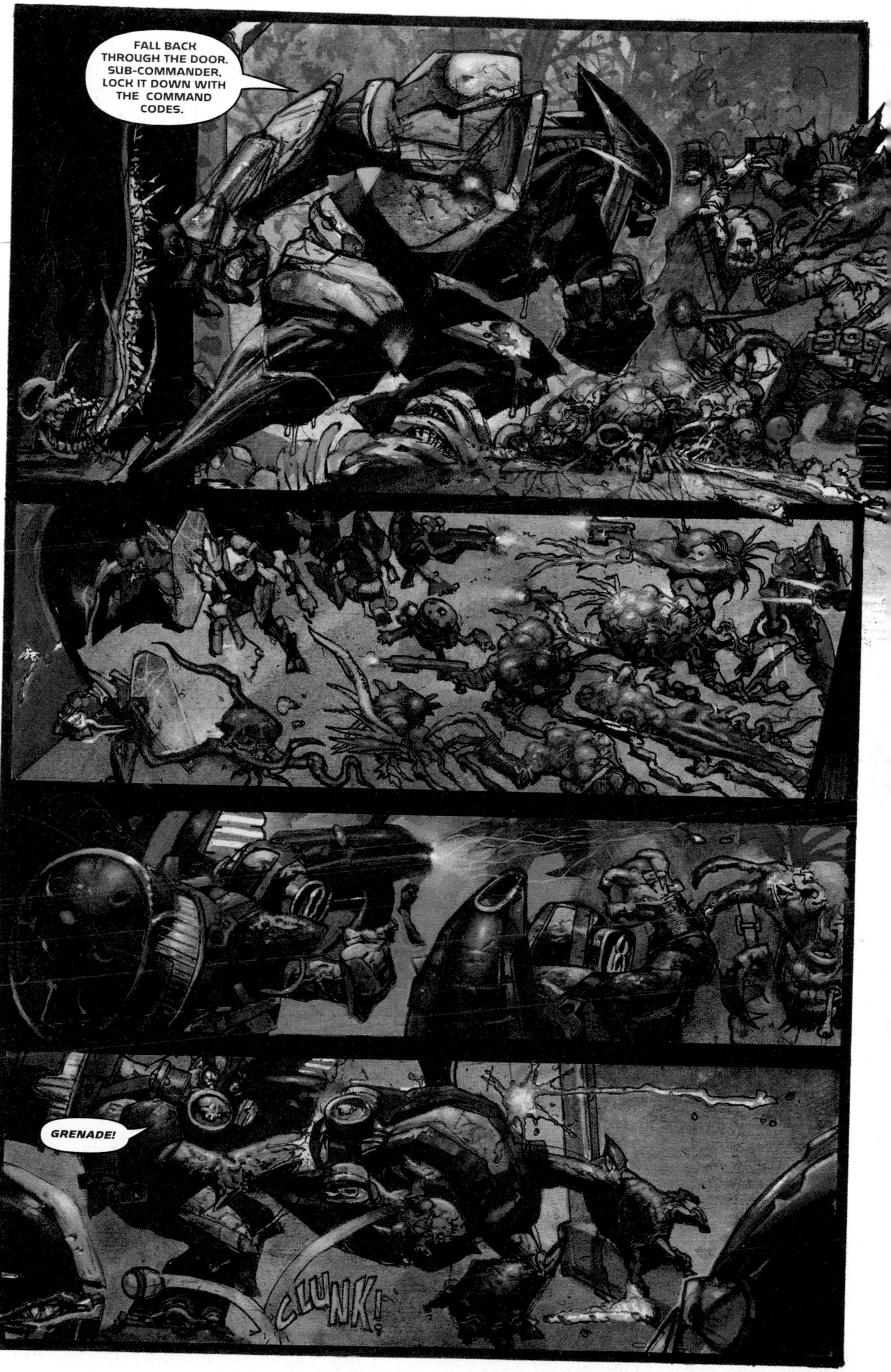
FALL BACK THROUGH THE DOOR. SUB-COMMANDER, LOCK IT DOWN WITH THE COMMAND CODES.
GRENADE!
CLUNK!

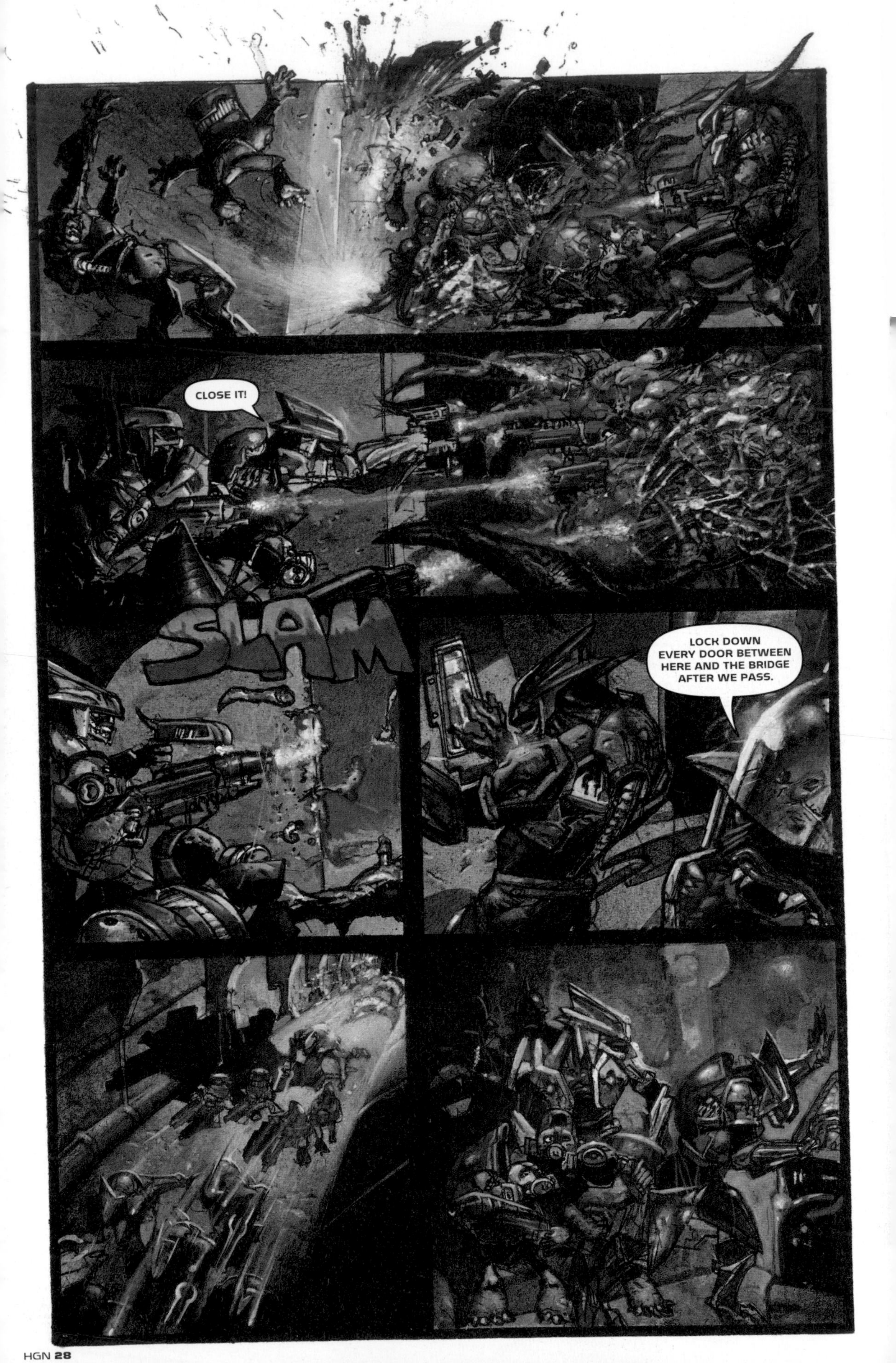
CLOSE IT!
SLAM
LOCK DOWN EVERY DOOR BETWEEN HERE AND THE BRIDGE AFTER WE PASS.

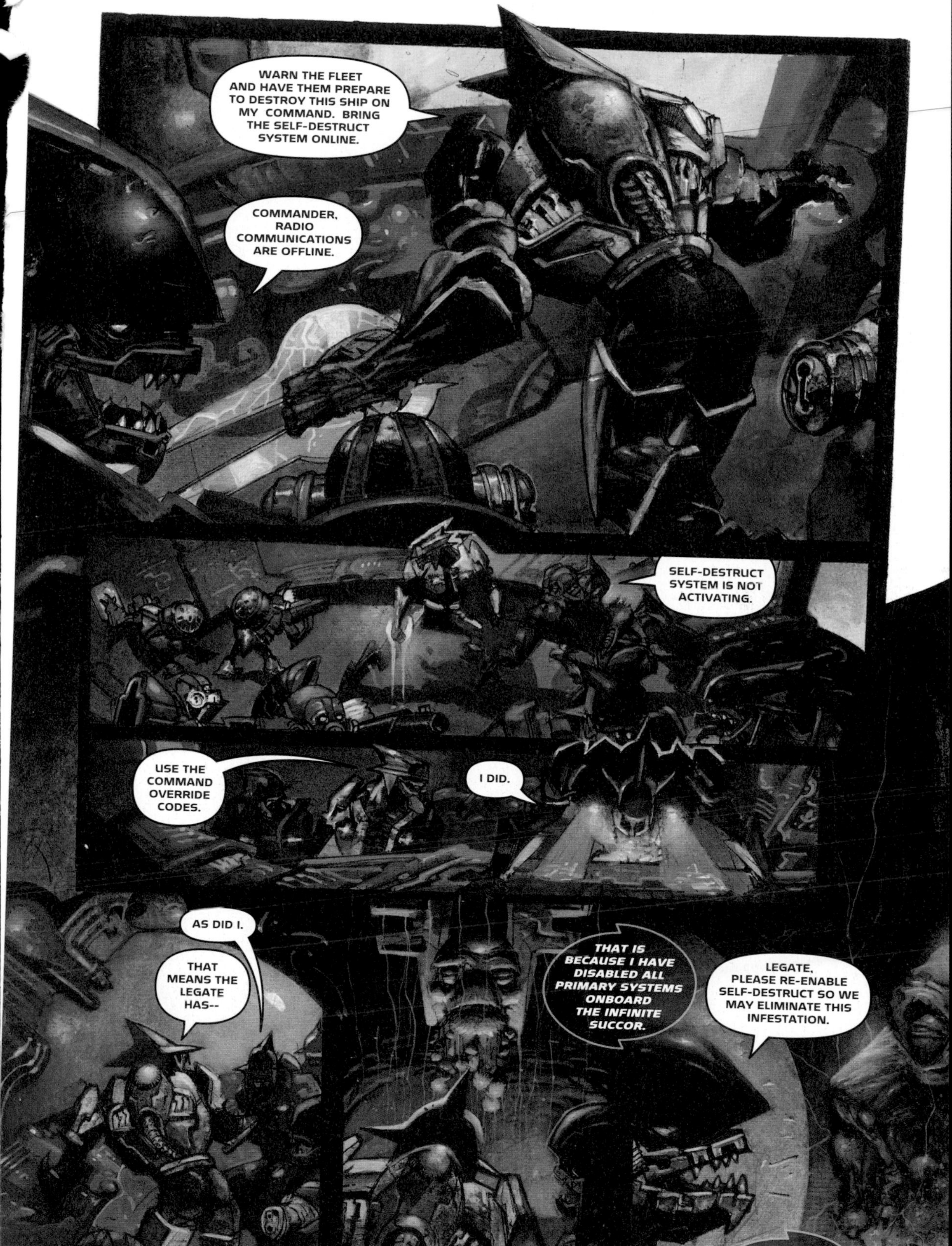
WARN THE FLEET AND HAVE THEM PREPARE TO DESTROY THIS SHIP ON MY COMMAND. BRING THE SELF-DESTRUCT SYSTEM ONLINE.
COMMANDER, RADIO COMMUNICATIONS ARE OFFLINE.
SELF-DESTRUCT SYSTEM IS NOT ACTIVATING.
USE THE COMMAND OVERRIDE CODES.
I DID.
AS DID I.
THAT MEANS THE LEGATE HAS--
THAT IS BECAUSE I HAVE DISABLED ALL PRIMARY SYSTEMS ONBOARD THE INFINITE SUCCOR.
LEGATE, PLEASE RE-ENABLE SELF-DESTRUCT SO WE MAY ELIMINATE THIS INFESTATION.
I WILL NOT, COMMANDER.

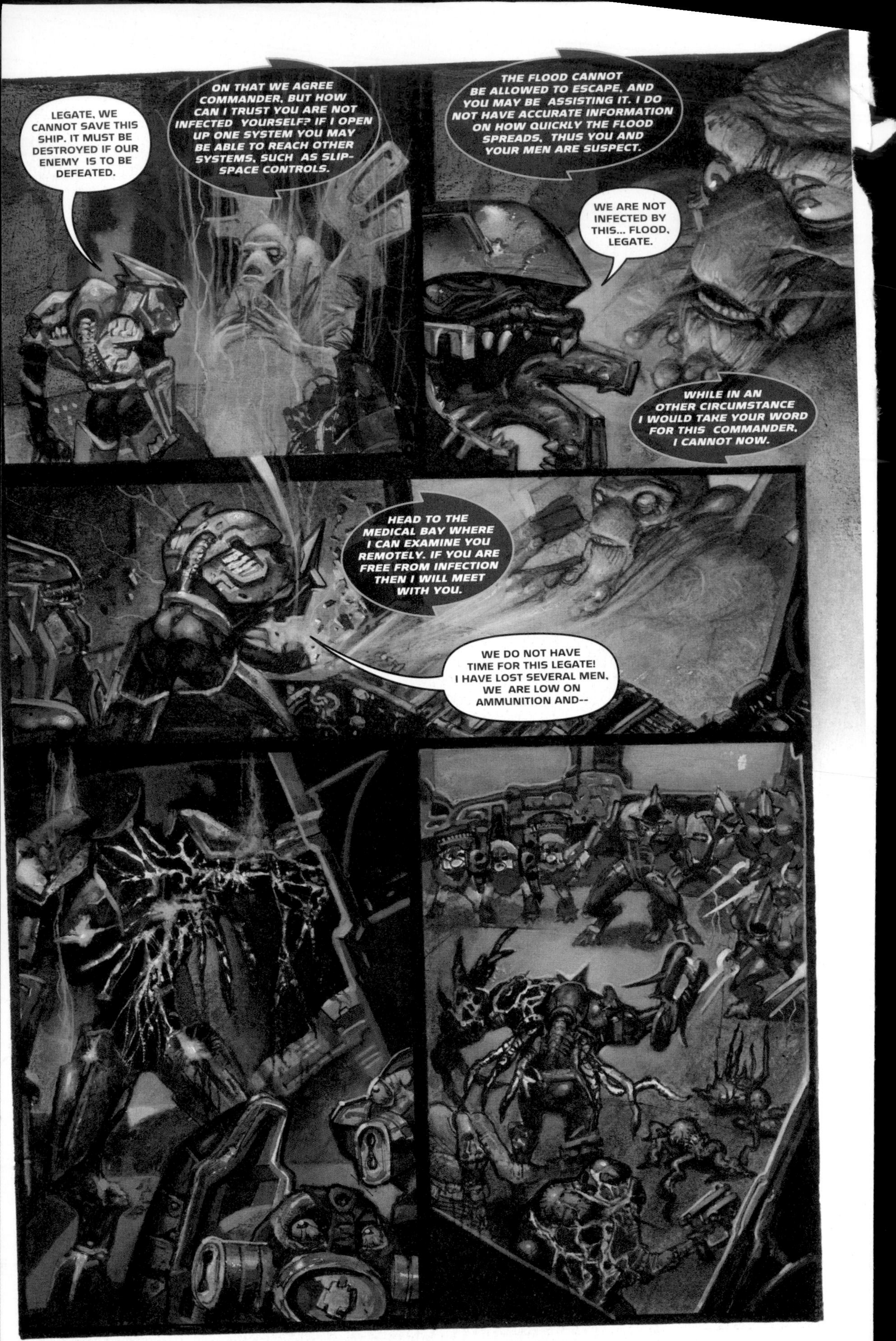
LEGATE, WE CANNOT SAVE THIS SHIP. IT MUST BE DESTROYED IF OUR ENEMY IS TO BE DEFEATED.
ON THAT WE AGREE COMMANDER, BUT HOW CAN I TRUST YOU ARE NOT INFECTED YOURSELF? IF I OPEN UP ONE SYSTEM YOU MAY BE ABLE TO REACH OTHER SYSTEMS, SUCH AS SLIP-SPACE CONTROLS.
THE FLOOD CANNOT BE ALLOWED TO ESCAPE, AND YOU MAY BE ASSISTING IT. I DO NOT HAVE ACCURATE INFORMATION ON HOW QUICKLY THE FLOOD SPREADS, THUS YOU AND YOUR MEN ARE SUSPECT.
WE ARE NOT INFECTED BY THIS... FLOOD, LEGATE.
WHILE IN AN OTHER CIRCUMSTANCE I WOULD TAKE YOUR WORD FOR THIS COMMANDER, I CANNOT NOW.
HEAD TO THE MEDICAL BAY WHERE I CAN EXAMINE YOU REMOTELY. IF YOU ARE FREE FROM INFECTION THEN I WILL MEET WITH YOU.
WE DO NOT HAVE TIME FOR THIS LEGATE! I HAVE LOST SEVERAL MEN, WE ARE LOW ON AMMUNITION AND--

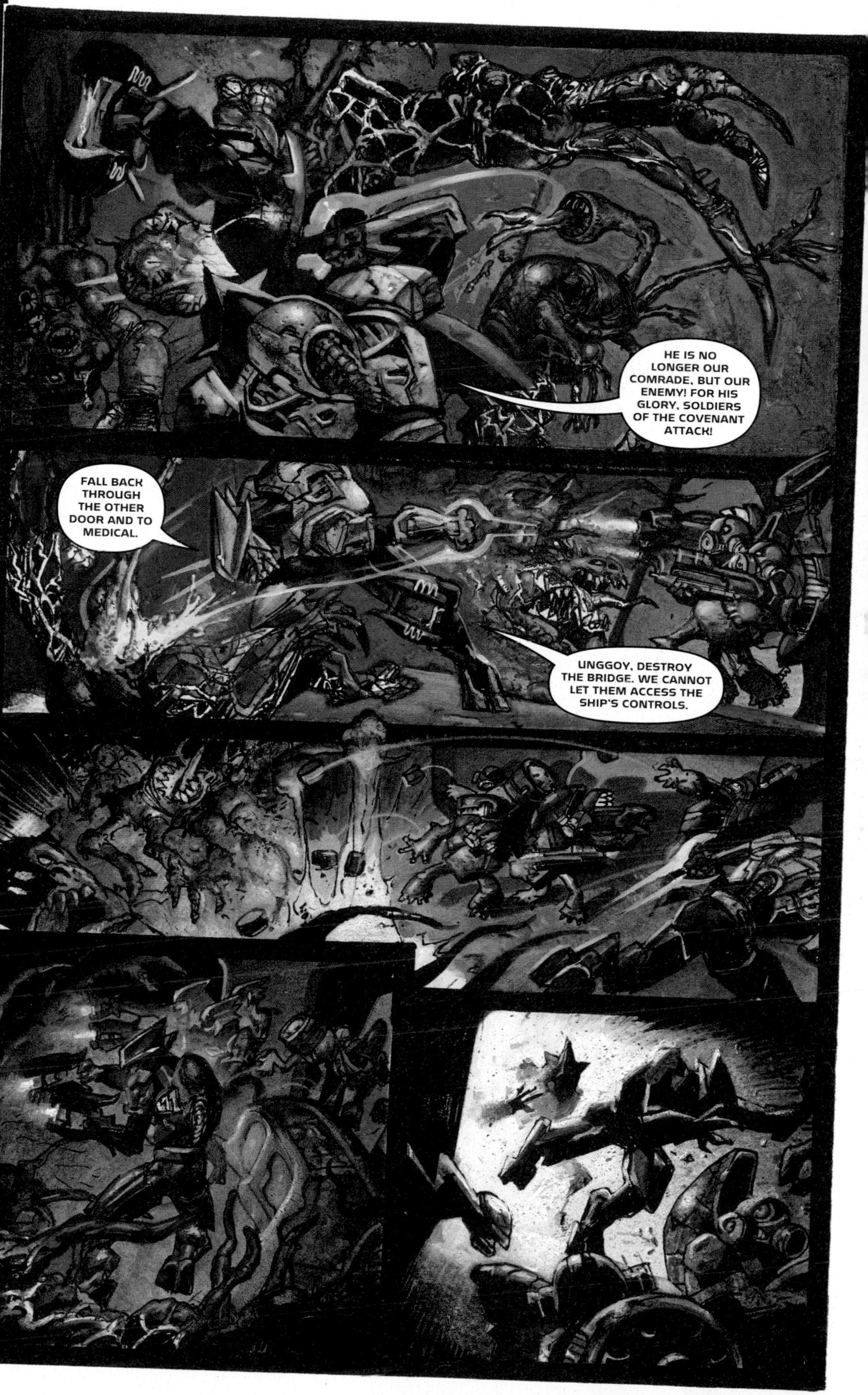
HE IS NO LONGER OUR COMRADE, BUT OUR ENEMY! FOR HIS GLORY, SOLDIERS OF THE COVENANT ATTACK!
FALL BACK THROUGH THE OTHER DOOR AND TO MEDICAL.
UNGGOY, DESTROY THE BRIDGE. WE CANNOT LET THEM ACCESS THE SHIP'S CONTROLS.

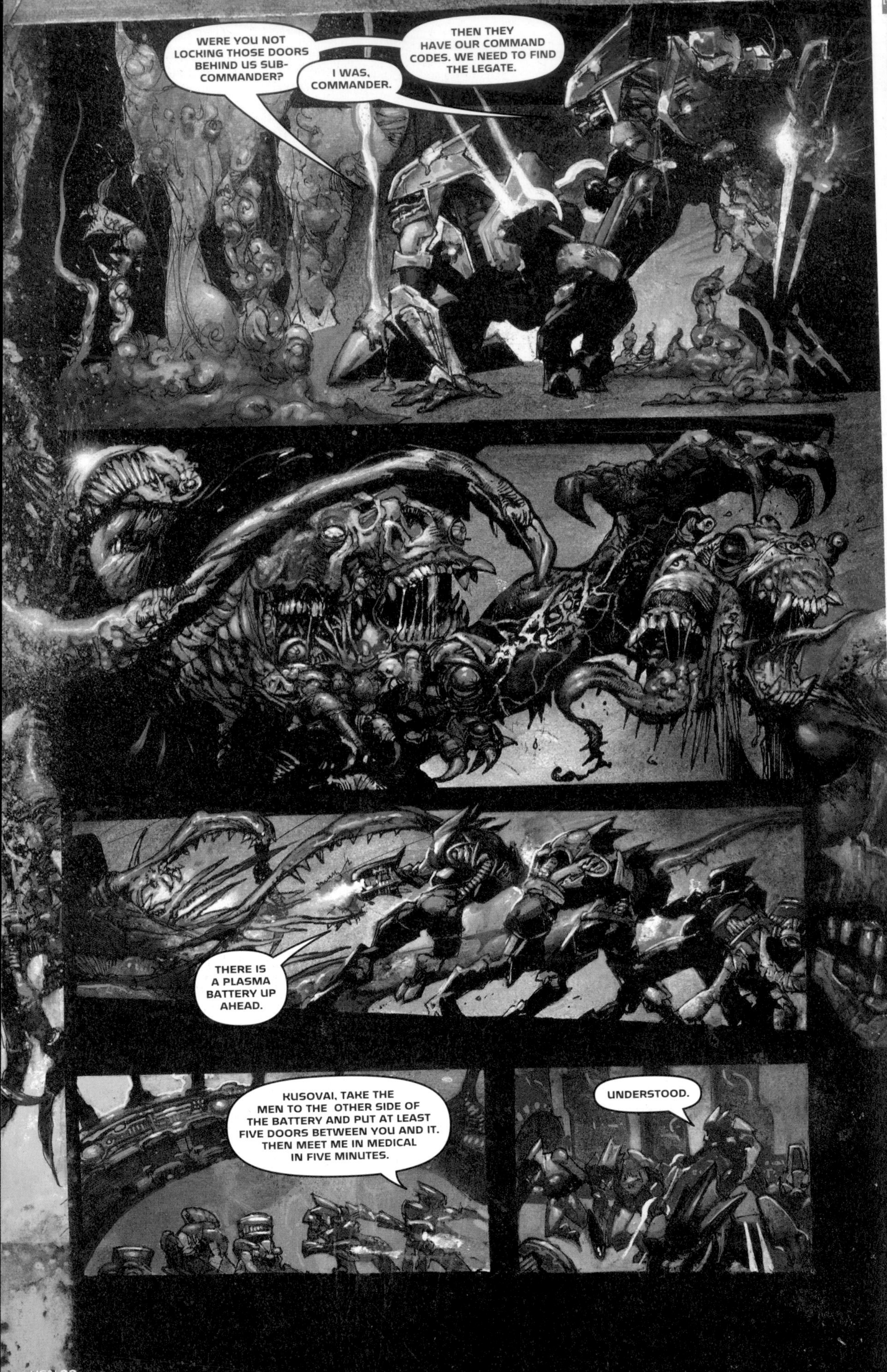
WERE YOU NOT LOCKING THOSE DOORS BEHIND US SUB-COMMANDER?
I WAS, COMMANDER.
THEN THEY HAVE OUR COMMAND CODES. WE NEED TO FIND THE LEGATE.
THERE IS A PLASMA BATTERY UP AHEAD.
KUSOVAI, TAKE THE MEN TO THE OTHER SIDE OF THE BATTERY AND PUT AT LEAST FIVE DOORS BETWEEN YOU AND IT. THEN MEET ME IN MEDICAL IN FIVE MINUTES.
UNDERSTOOD.

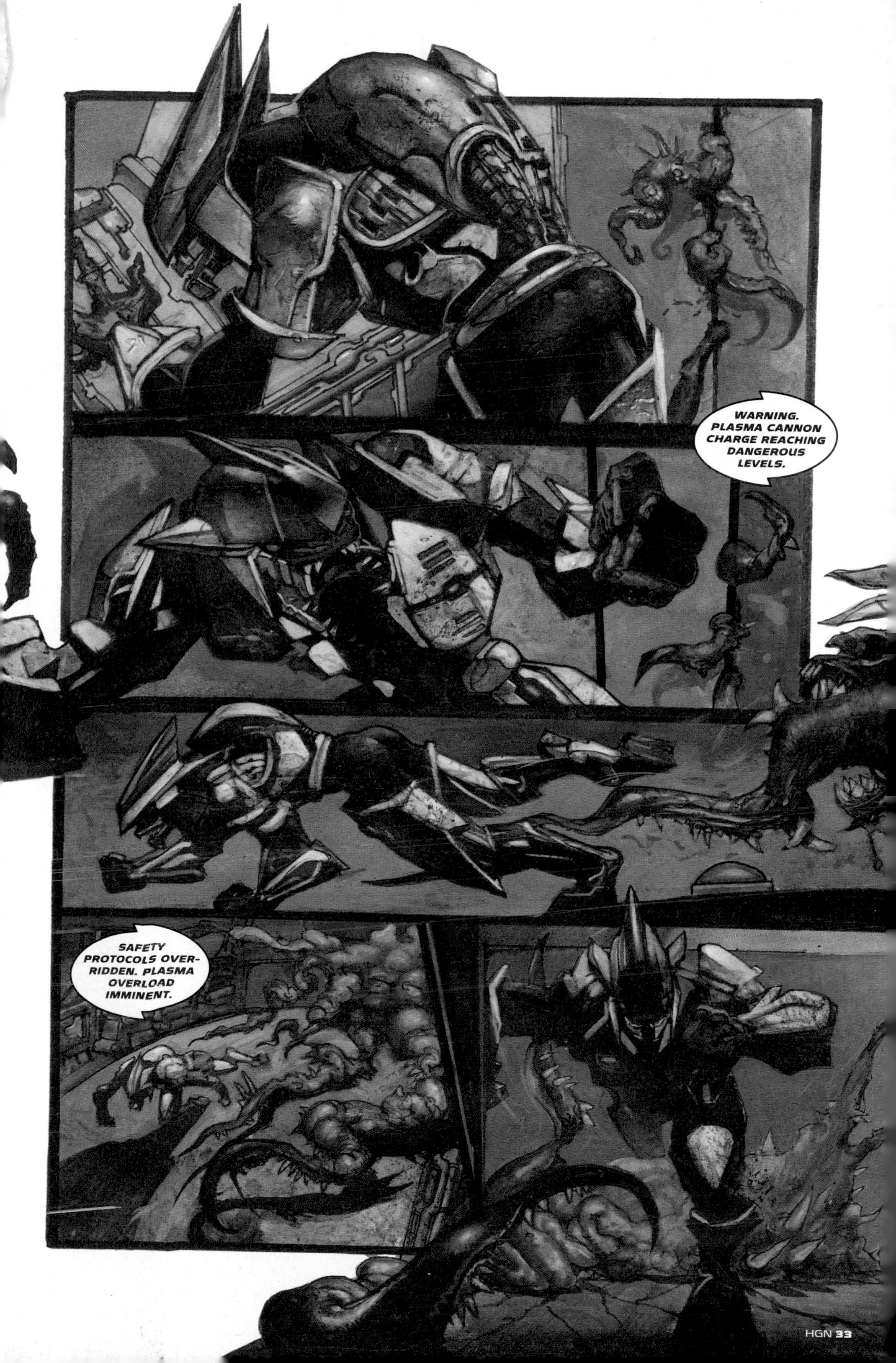
WARNING. PLASMA CANNON CHARGE REACHING DANGEROUS LEVELS.
SAFETY PROTOCOLS OVER-RIDDEN. PLASMA OVERLOAD IMMINENT.

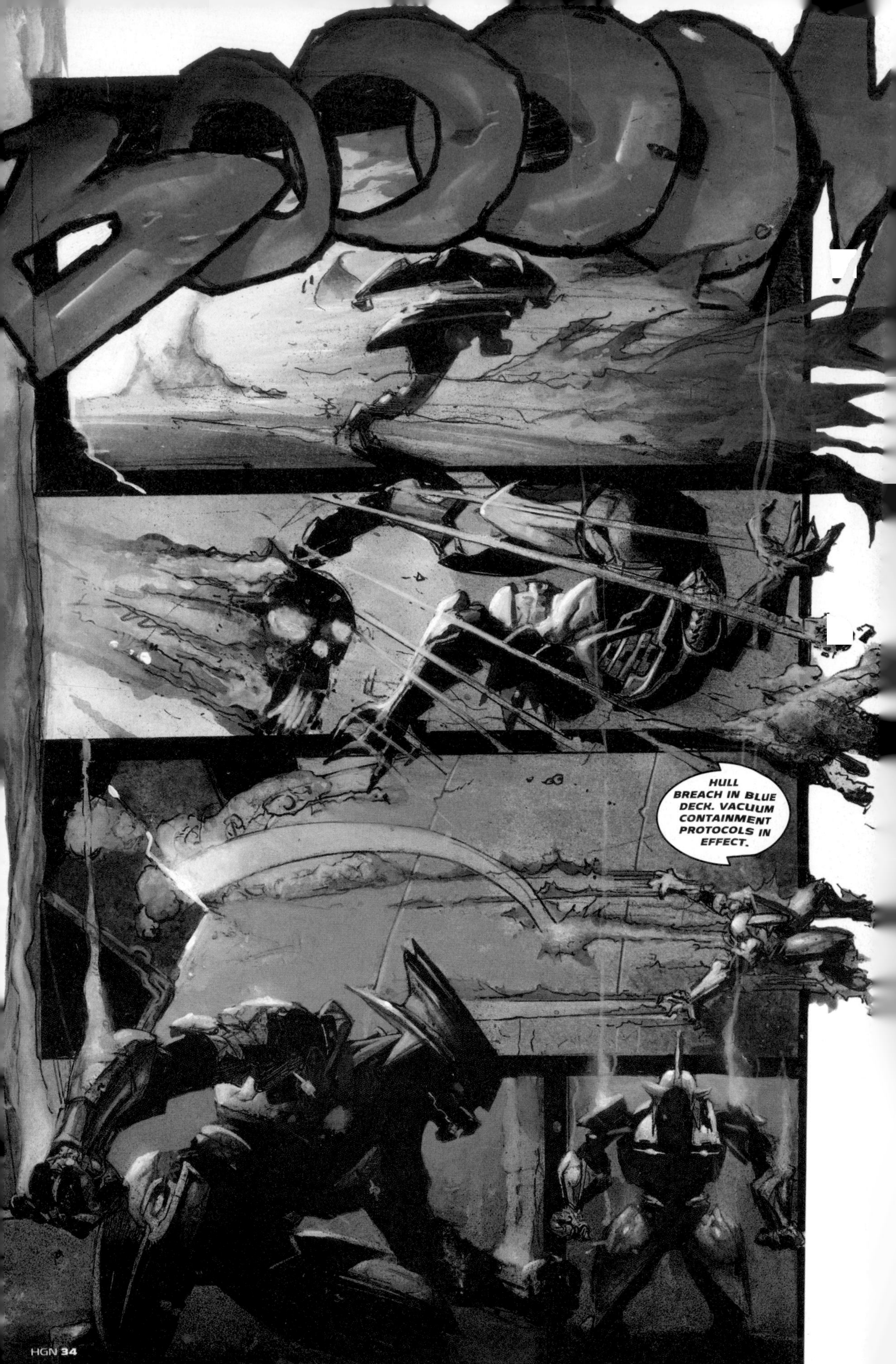
HULL BREACH IN BLUE DECK. VACUUM CONTAINMENT PROTOCOLS IN EFFECT.

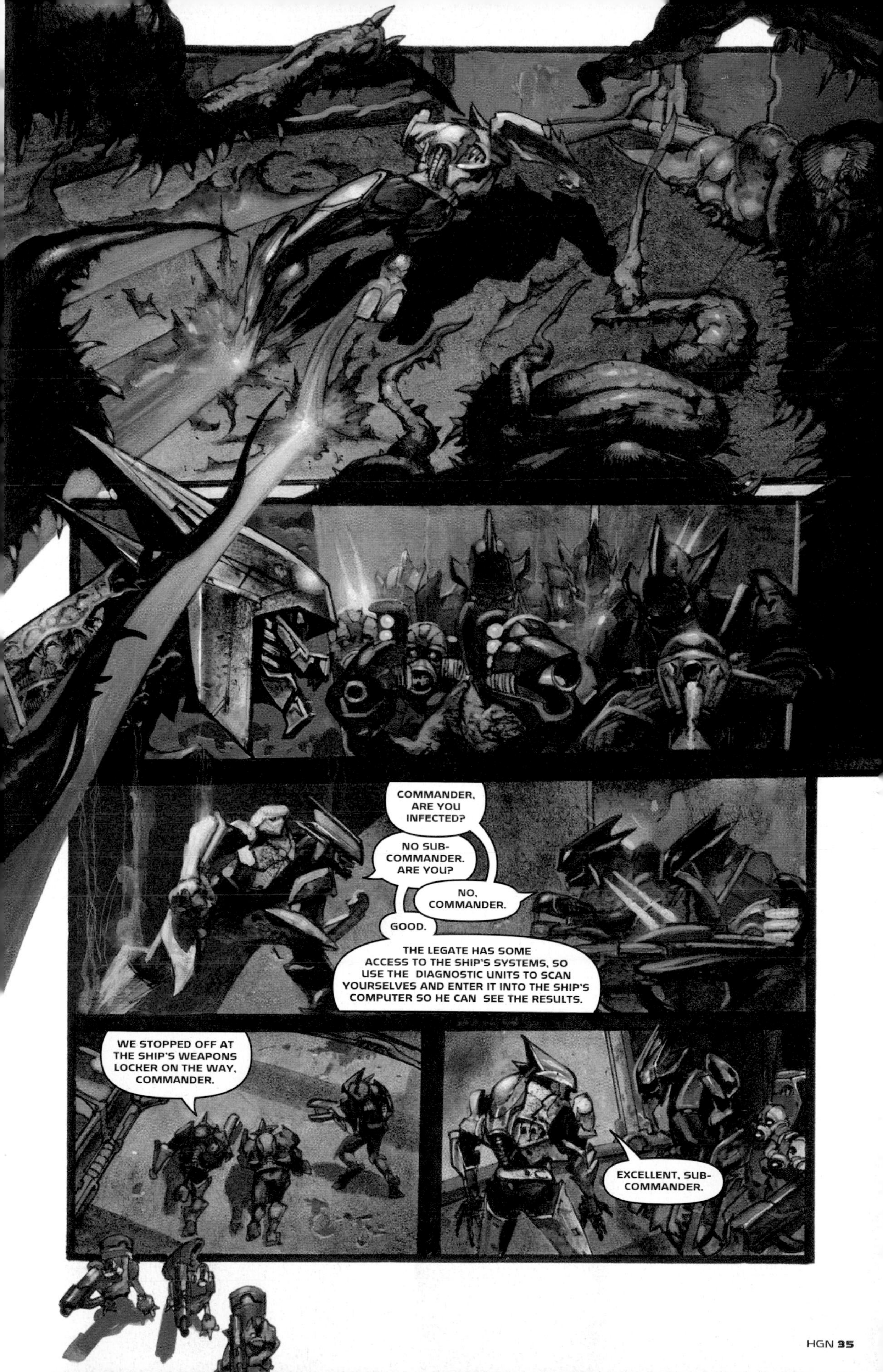
COMMANDER, ARE YOU INFECTED?
NO SUB-COMMANDER. ARE YOU?
NO, COMMANDER.
GOOD.
THE LEGATE HAS SOME ACCESS TO THE SHIP'S SYSTEMS, SO USE THE DIAGNOSTIC UNITS TO SCAN YOURSELVES AND ENTER IT INTO THE SHIP'S COMPUTER SO HE CAN SEE THE RESULTS.
WE STOPPED OFF AT THE SHIP'S WEAPONS LOCKER ON THE WAY, COMMANDER.
EXCELLENT, SUB-COMMANDER.

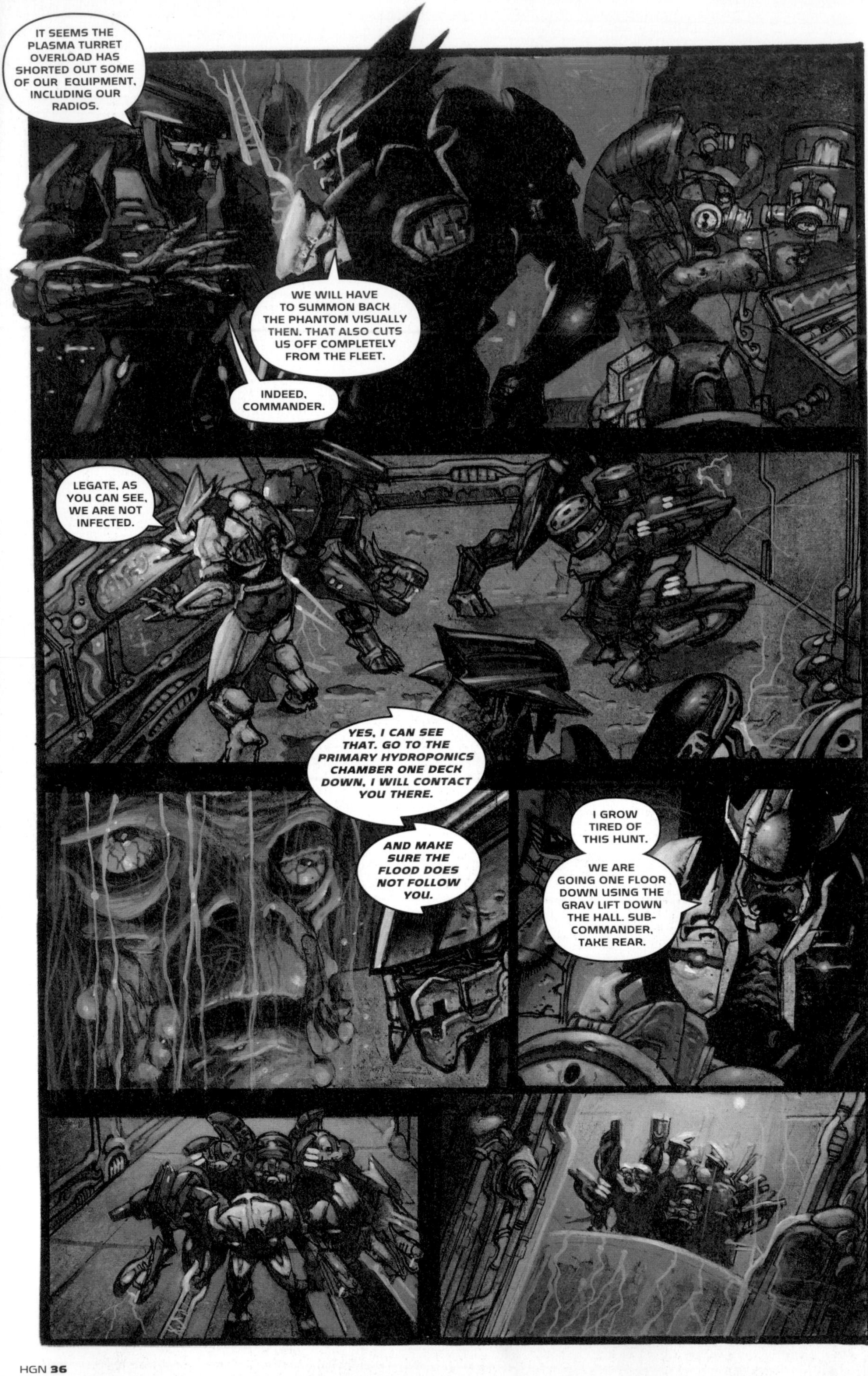
IT SEEMS THE PLASMA TURRET OVERLOAD HAS SHORTED OUT SOME OF OUR EQUIPMENT, INCLUDING OUR RADIOS.
WE WILL HAVE TO SUMMON BACK THE PHANTOM VISUALLY THEN. THAT ALSO CUTS US OFF COMPLETELY FROM THE FLEET.
INDEED, COMMANDER.
LEGATE, AS YOU CAN SEE, WE ARE NOT INFECTED.
YES, I CAN SEE THAT. GO TO THE PRIMARY HYDROPONICS CHAMBER ONE DECK DOWN, I WILL CONTACT YOU THERE.
AND MAKE SURE THE FLOOD DOES NOT FOLLOW YOU.
I GROW TIRED OF THIS HUNT.
WE ARE GOING ONE FLOOR DOWN USING THE GRAV LIFT DOWN THE HALL. SUB-COMMANDER, TAKE REAR.

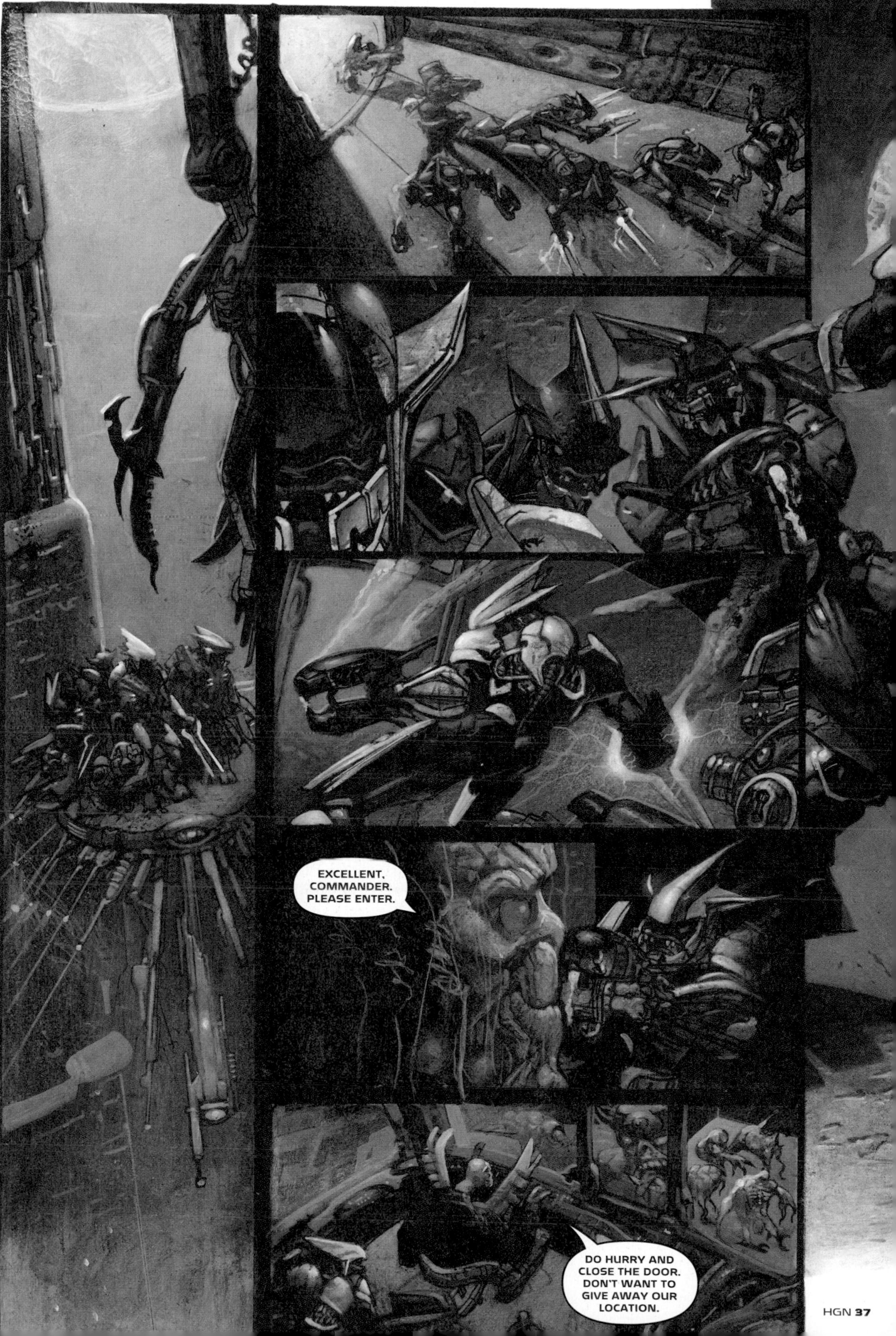
EXCELLENT, COMMANDER. PLEASE ENTER.
DO HURRY AND CLOSE THE DOOR. DON'T WANT TO GIVE AWAY OUR LOCATION.

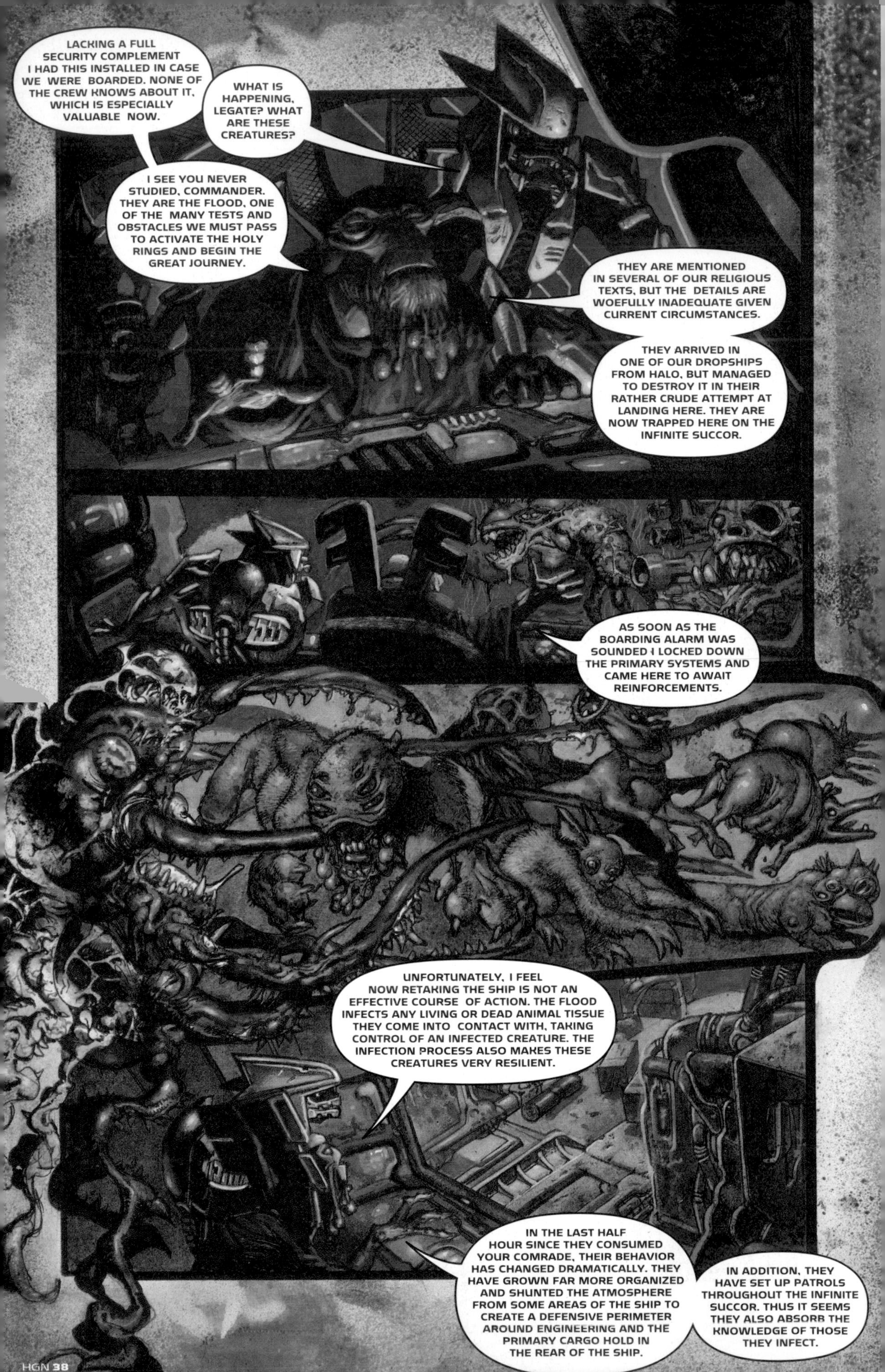
LACKING A FULL SECURITY COMPLEMENT I HAD THIS INSTALLED IN CASE WE WERE BOARDED. NONE OF THE CREW KNOWS ABOUT IT, WHICH IS ESPECIALLY VALUABLE NOW.
WHAT IS HAPPENING, LEGATE? WHAT ARE THESE CREATURES?
I SEE YOU NEVER STUDIED, COMMANDER. THEY ARE THE FLOOD, ONE OF THE MANY TESTS AND OBSTACLES WE MUST PASS TO ACTIVATE THE HOLY RINGS AND BEGIN THE GREAT JOURNEY.
THEY ARE MENTIONED IN SEVERAL OF OUR RELIGIOUS TEXTS, BUT THE DETAILS ARE WOEFULLY INADEQUATE GIVEN CURRENT CIRCUMSTANCES.
THEY ARRIVED IN ONE OF OUR DROPSHIPS FROM HALO, BUT MANAGED TO DESTROY IT IN THEIR RATHER CRUDE ATTEMPT AT LANDING HERE. THEY ARE NOW TRAPPED HERE ON THE INFINITE SUCCOR.
AS SOON AS THE BOARDING ALARM WAS SOUNDED I LOCKED DOWN THE PRIMARY SYSTEMS AND CAME HERE TO AWAIT REINFORCEMENTS.
UNFORTUNATELY, I FEEL NOW RETAKING THE SHIP IS NOT AN EFFECTIVE COURSE OF ACTION. THE FLOOD INFECTS ANY LIVING OR DEAD ANIMAL TISSUE THEY COME INTO CONTACT WITH, TAKING CONTROL OF AN INFECTED CREATURE. THE INFECTION PROCESS ALSO MAKES THESE CREATURES VERY RESILIENT.
IN THE LAST HALF HOUR SINCE THEY CONSUMED YOUR COMRADE, THEIR BEHAVIOR HAS CHANGED DRAMATICALLY. THEY HAVE GROWN FAR MORE ORGANIZED AND SHUNTED THE ATMOSPHERE FROM SOME AREAS OF THE SHIP TO CREATE A DEFENSIVE PERIMETER AROUND ENGINEERING AND THE PRIMARY CARGO HOLD IN THE REAR OF THE SHIP.
IN ADDITION, THEY HAVE SET UP PATROLS THROUGHOUT THE INFINITE SUCCOR. THUS IT SEEMS THEY ALSO ABSORB THE KNOWLEDGE OF THOSE THEY INFECT.

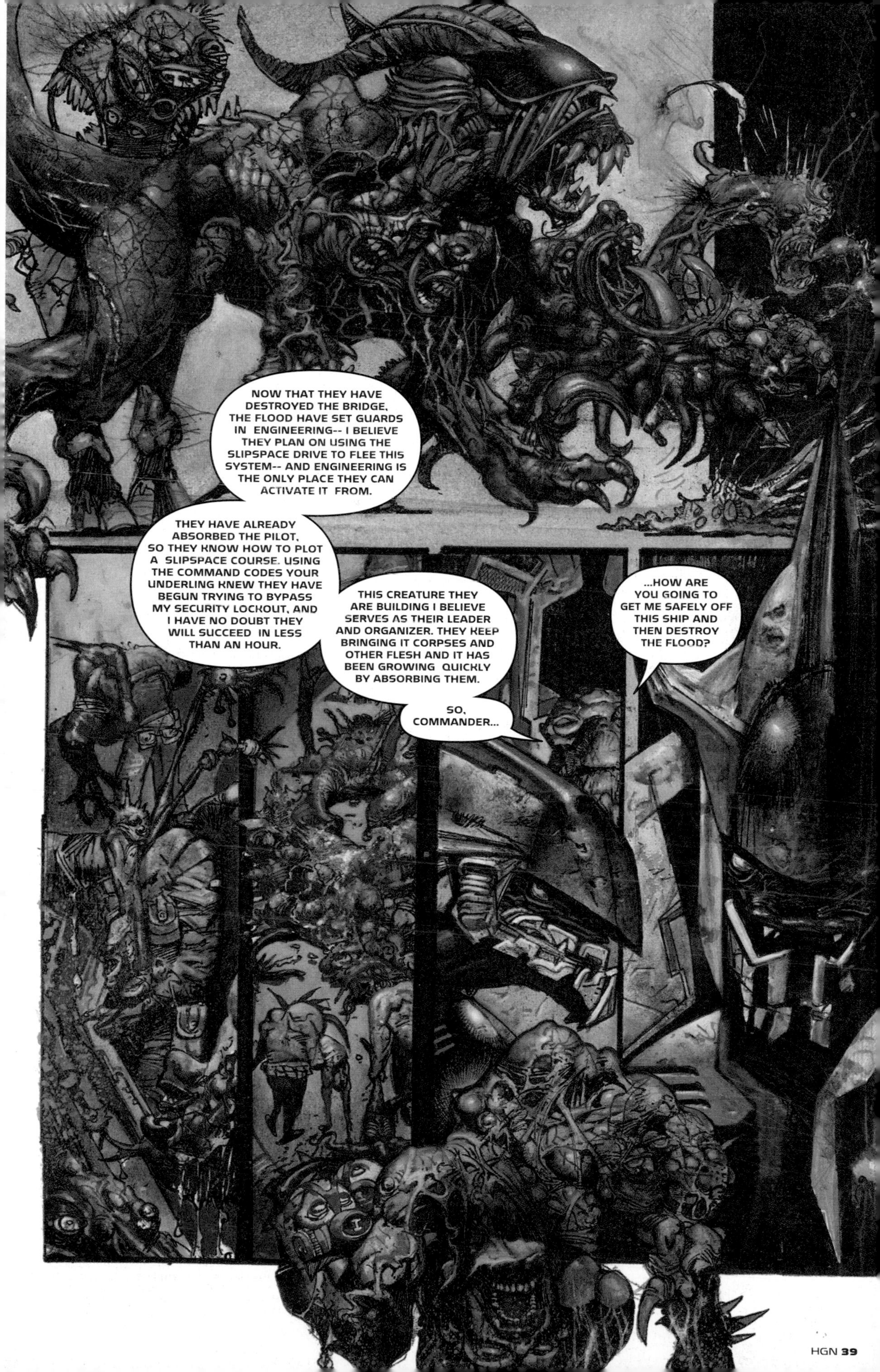
NOW THAT THEY HAVE DESTROYED THE BRIDGE, THE FLOOD HAVE SET GUARDS IN ENGINEERING-- I BELIEVE THEY PLAN ON USING THE SLIPSPACE DRIVE TO FLEE THIS SYSTEM-- AND ENGINEERING IS THE ONLY PLACE THEY CAN ACTIVATE IT FROM.
THEY HAVE ALREADY ABSORBED THE PILOT, SO THEY KNOW HOW TO PLOT A SLIPSPACE COURSE. USING THE COMMAND CODES YOUR UNDERLING KNEW THEY HAVE BEGUN TRYING TO BYPASS MY SECURITY LOCKOUT, AND I HAVE NO DOUBT THEY WILL SUCCEED IN LESS THAN AN HOUR.
THIS CREATURE THEY ARE BUILDING I BELIEVE SERVES AS THEIR LEADER AND ORGANIZER. THEY KEEP BRINGING IT CORPSES AND OTHER FLESH AND IT HAS BEEN GROWING QUICKLY BY ABSORBING THEM.
SO, COMMANDER...
...HOW ARE YOU GOING TO GET ME SAFELY OFF THIS SHIP AND THEN DESTROY THE FLOOD?

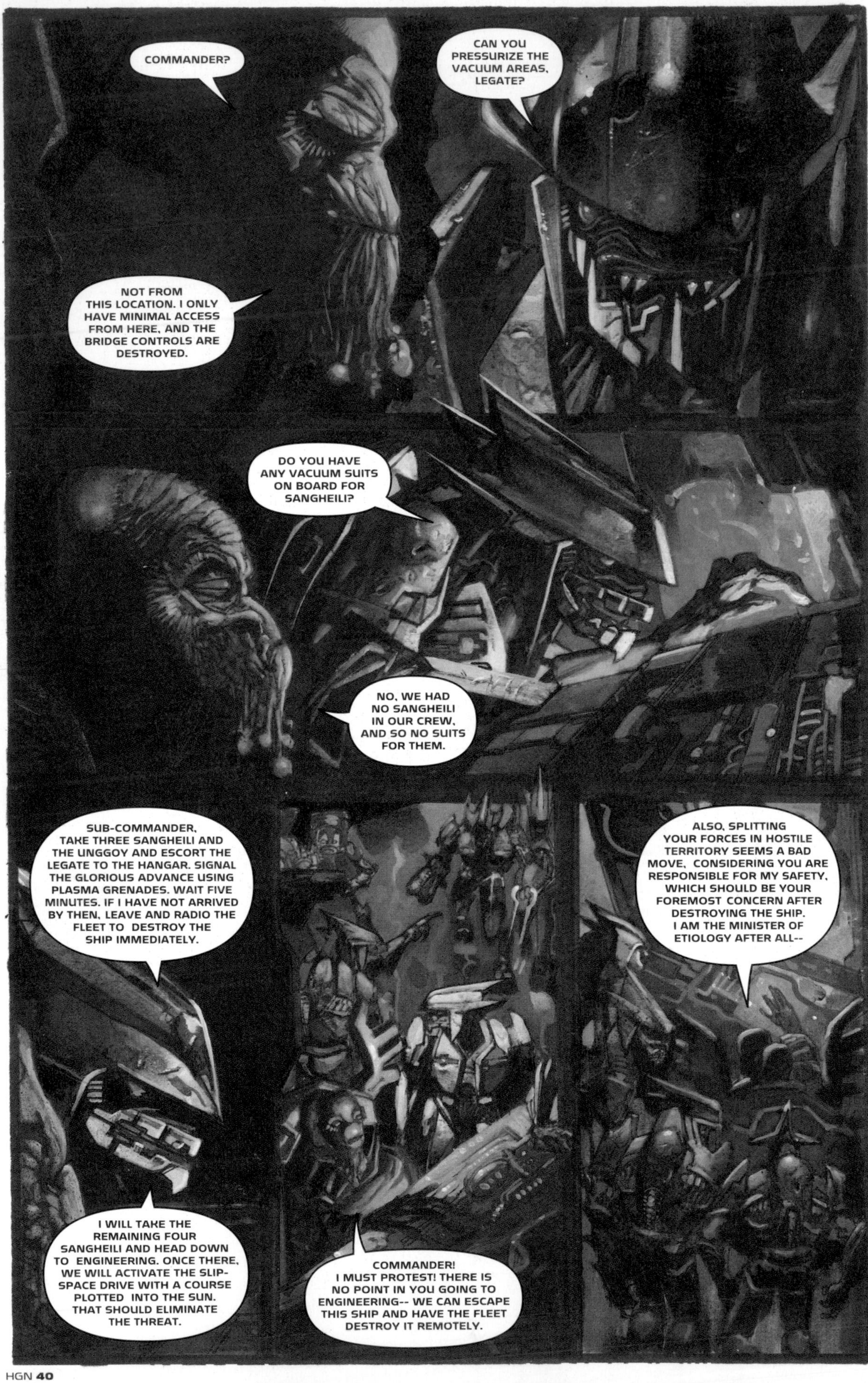
COMMANDER?
CAN YOU PRESSURIZE THE VACUUM AREAS, LEGATE?
NOT FROM THIS LOCATION. I ONLY HAVE MINIMAL ACCESS FROM HERE, AND THE BRIDGE CONTROLS ARE DESTROYED.
DO YOU HAVE ANY VACUUM SUITS ON BOARD FOR SANGHEILI?
NO, WE HAD NO SANGHEILI IN OUR CREW, AND SO NO SUITS FOR THEM.
SUB-COMMANDER, TAKE THREE SANGHEILI AND THE UNGGOY AND ESCORT THE LEGATE TO THE HANGAR. SIGNAL THE GLORIOUS ADVANCE USING PLASMA GRENADES. WAIT FIVE MINUTES. IF I HAVE NOT ARRIVED BY THEN, LEAVE AND RADIO THE FLEET TO DESTROY THE SHIP IMMEDIATELY.
I WILL TAKE THE REMAINING FOUR SANGHEILI AND HEAD DOWN TO ENGINEERING. ONCE THERE, WE WILL ACTIVATE THE SLIP-SPACE DRIVE WITH A COURSE PLOTTED INTO THE SUN. THAT SHOULD ELIMINATE THE THREAT.
COMMANDER! I MUST PROTEST! THERE IS NO POINT IN YOU GOING TO ENGINEERING-- WE CAN ESCAPE THIS SHIP AND HAVE THE FLEET DESTROY IT REMOTELY.
ALSO, SPLITTING YOUR FORCES IN HOSTILE TERRITORY SEEMS A BAD MOVE, CONSIDERING YOU ARE RESPONSIBLE FOR MY SAFETY, WHICH SHOULD BE YOUR FOREMOST CONCERN AFTER DESTROYING THE SHIP. I AM THE MINISTER OF ETIOLOGY AFTER ALL--

LEGATE, IT WILL TAKE FIVE MINUTES TO REACH THE HANGAR, FIVE TO BOARD THE PHANTOM DUE TO OUR LACK OF RADIO COMMS, AND ANOTHER FIFTEEN TO GET THE FLEET INTO FIRING POSITION WITH THE PROPER AUTHORIZATIONS IN PLACE.
IT WOULD BE A SIMPLE MATTER TO MAKE IT APPEAR YOU DIED IN THE FLOOD ATTACK. NOW GIVE ME YOUR COMMAND CODES.
NOW YOU WILL BE QUIET AND LET MY MEN DO THEIR DUTY. OUR PRIME CONCERN IS THE SAFETY OF THE COVENANT, NOT YOU.

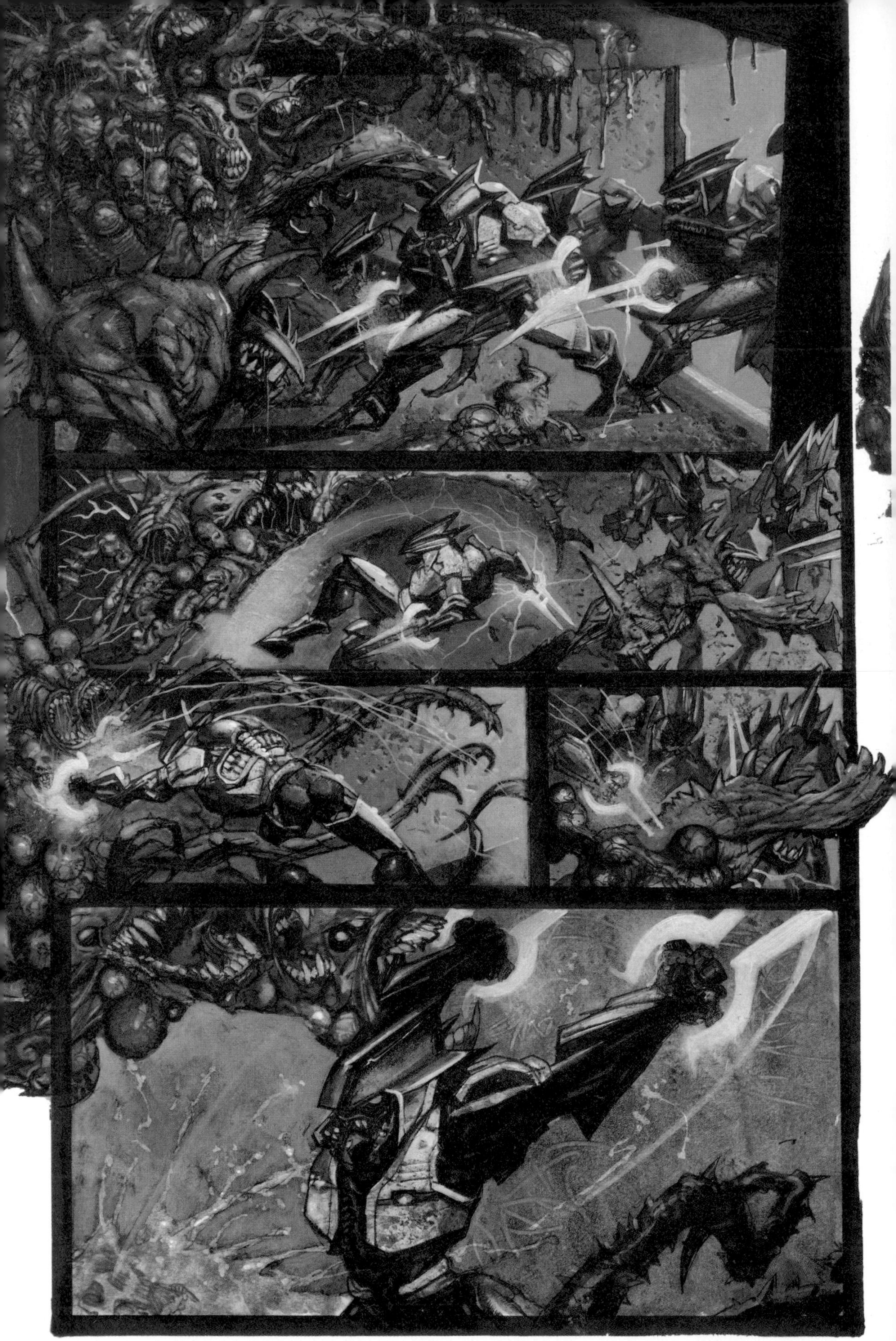

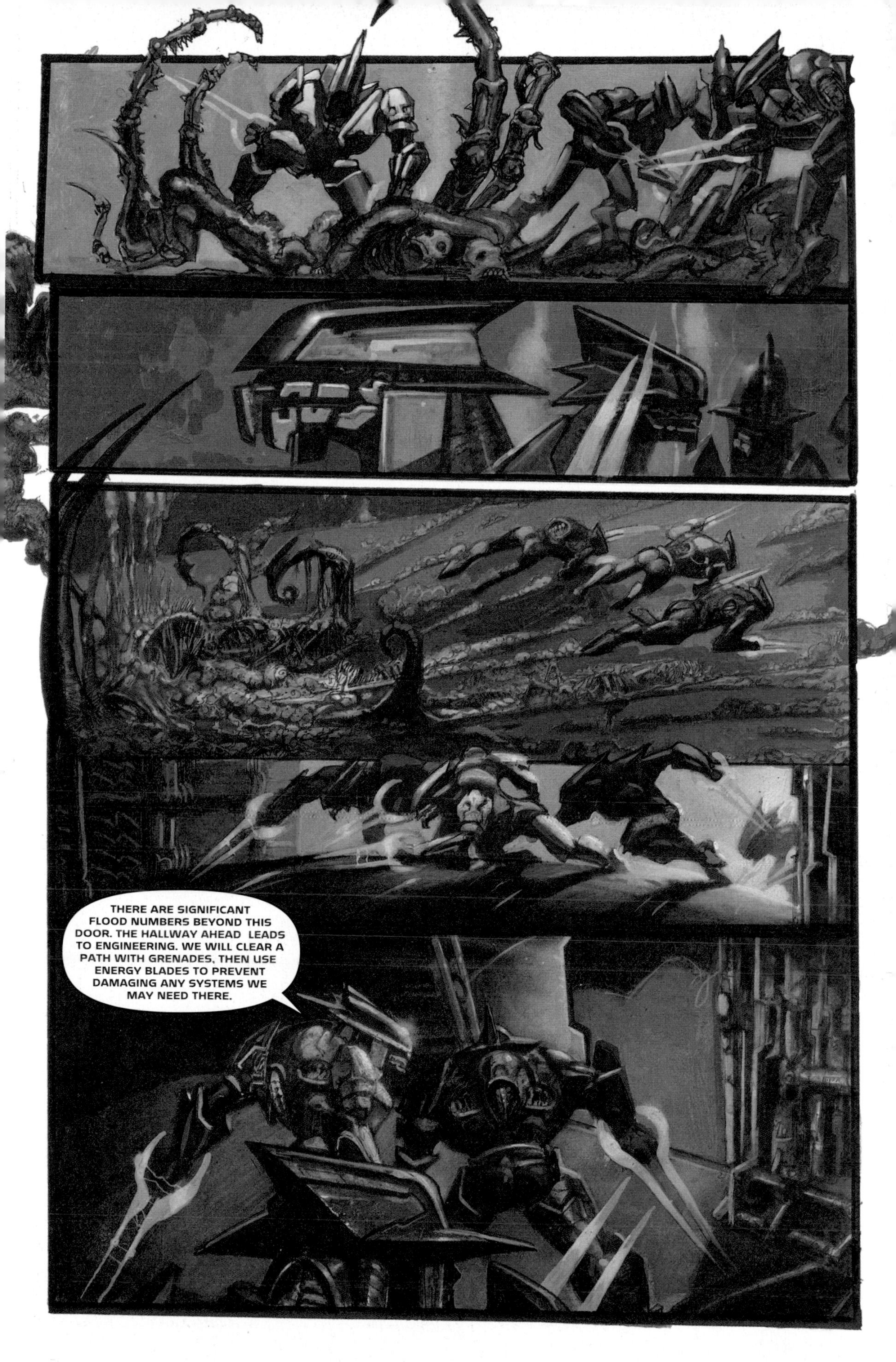
THERE ARE SIGNIFICANT FLOOD NUMBERS BEYOND THIS DOOR. THE HALLWAY AHEAD LEADS TO ENGINEERING. WE WILL CLEAR A PATH WITH GRENADES, THEN USE ENERGY BLADES TO PREVENT DAMAGING ANY SYSTEMS WE MAY NEED THERE.

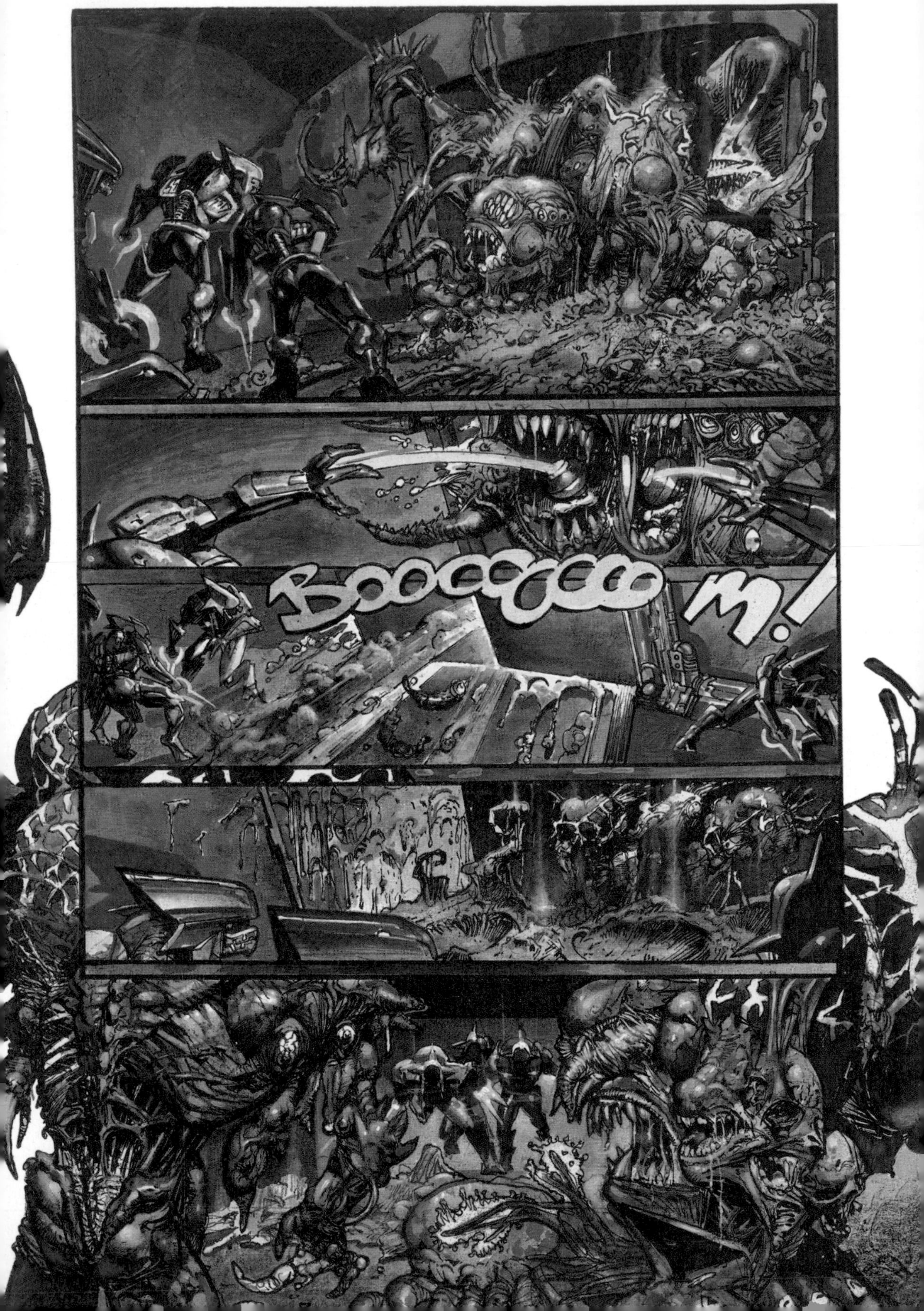
BOOOOOOOOM!

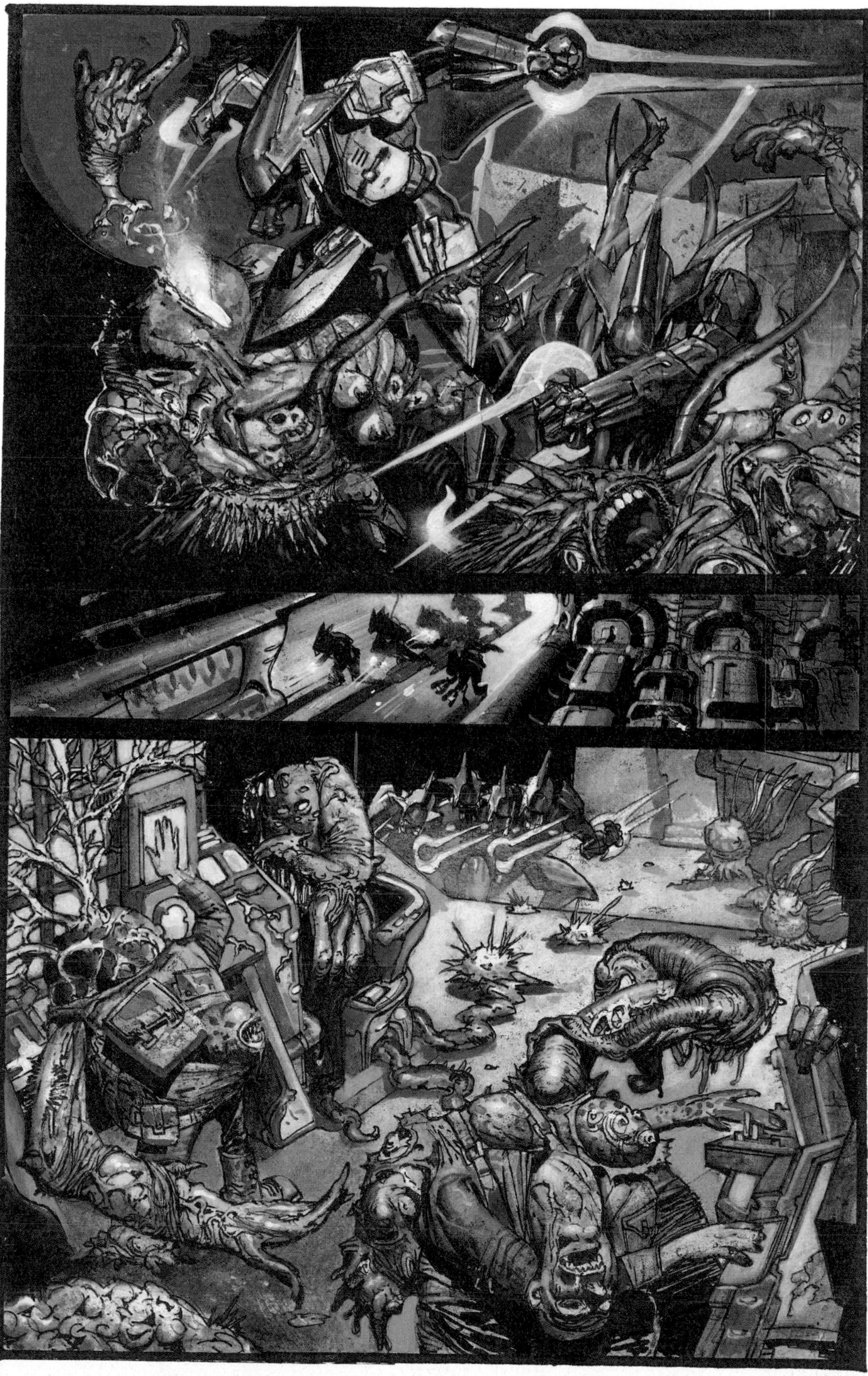

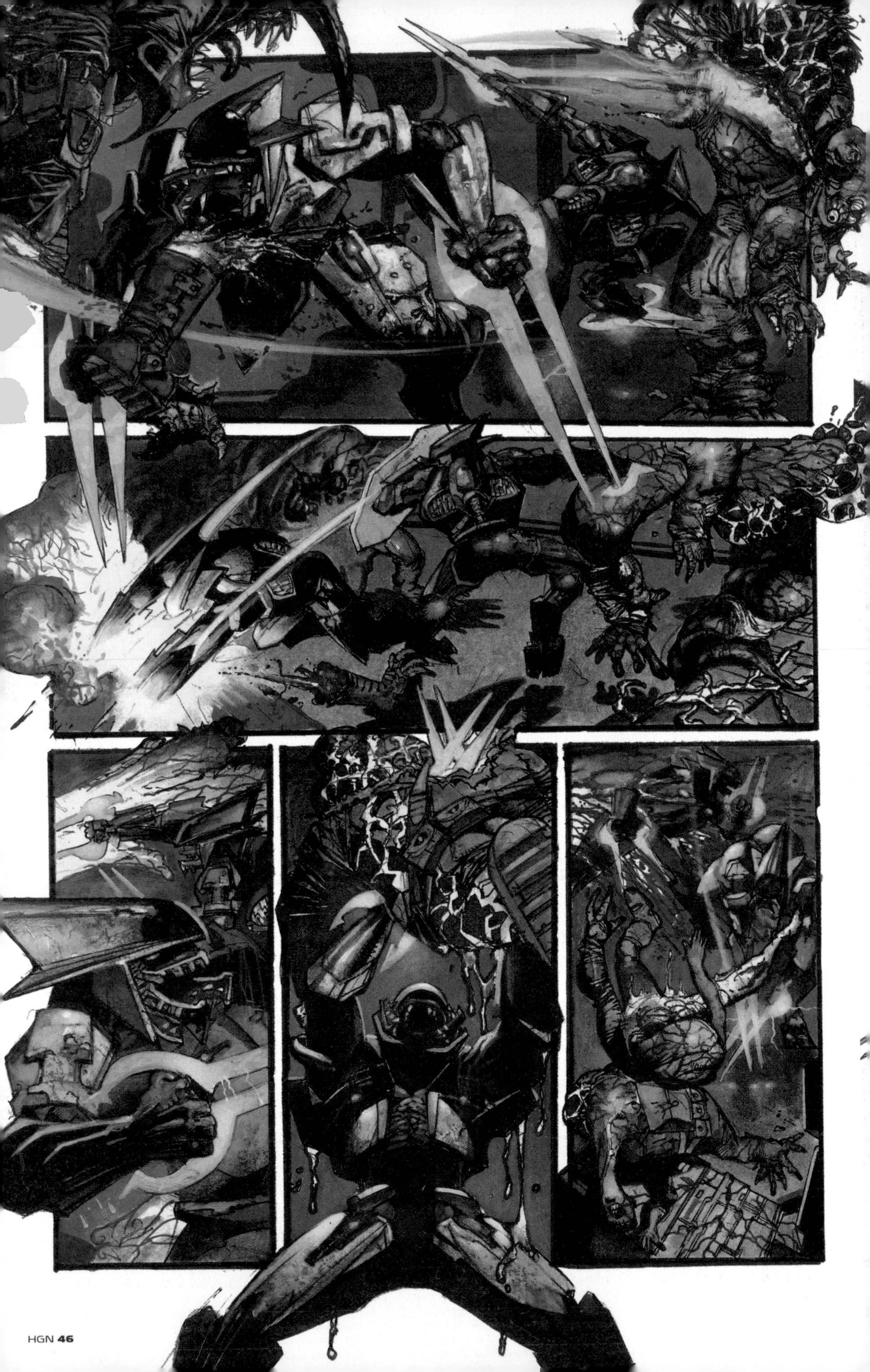

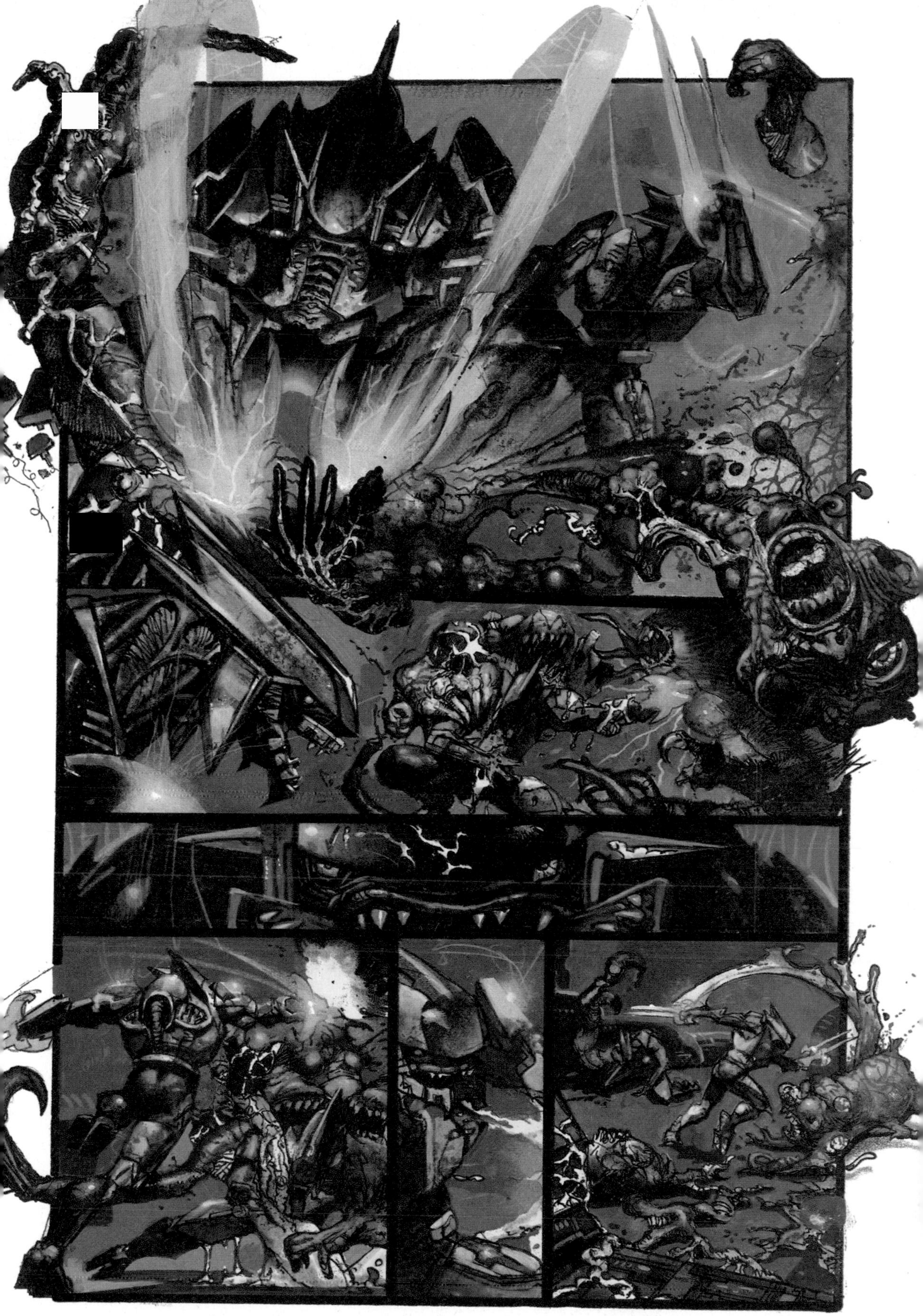

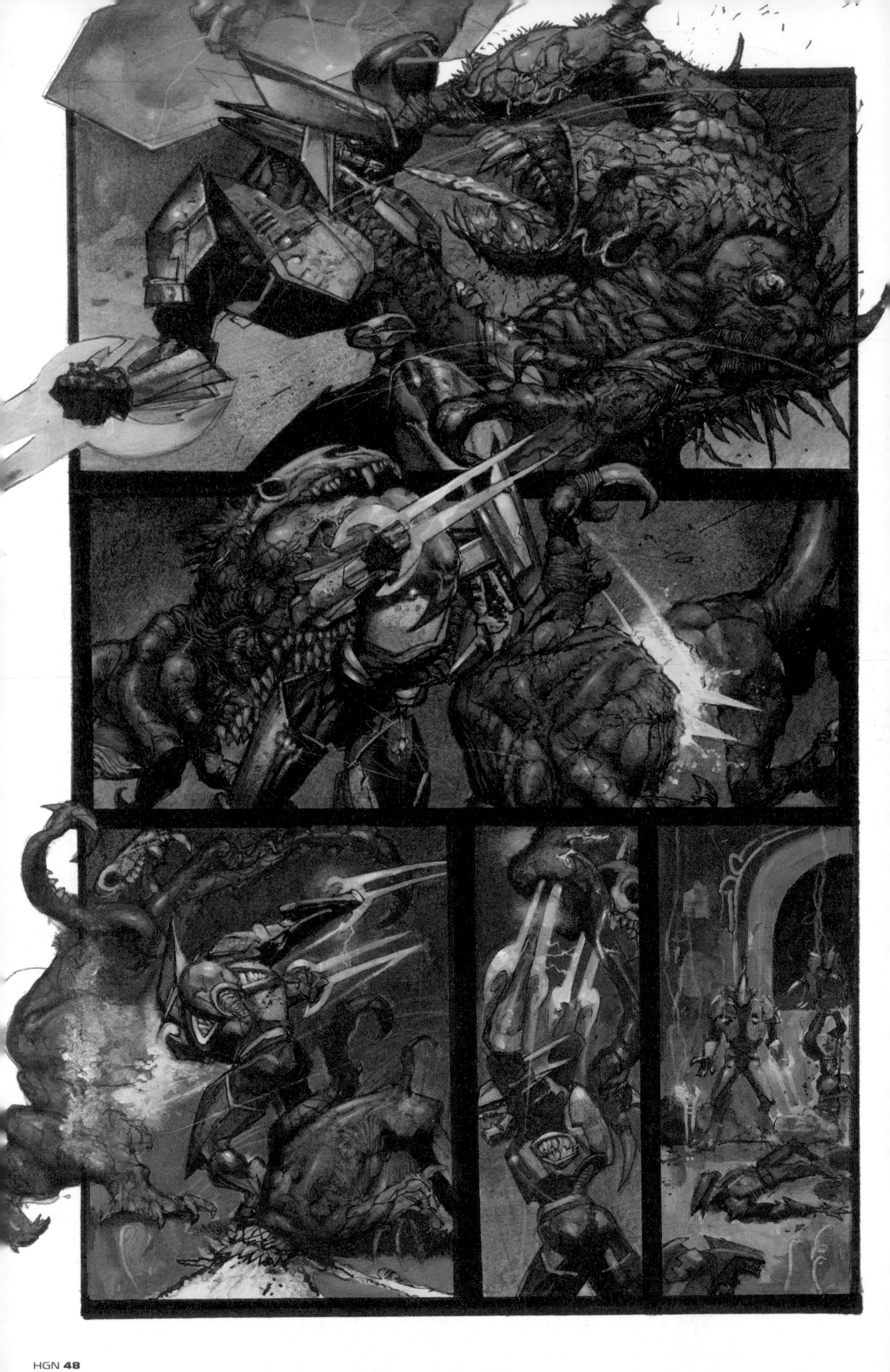

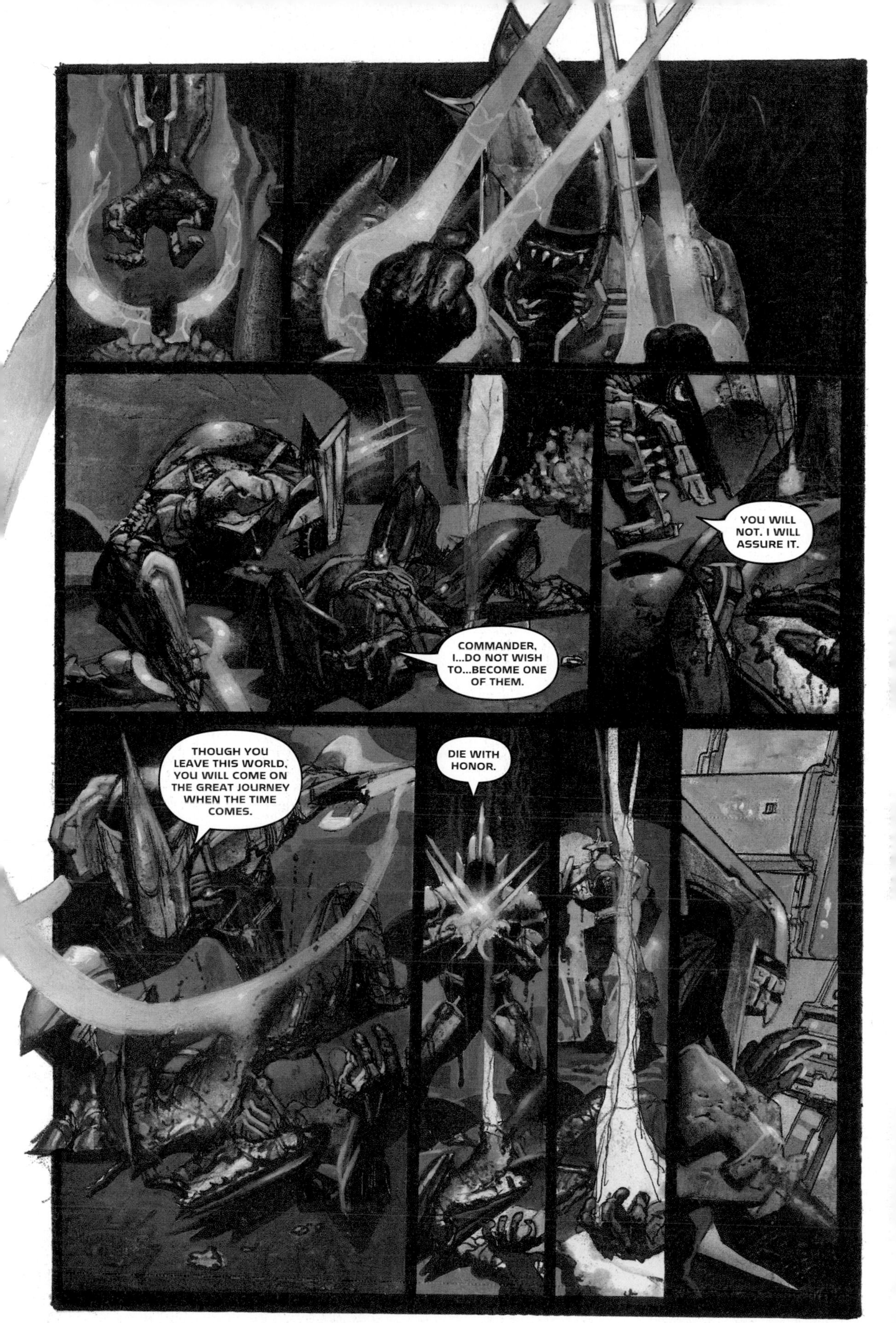
COMMANDER, I...DO NOT WISH TO...BECOME ONE OF THEM.
YOU WILL NOT. I WILL ASSURE IT.
THOUGH YOU LEAVE THIS WORLD, YOU WILL COME ON THE GREAT JOURNEY WHEN THE TIME COMES.
DIE WITH HONOR.

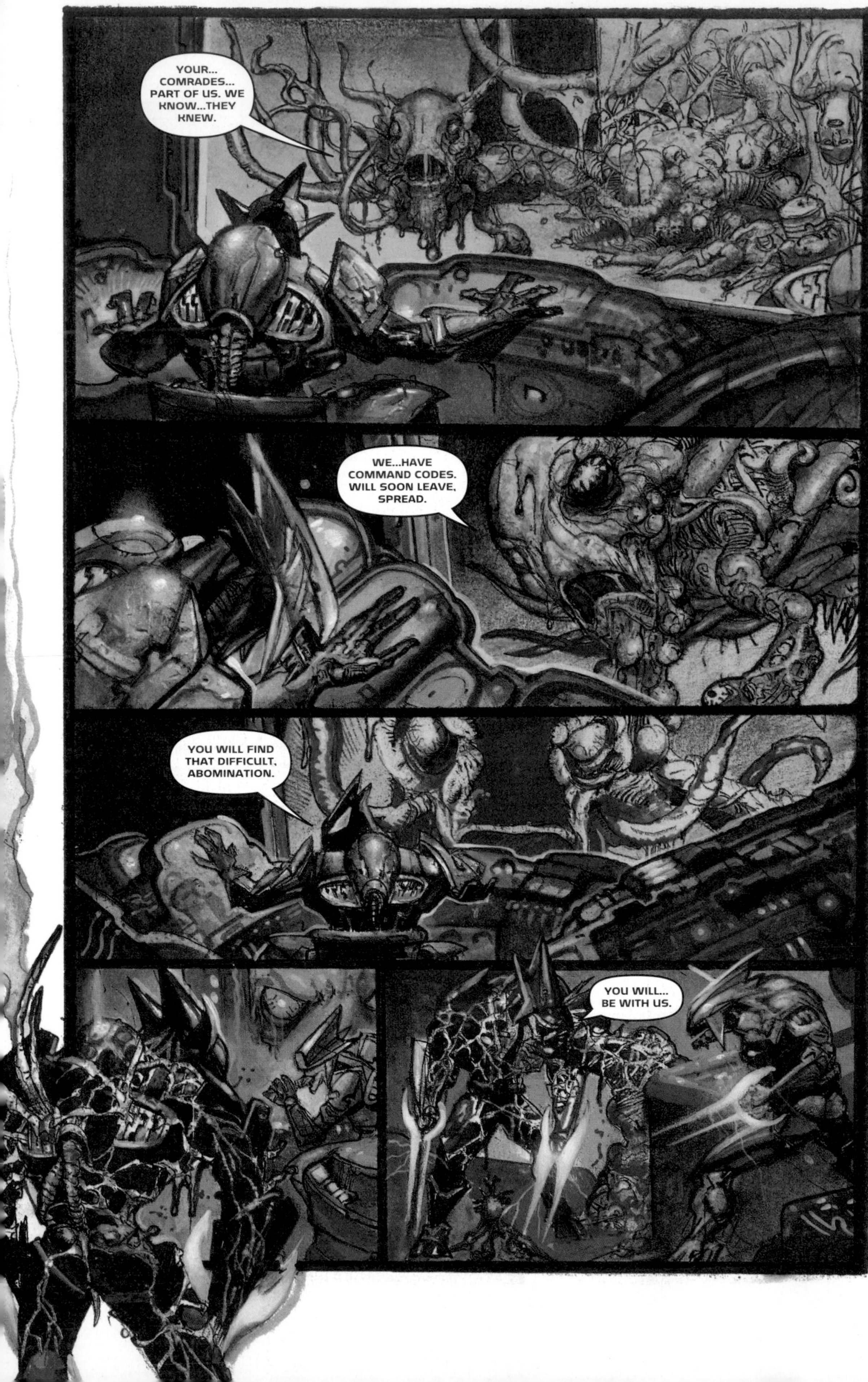
YOUR... COMRADES... PART OF US. WE KNOW...THEY KNEW.
WE...HAVE COMMAND CODES. WILL SOON LEAVE, SPREAD.
YOU WILL FIND THAT DIFFICULT, ABOMINATION.
YOU WILL... BE WITH US.

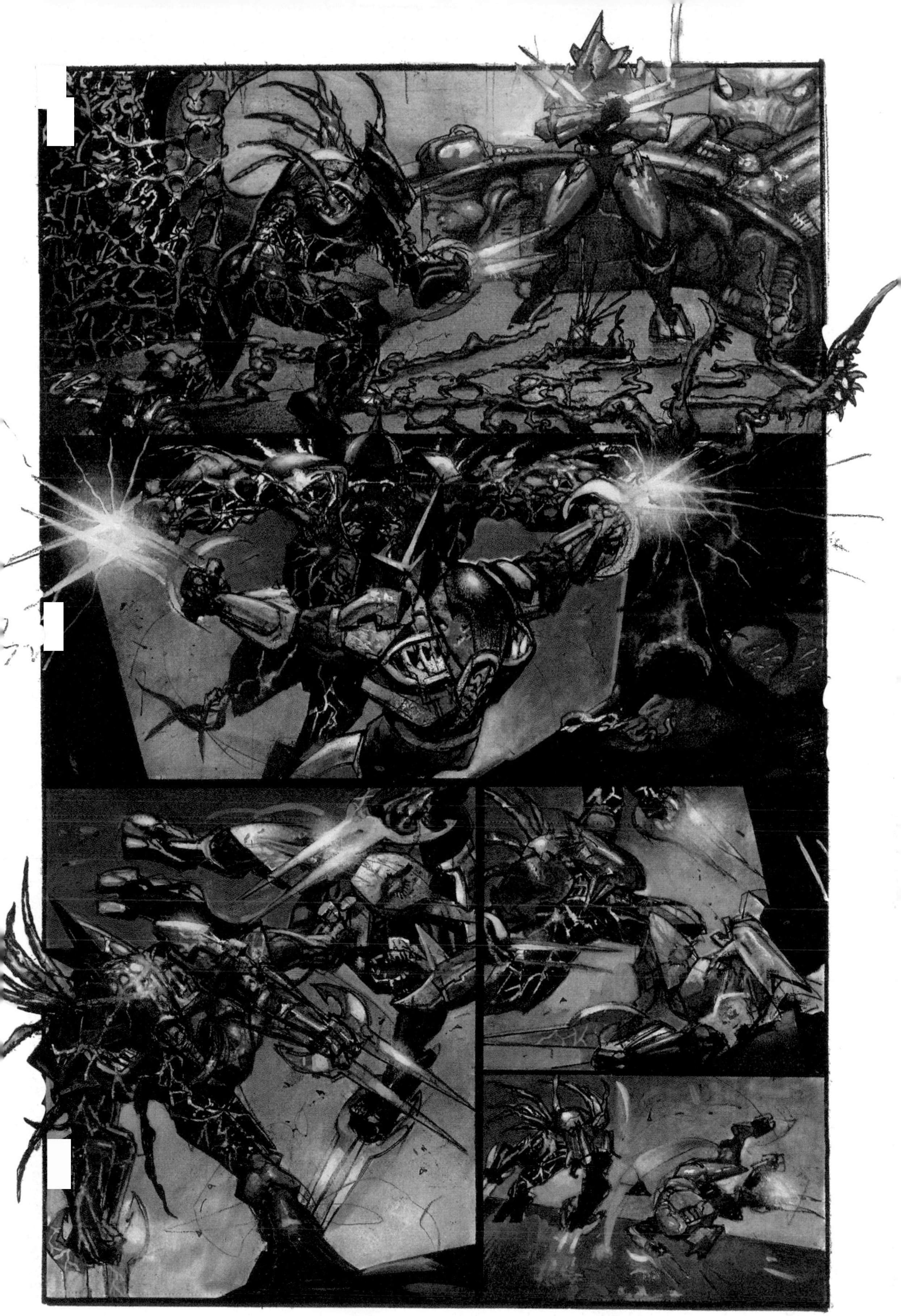

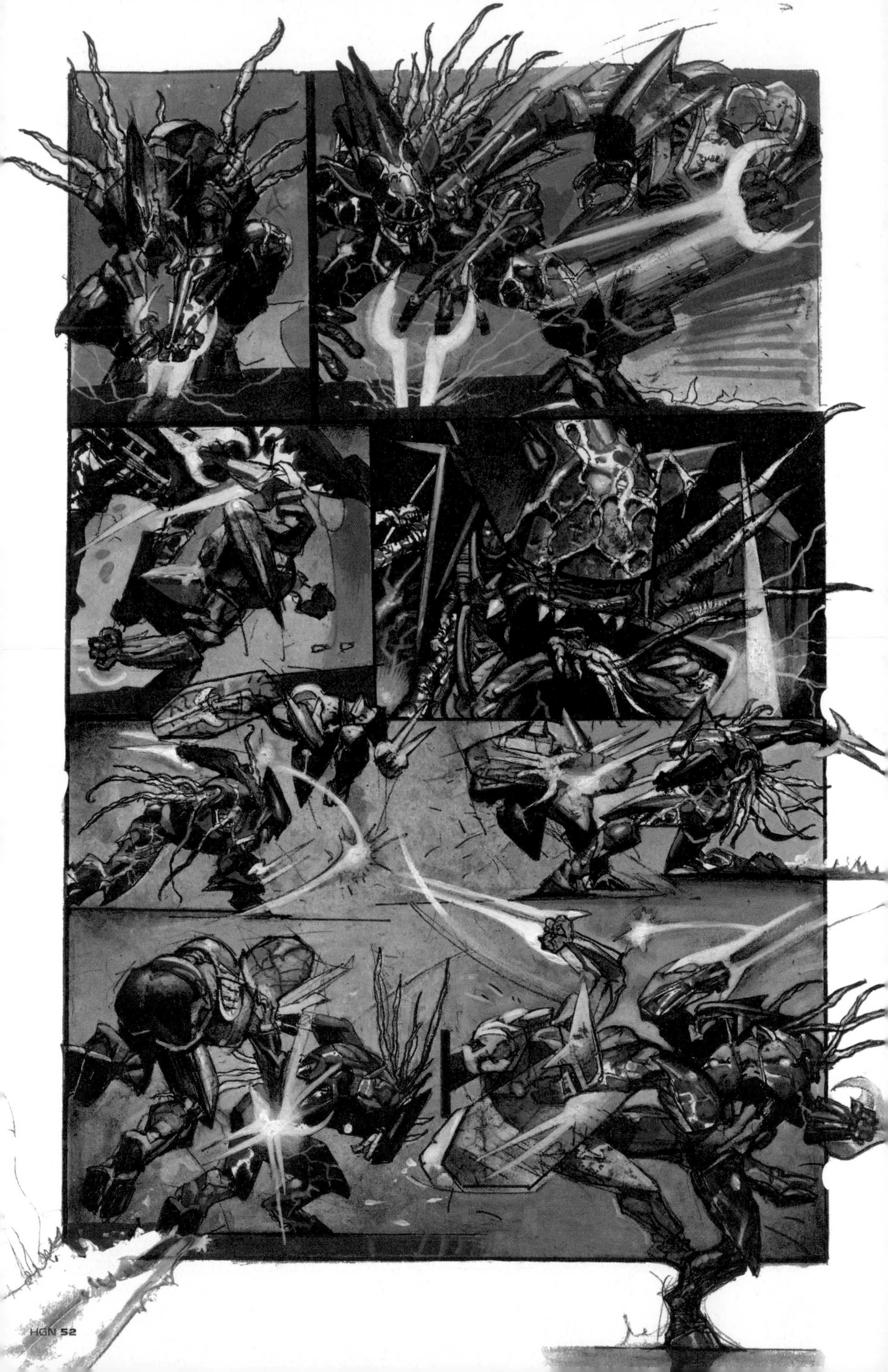

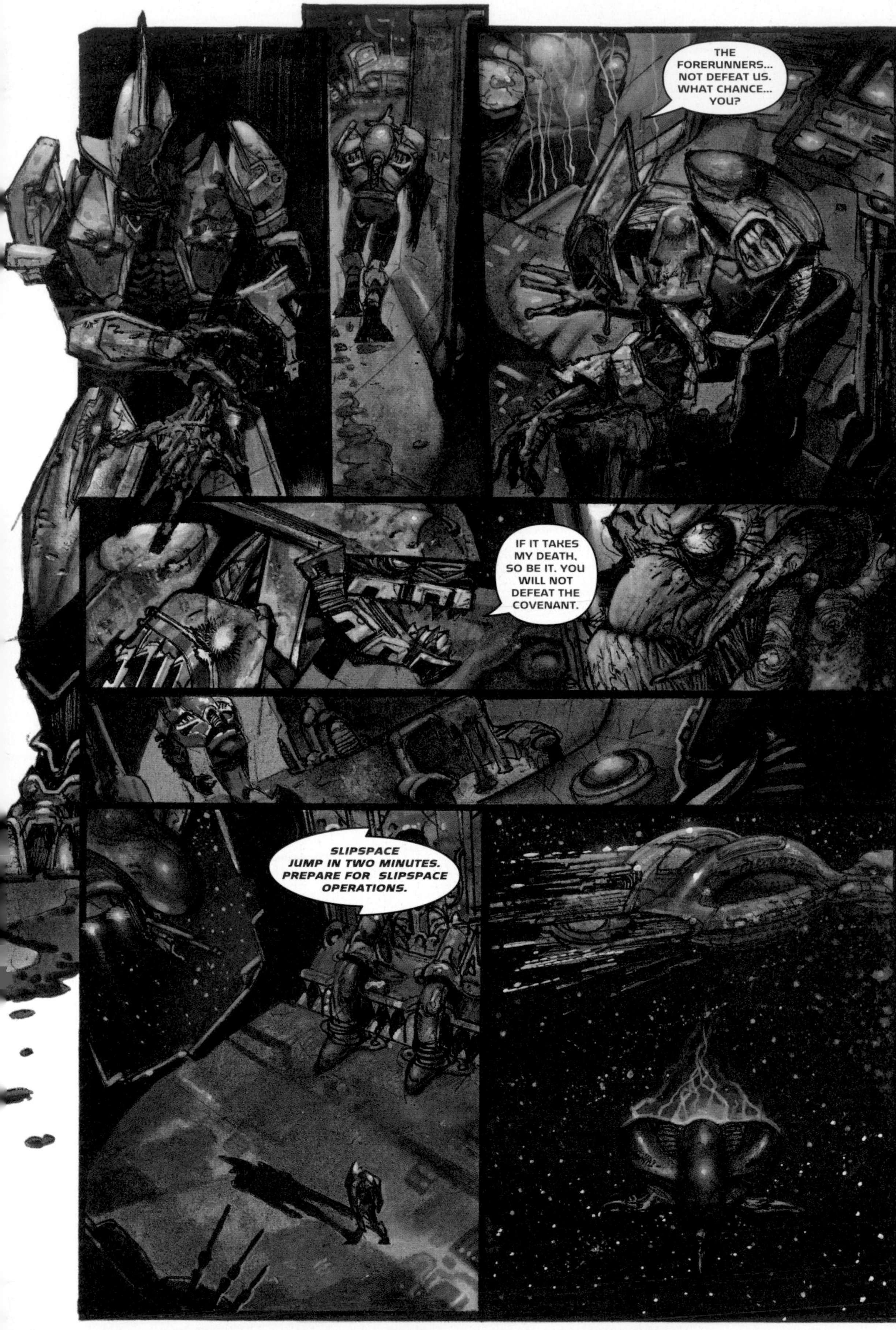
THE FORERUNNERS... NOT DEFEAT US. WHAT CHANCE... YOU?
IF IT TAKES MY DEATH, SO BE IT. YOU WILL NOT DEFEAT THE COVENANT.
SLIPSPACE JUMP IN TWO MINUTES. PREPARE FOR SLIPSPACE OPERATIONS.

Writing for HALO. Wow. What a responsibility. I have to imagine it feels something like writing for other major facets of our culture's entertainment, like Star Wars, but HALO has an added wrinkle. The people who love it have not just read or seen the adventures of Master Chief in the HALO universe; on some level they have lived it. They have been Master Chief and the Arbiter, seeing the universe through the eyes of one of its inhabitants instead of an omniscient third party. And because every person who has played a HALO game feels some ownership or connection to the primary characters, having trudged with them through the halls of the Library, the decks of the Pillar of Autumn, or the streets of Mombassa. The fans of HALO are just not a passive audience, but part of the story. That creates a connection that merely watching or reading a story unfold cannot emulate, and thus it creates a monumental task for a writer. You must not only write an entertaining and engaging story, but also do so in a way that makes all those people who invested part of themselves in the characters and universe feel that their part in it was respected and worthwhile. That the characters they know as a part of themselves are portrayed aptly. A heady task to be sure.

Luckily, in this story this difficulty was ameliorated by the fact the main character of the story was the SpecOps Commander, a character seen by players so they were familiar with him, but not as intimately as Master Chief or the Arbiter. I was given the chance to develop the background of an already existing character who was extremely interesting to begin with, which when working with a universe as complex as the HALO universe is always a challenge since you have so much background material to synch up with and yet still bring something new to the table to expand that universe. The SpecOps Commander's characterization must be matched up with what has been seen before, and then expanded upon as time and story allow.

– Lee Hammock

Lee Hammock is currently employed as a video game designer, but also works as a freelance comic book, trading card, role playing game, and newsletter writer. He's worked for **DC Comics**, spent time as a full time freelance writer, and is an all around professional geek. A graduate of the University of Georgia, he now lives in Raleigh, North Carolina.

Simon Bisley was chosen as the artist because he is one of the best action storytellers in the comics industry. Not since his amazing work with **Batman/Judge Dredd: Judgement On Gotham,** published almost fifteen years ago, has the Biz been involved in such a frenzied kinetic painting project as this one. His unique vision contributes thrills, energy and humor to the story, plus a majestic interpretation of the fighting Elite (ergonomically designed with backsides drawn as close to perfection as possible). By day he is mostly asleep. At midday, he paints in a cellar somewhere in Oxfordshire, England. And sometimes, as night falls, whenever he is not holding a paintbrush he can be heard banging loudly on the drums as he plays with his band.

ARMOR TESTING

JAY FAERBER, ED LEE, AND ANDREW ROBINSON

At the beginning of this project we had a meeting where we brainstormed about stuff we wanted to see – not just purely visual stuff, but interesting stuff that was totally outside the scope of the game. It just so happens that that initial meeting came right on the heels of several of us reading *Skunk Works* (a memoir about secret military projects at Lockheed). Some of the kernels from that initial meeting were duct-taped together and then pared down into a serviceable story. We wanted something that linked directly to the game, but would also make sense without that bridge. During development we had this idea that the armor had "just came up from Songnam" was going to be variable dialog (i.e. that it could've come up from Pittsburgh, Shanghai, or Essen as well – depending on what difficulty level you were playing on). But the idea that the Mjolnir/Spartan II Project is bigger than John-117, that dear old *Ma-117* didn't just knit him that suit of Mark V Mjolnir Assault Armor when he was a wee bairn, is something that never came across very well in the games – and at times seemed to be at direct odds with other aspects of the fiction.

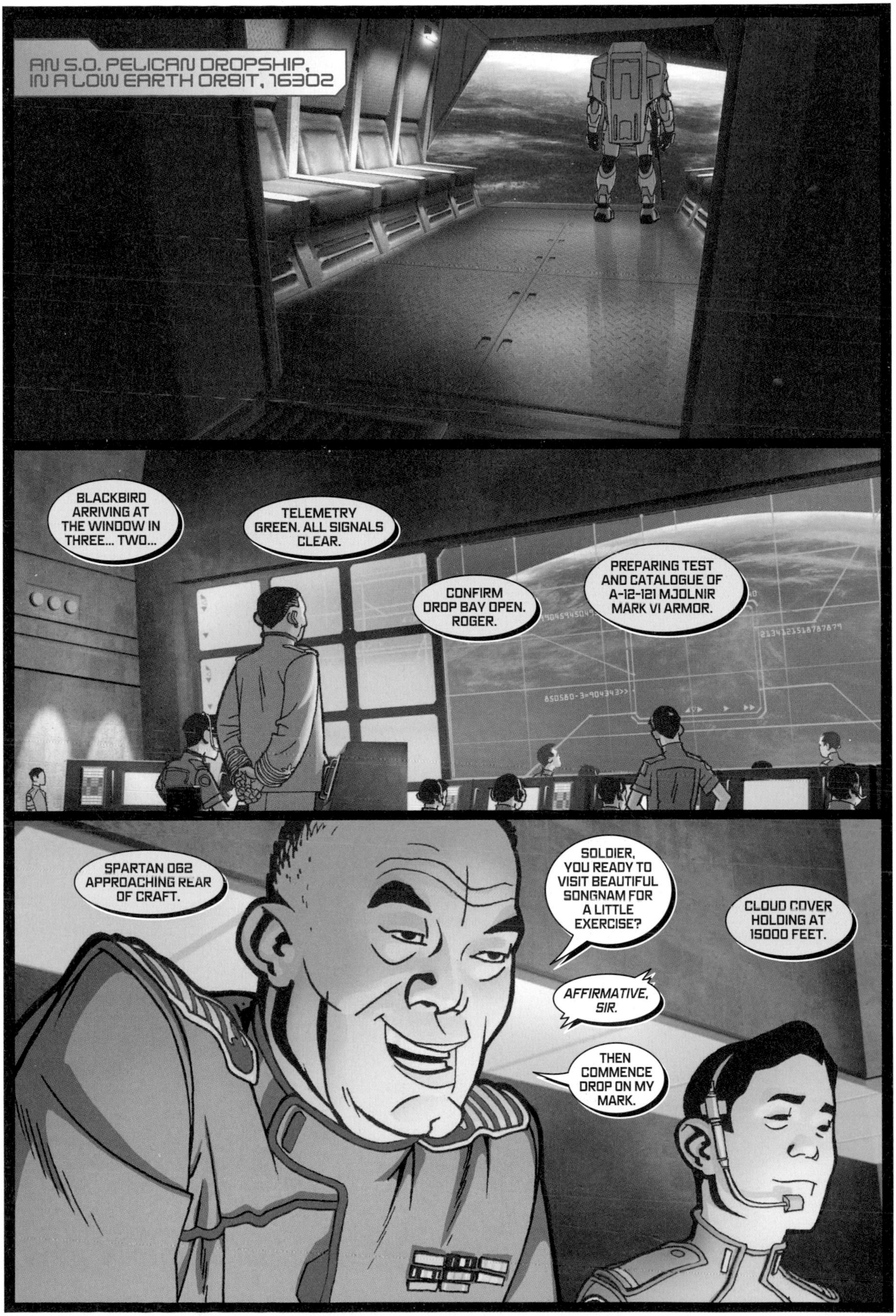
AN S.O. PELICAN DROPSHIP,
IN A LOW EARTH ORBIT, 16302
BLACKBIRD ARRIVING AT THE WINDOW IN THREE... TWO...
TELEMETRY GREEN. ALL SIGNALS CLEAR.
CONFIRM DROP BAY OPEN. ROGER.
PREPARING TEST AND CATALOGUE OF A-12-121 MJOLNIR MARK VI ARMOR.
SPARTAN 062 APPROACHING REAR OF CRAFT.
SOLDIER, YOU READY TO VISIT BEAUTIFUL SONGNAM FOR A LITTLE EXERCISE?
AFFIRMATIVE, SIR.
THEN COMMENCE DROP ON MY MARK.
CLOUD COVER HOLDING AT 15000 FEET.

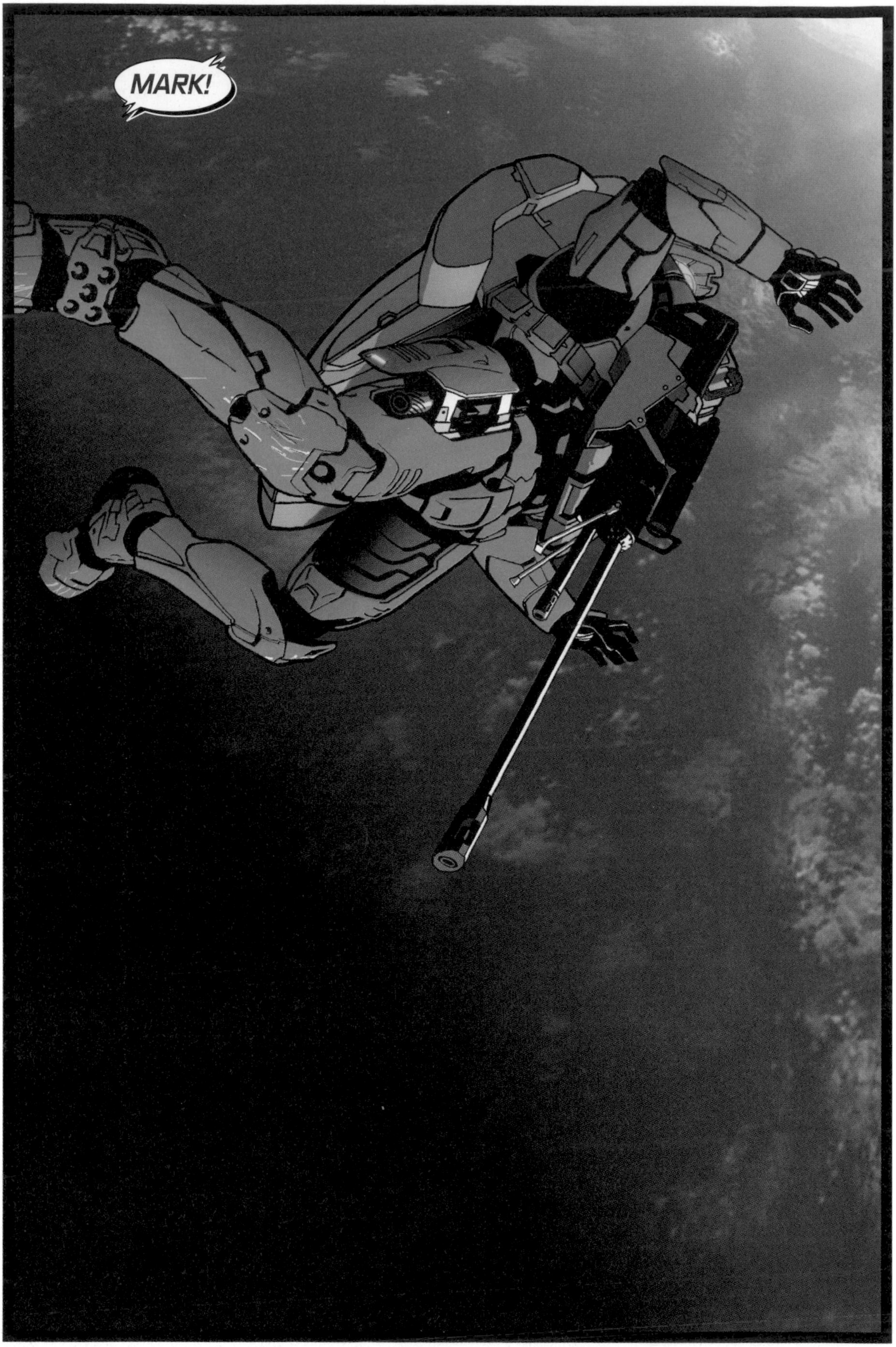
MARK!

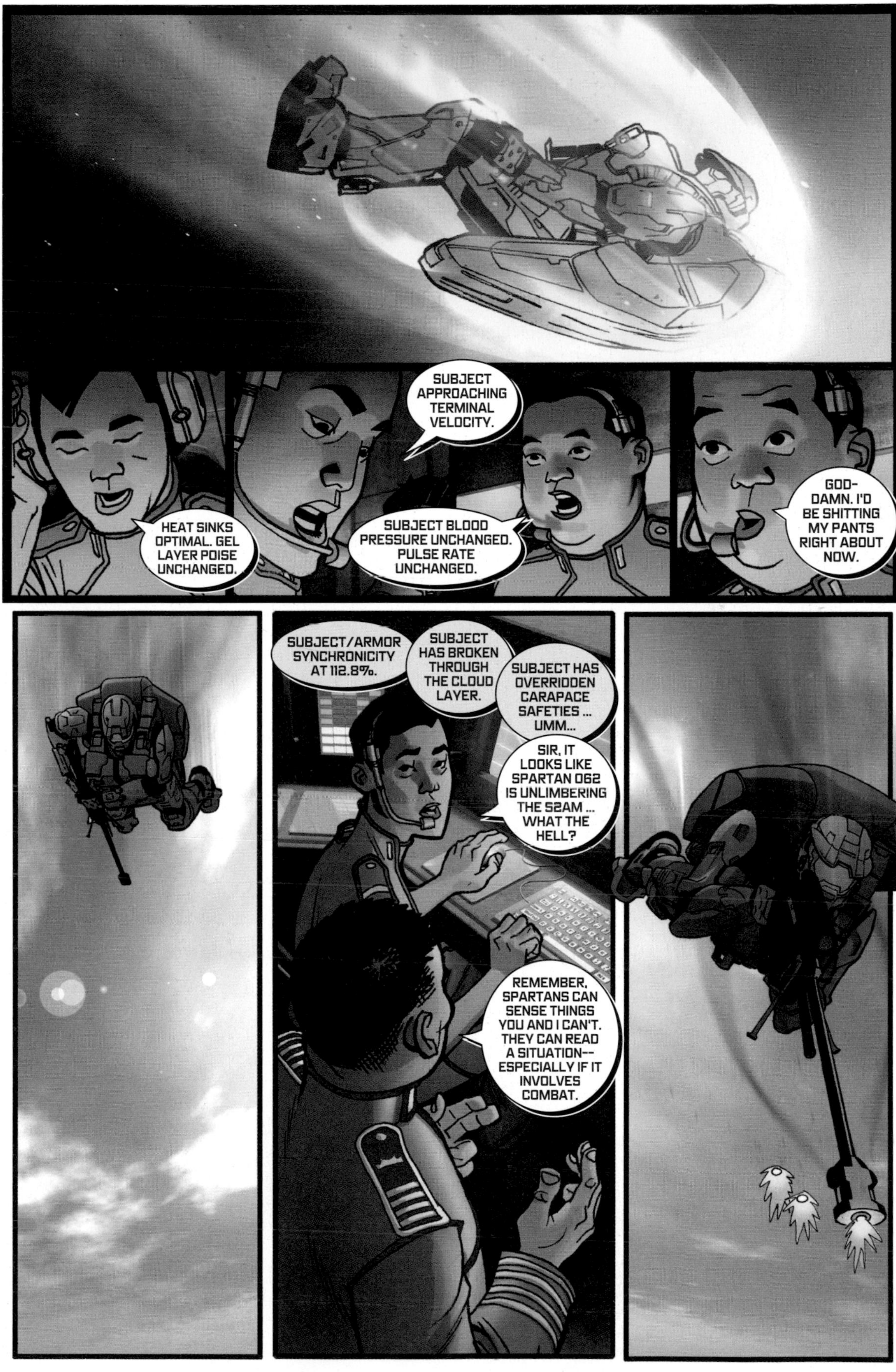
HEAT SINKS OPTIMAL. GEL LAYER POISE UNCHANGED.
SUBJECT APPROACHING TERMINAL VELOCITY.
SUBJECT BLOOD PRESSURE UNCHANGED. PULSE RATE UNCHANGED.
GOD-DAMN. I'D BE SHITTING MY PANTS RIGHT ABOUT NOW.
SUBJECT/ARMOR SYNCHRONICITY AT 112.8%.
SUBJECT HAS BROKEN THROUGH THE CLOUD LAYER.
SUBJECT HAS OVERRIDDEN CARAPACE SAFETIES ... UMM...
SIR, IT LOOKS LIKE SPARTAN 062 IS UNLIMBERING THE S2AM ... WHAT THE HELL?
REMEMBER, SPARTANS CAN SENSE THINGS YOU AND I CAN'T. THEY CAN READ A SITUATION-- ESPECIALLY IF IT INVOLVES COMBAT.

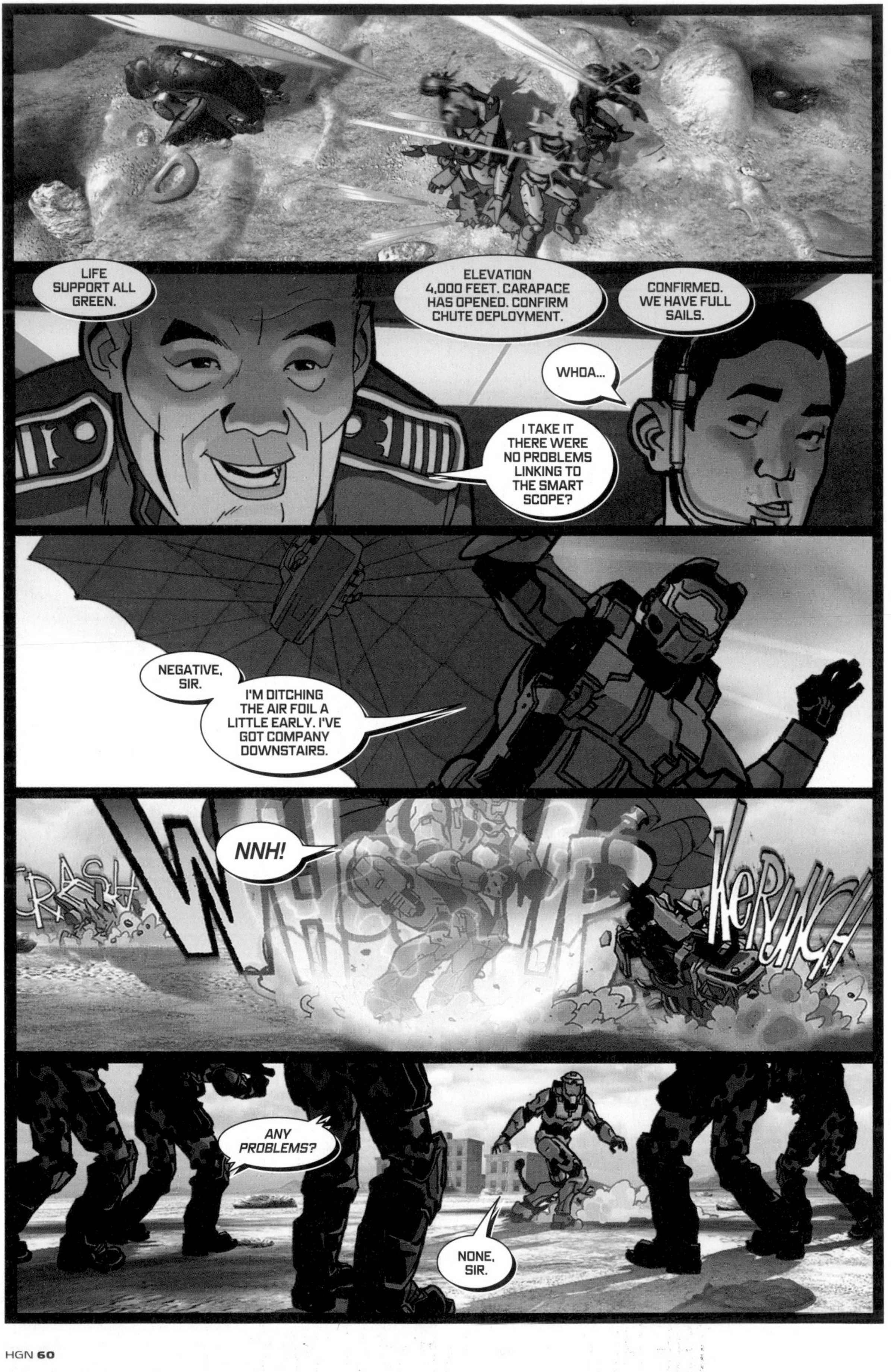
LIFE SUPPORT ALL GREEN.
ELEVATION 4,000 FEET. CARAPACE HAS OPENED. CONFIRM CHUTE DEPLOYMENT.
CONFIRMED. WE HAVE FULL SAILS.
WHOA...
I TAKE IT THERE WERE NO PROBLEMS LINKING TO THE SMART SCOPE?
NEGATIVE, SIR.
I'M DITCHING THE AIR FOIL A LITTLE EARLY. I'VE GOT COMPANY DOWNSTAIRS.
CRASH
NNH!
KERUNCH
ANY PROBLEMS?
NONE, SIR.

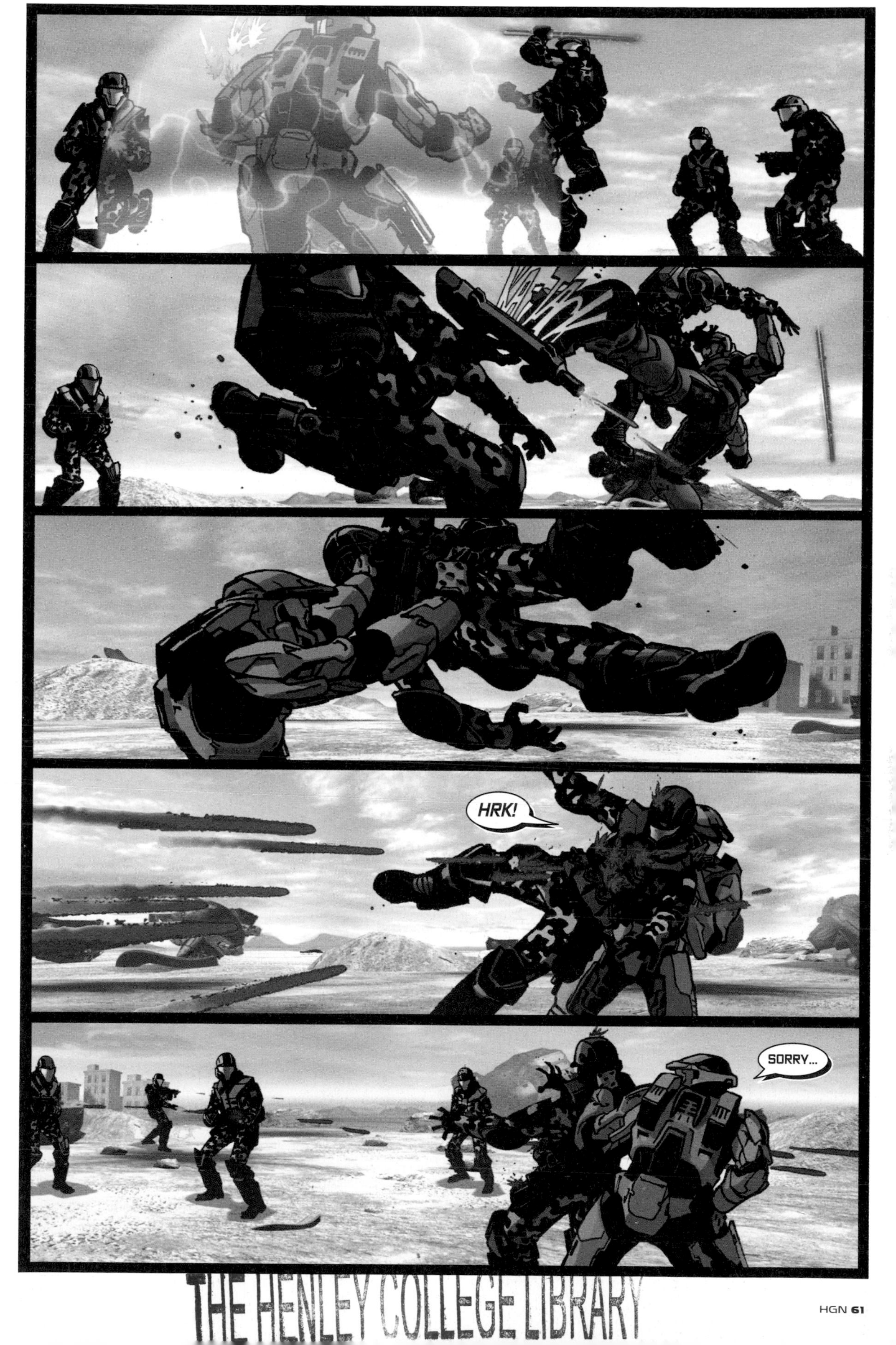
HRK!
SORRY...

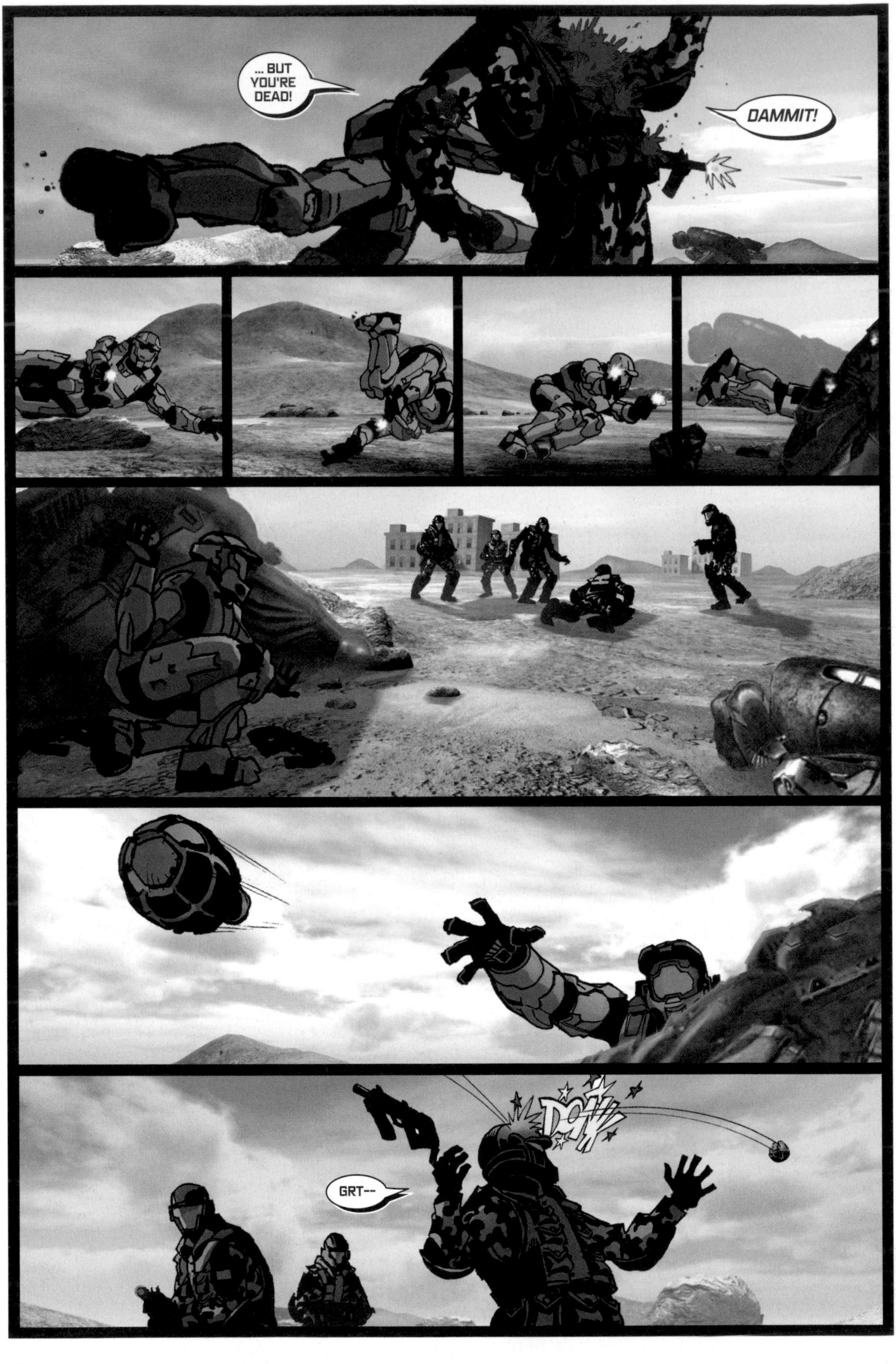
... BUT YOU'RE DEAD!
DAMMIT!
GRT--

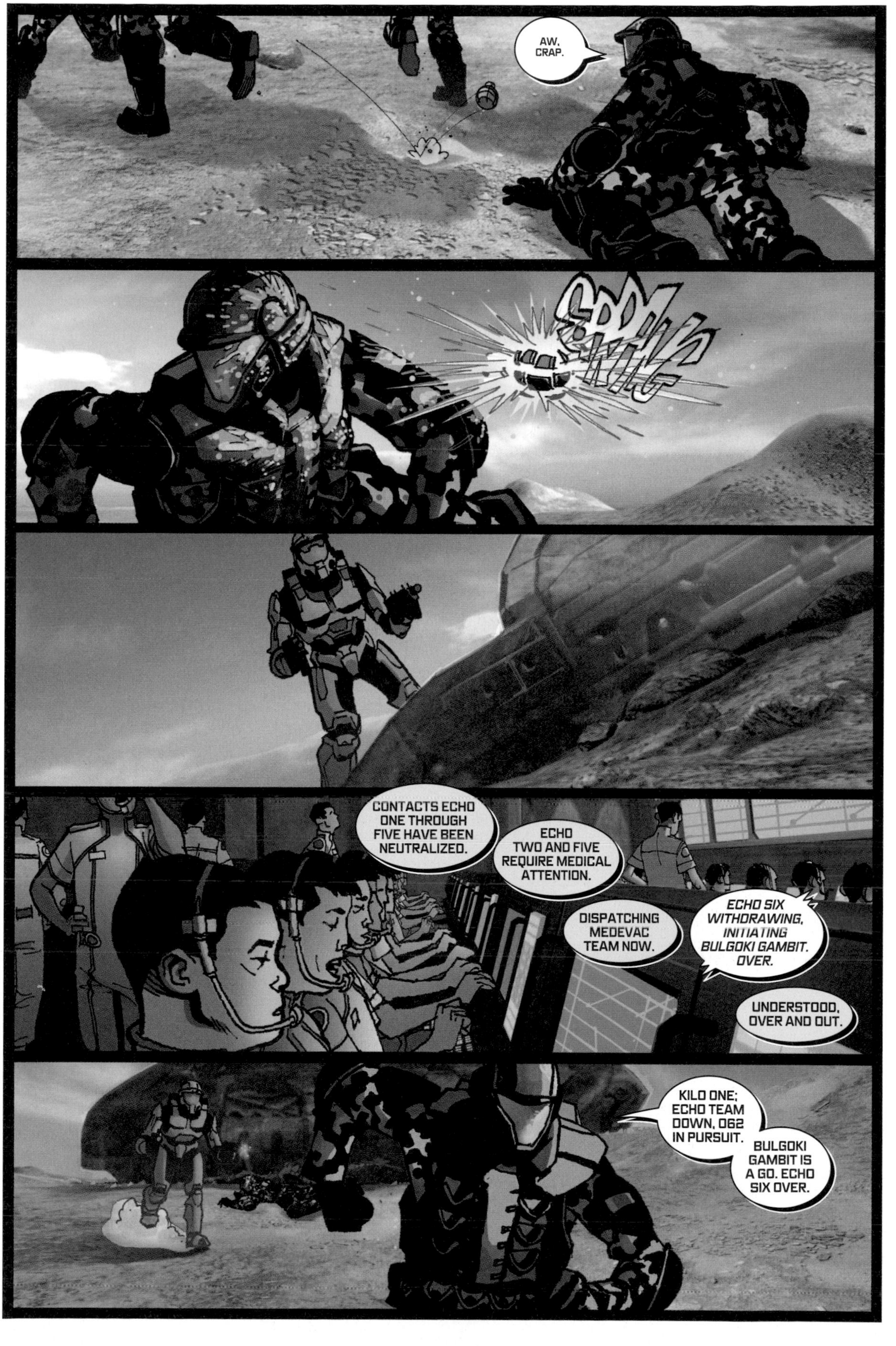
AW, CRAP.
SPANG
CONTACTS ECHO ONE THROUGH FIVE HAVE BEEN NEUTRALIZED.
ECHO TWO AND FIVE REQUIRE MEDICAL ATTENTION.
DISPATCHING MEDEVAC TEAM NOW.
ECHO SIX WITHDRAWING, INITIATING BULGOKI GAMBIT. OVER.
UNDERSTOOD, OVER AND OUT.
KILO ONE; ECHO TEAM DOWN, 062 IN PURSUIT.
BULGOKI GAMBIT IS A GO. ECHO SIX OVER.

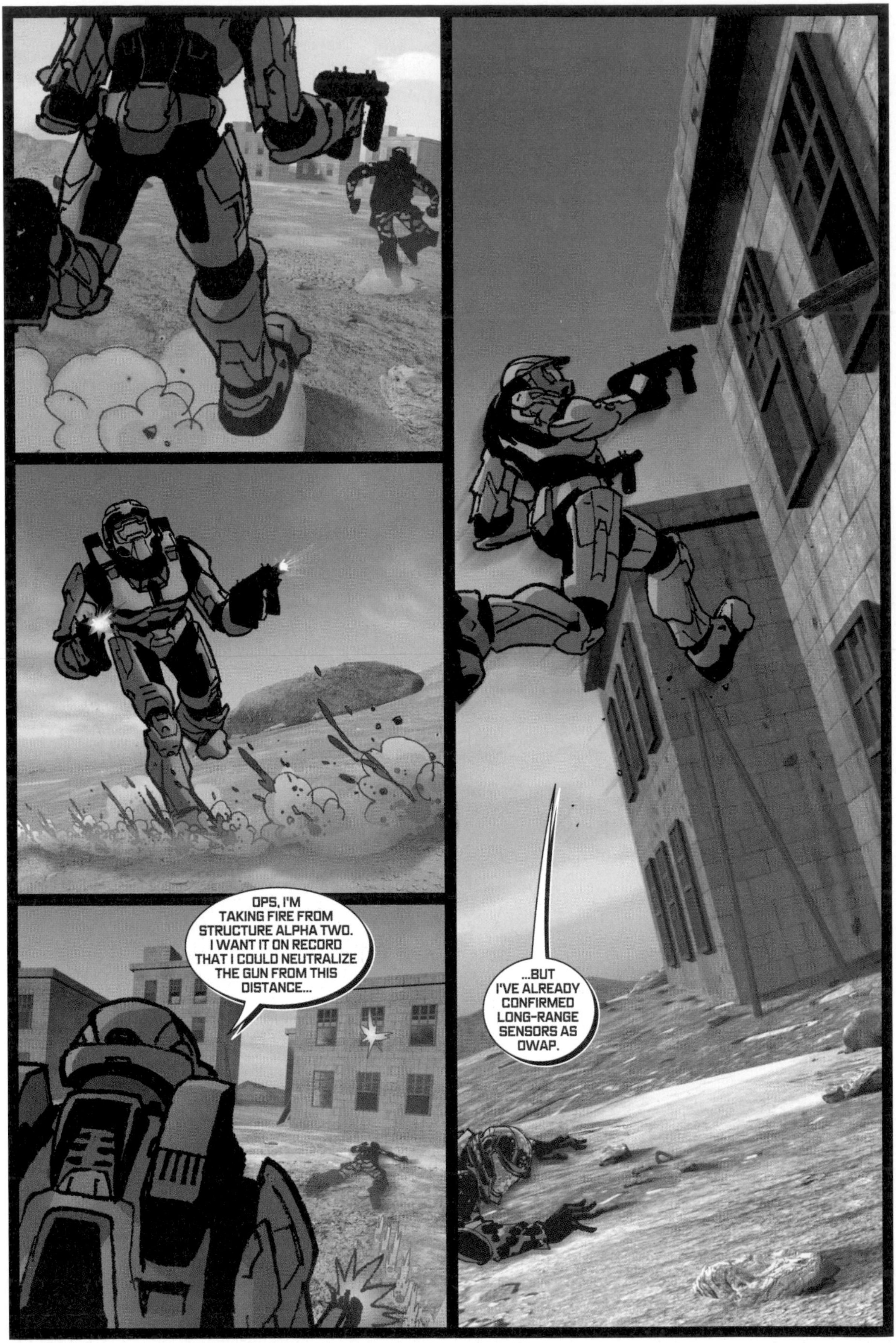
OPS, I'M TAKING FIRE FROM STRUCTURE ALPHA TWO. I WANT IT ON RECORD THAT I COULD NEUTRALIZE THE GUN FROM THIS DISTANCE...
...BUT I'VE ALREADY CONFIRMED LONG-RANGE SENSORS AS OWAP.

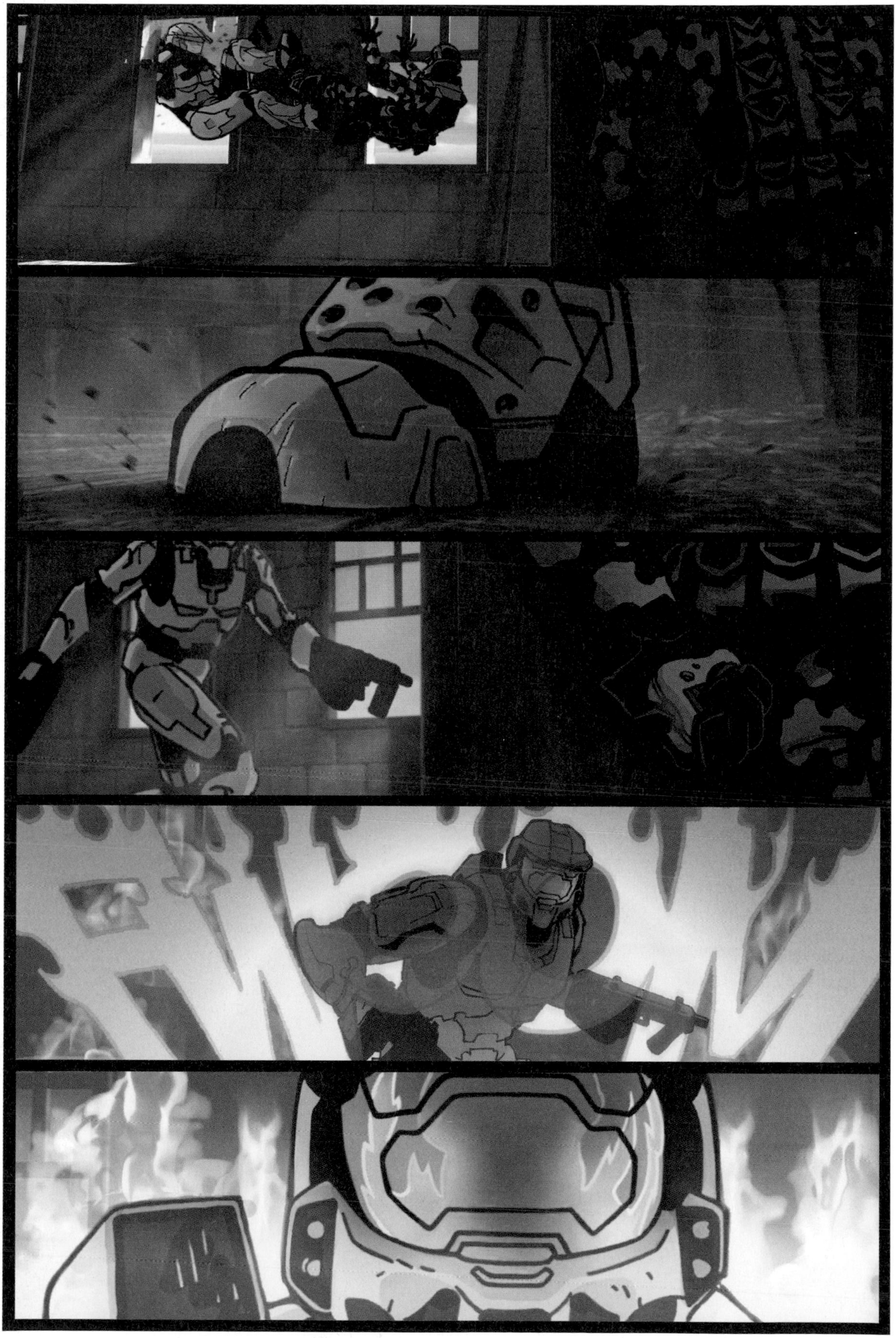

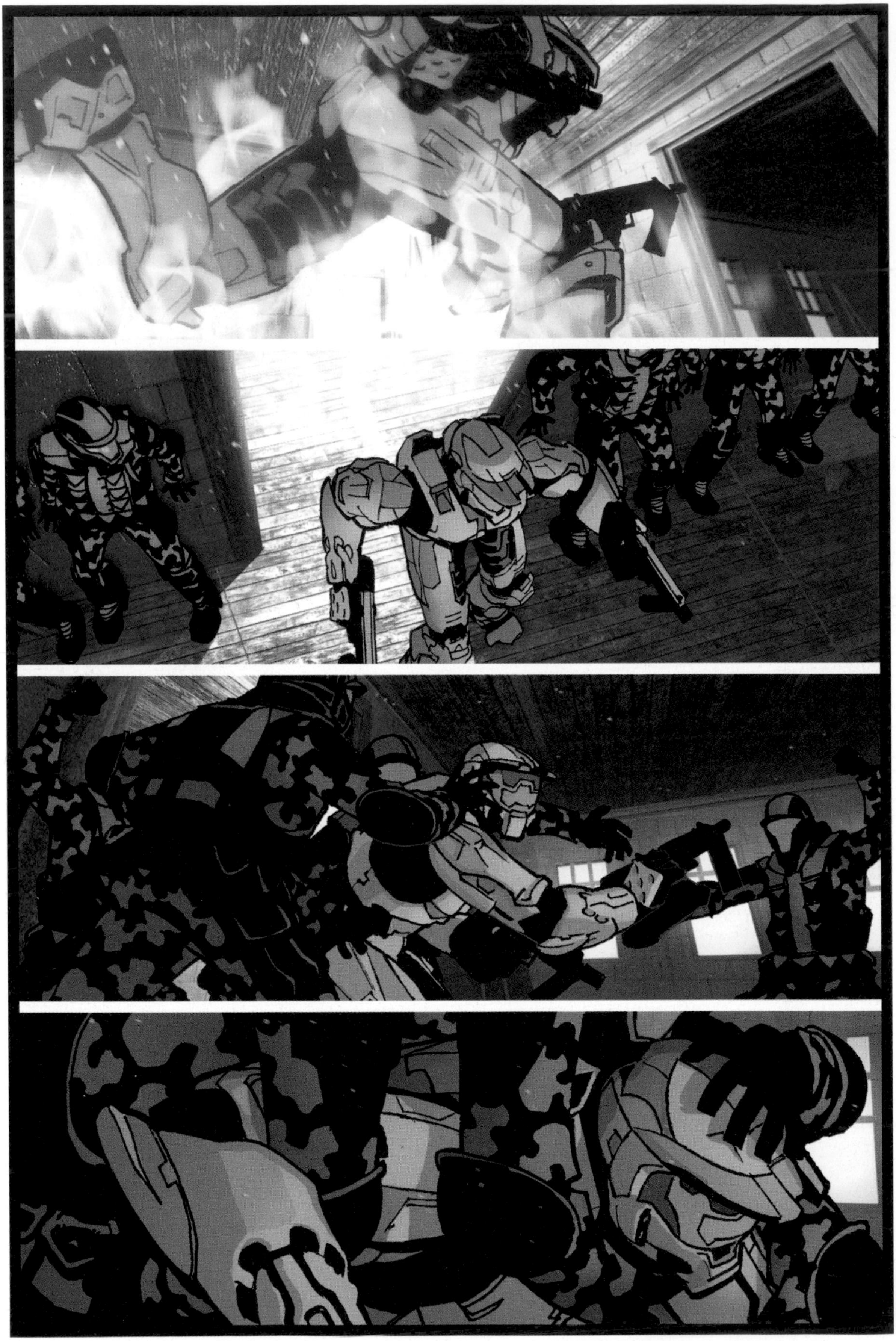

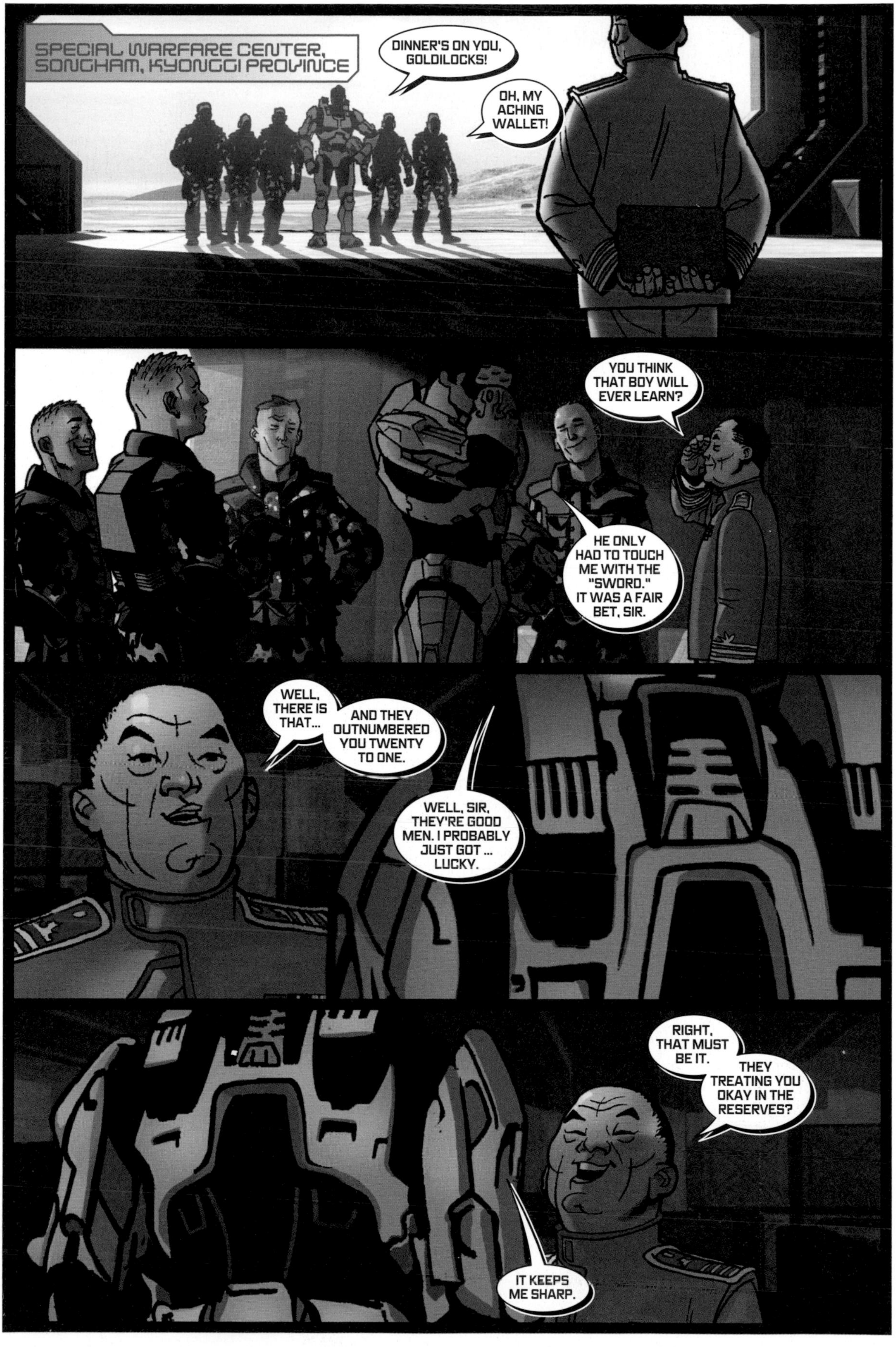
SPECIAL WARFARE CENTER, SONGHAM, KYONGGI PROVINCE
DINNER'S ON YOU, GOLDILOCKS!
OH, MY ACHING WALLET!
YOU THINK THAT BOY WILL EVER LEARN?
HE ONLY HAD TO TOUCH ME WITH THE "SWORD." IT WAS A FAIR BET, SIR.
WELL, THERE IS THAT...
AND THEY OUTNUMBERED YOU TWENTY TO ONE.
WELL, SIR, THEY'RE GOOD MEN. I PROBABLY JUST GOT ... LUCKY.
RIGHT, THAT MUST BE IT.
THEY TREATING YOU OKAY IN THE RESERVES?
IT KEEPS ME SHARP.

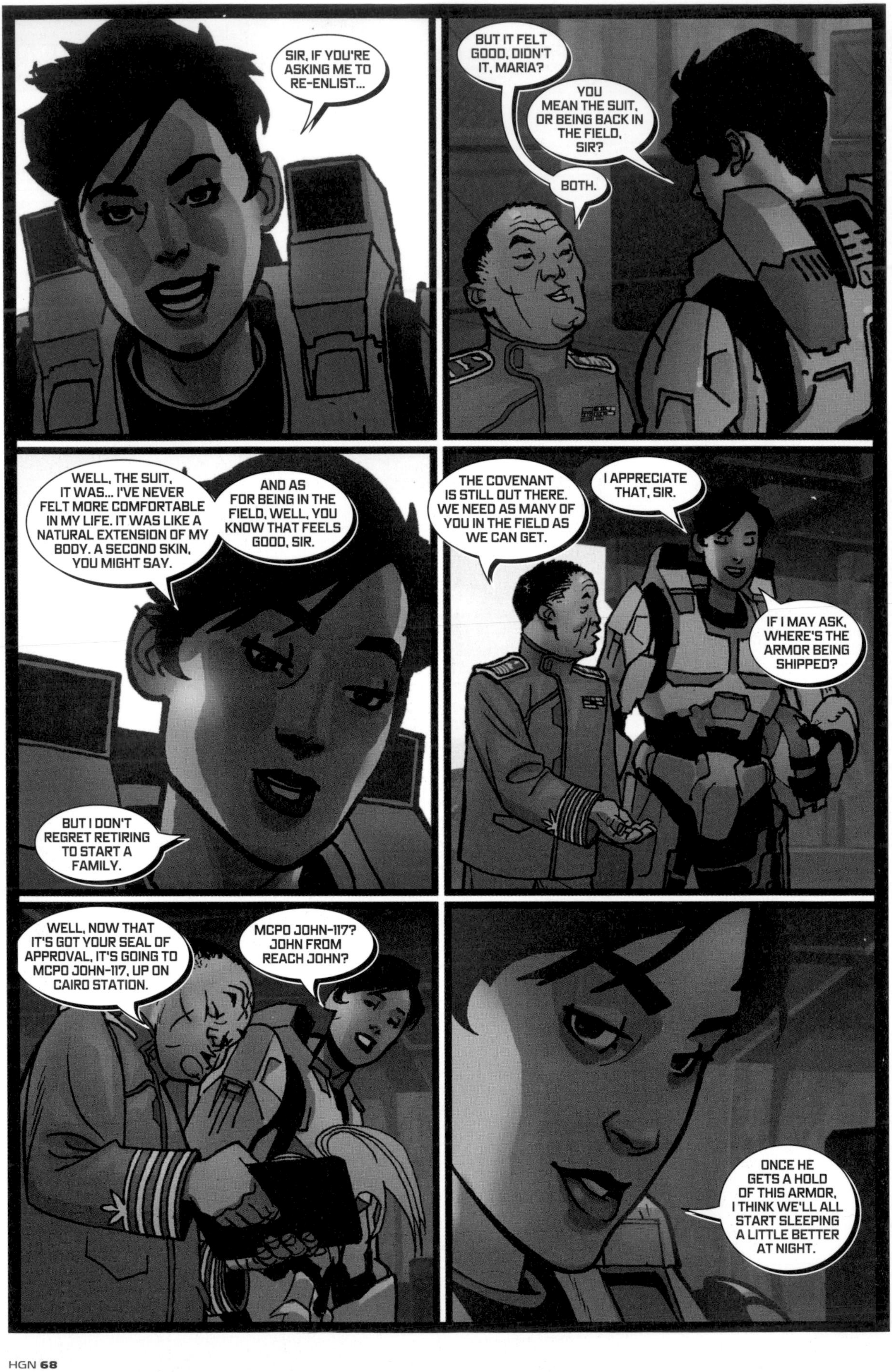
SIR, IF YOU'RE ASKING ME TO RE-ENLIST...
BUT IT FELT GOOD, DIDN'T IT, MARIA?
YOU MEAN THE SUIT, OR BEING BACK IN THE FIELD, SIR?
BOTH.
WELL, THE SUIT, IT WAS... I'VE NEVER FELT MORE COMFORTABLE IN MY LIFE. IT WAS LIKE A NATURAL EXTENSION OF MY BODY. A SECOND SKIN, YOU MIGHT SAY.
AND AS FOR BEING IN THE FIELD, WELL, YOU KNOW THAT FEELS GOOD, SIR.
BUT I DON'T REGRET RETIRING TO START A FAMILY.
THE COVENANT IS STILL OUT THERE. WE NEED AS MANY OF YOU IN THE FIELD AS WE CAN GET.
I APPRECIATE THAT, SIR.
IF I MAY ASK, WHERE'S THE ARMOR BEING SHIPPED?
WELL, NOW THAT IT'S GOT YOUR SEAL OF APPROVAL, IT'S GOING TO MCPO JOHN-117, UP ON CAIRO STATION.
MCPO JOHN-117? JOHN FROM REACH JOHN?
ONCE HE GETS A HOLD OF THIS ARMOR, I THINK WE'LL ALL START SLEEPING A LITTLE BETTER AT NIGHT.

I've been writing comic books since around 1998 - professionally, at least. I've actually been writing comics as long as I can remember. When I was a kid, I'd write and draw my own comics. They featured original characters, and when I say "original," I mean they were blatant rip-offs of whatever was influencing me at the time. Anything from comic books to cartoons to movies to video games. Since I became a professional writer, I've had the chance to be involved - however peripherally - with some amazing pop culture icons. I can't begin to describe how cool it was to get the call to pitch for a Halo comic book.

One of the favorite pastimes amongst comic book creators is to bemoan the current state of the industry - the fact that comics don't sell as well as they did when we were kids, and you could pick them up in any corner grocery story or pharmacy. It's a popular theory that video games have contributed to the erosion of the comic book audience. Who wants to read about a super-powered adventurer in a comic book when you can become one in a video game?

And now here I am, writing a comic book based on a video game. It's the best of both worlds! Personally, I don't subscribe to the theory that video games are stealing the audience from comics. In fact, I think there's a huge crossover appeal between the two mediums, and I bet this specific project will help expose even more Halo fans to comics, and vice versa.

Comics and video games -- two fantastic mediums that complement each other perfectly.

– Jay Faerber

Ed Lee and Andrew Robinson were the chosen ones for the art team in this story. Andrew's extensive background working in comics such as **Starman, Hawkman,** and his original work, **Dusty Lonestar** have provided the dynamic sketches, inks and color that served as the base for this action-oriented storytelling piece. He is based in Los Angeles, and is being kept busy at the moment by his art exhibitions.

Ed, a very prolific and highly skilled artist/animator whose background is in movie animation and illustration, applied Andrew's art to a new and exciting level. Giving it new intensity and depth via computer enhancement, the end results bring a fresher and more exciting visual feel created by this hybrid of technique and talent. Ed is currently teaching animation in Dongseo University in Busan, South Korea, and is constantly updating his website with amazing work.

BREAKING QUARANTINE

TSUTOMU NIHEI

One of the jobs that we set out to do with this book was to carve in stone certain events from the extended universe that deviated from our original vision of the story. Sergeant Johnson's escape from the Flood was one of those. And, aside from being beautiful and exciting, that is exactly what "Breaking Quarantine" is all about. Johnson's adventure was one of the side stories that had to be left to the player's imagination. We had the benefit of fantastic communication with the artist/writer for "Breaking Quarantine" - despite the fact that he lives on the other side of the planet and does not speak very much English. He did have the benefit of being the most hardcore fan* of the game in Japan and owning a summer home in my head (apparently). Nihei-san sent in his "proposal" before we could even get references for his story to the post. We sent them along anyway, not because he needed them, but because we thought he might just like to have them. As with all of these stories, I wish we had more space (and time and money and...).

* Not the best player in Japan, just the most hardcore fan. (^o^)

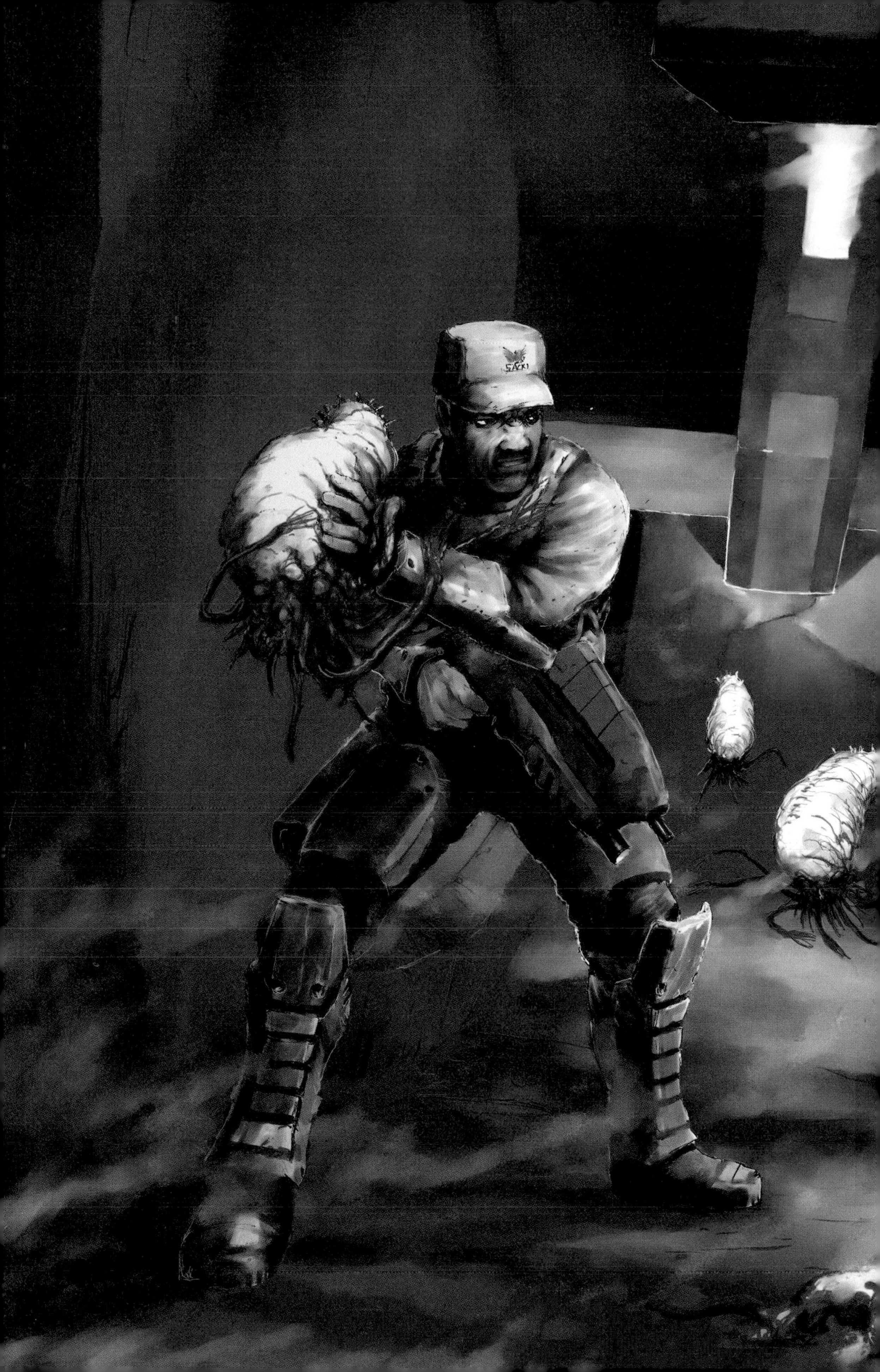

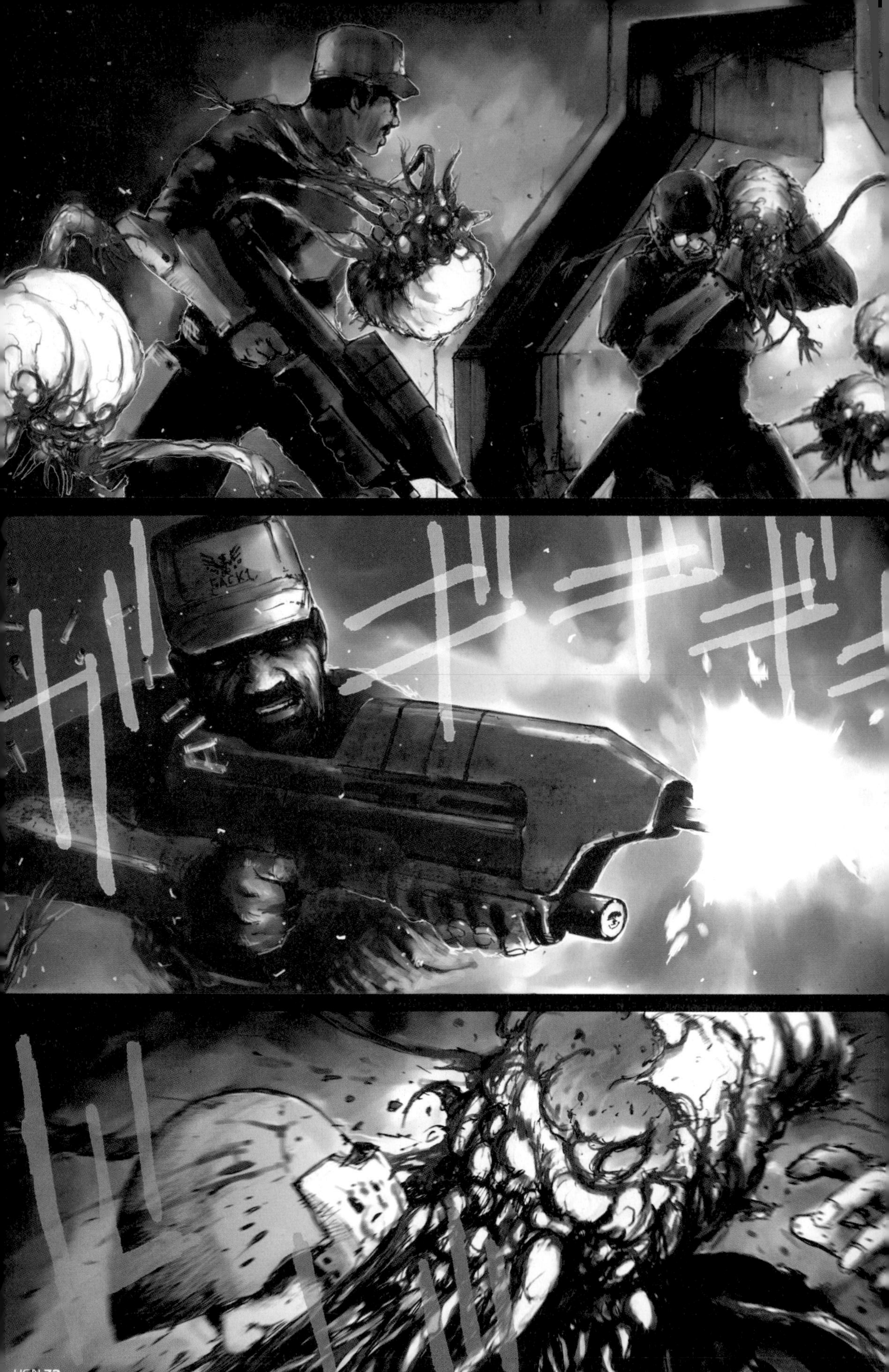

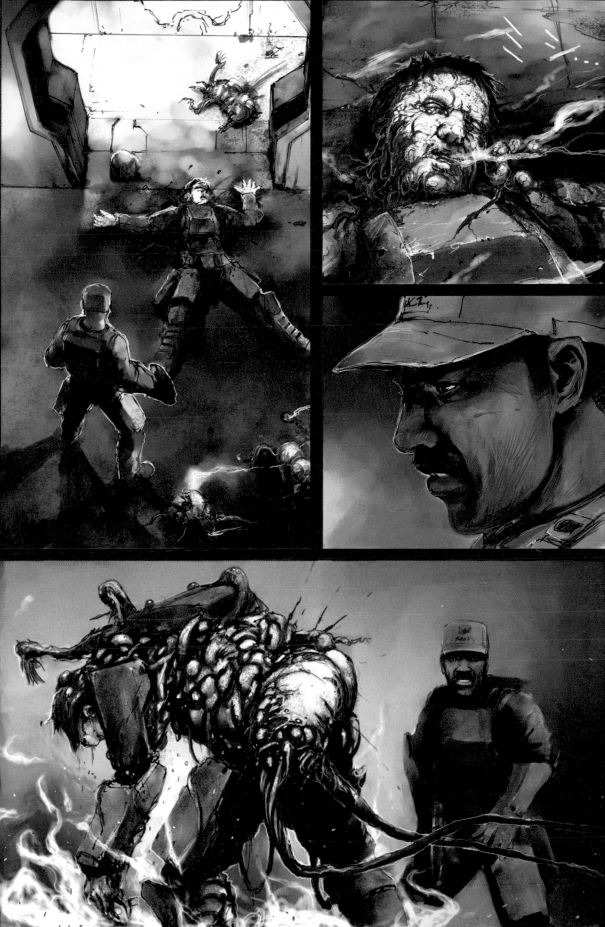

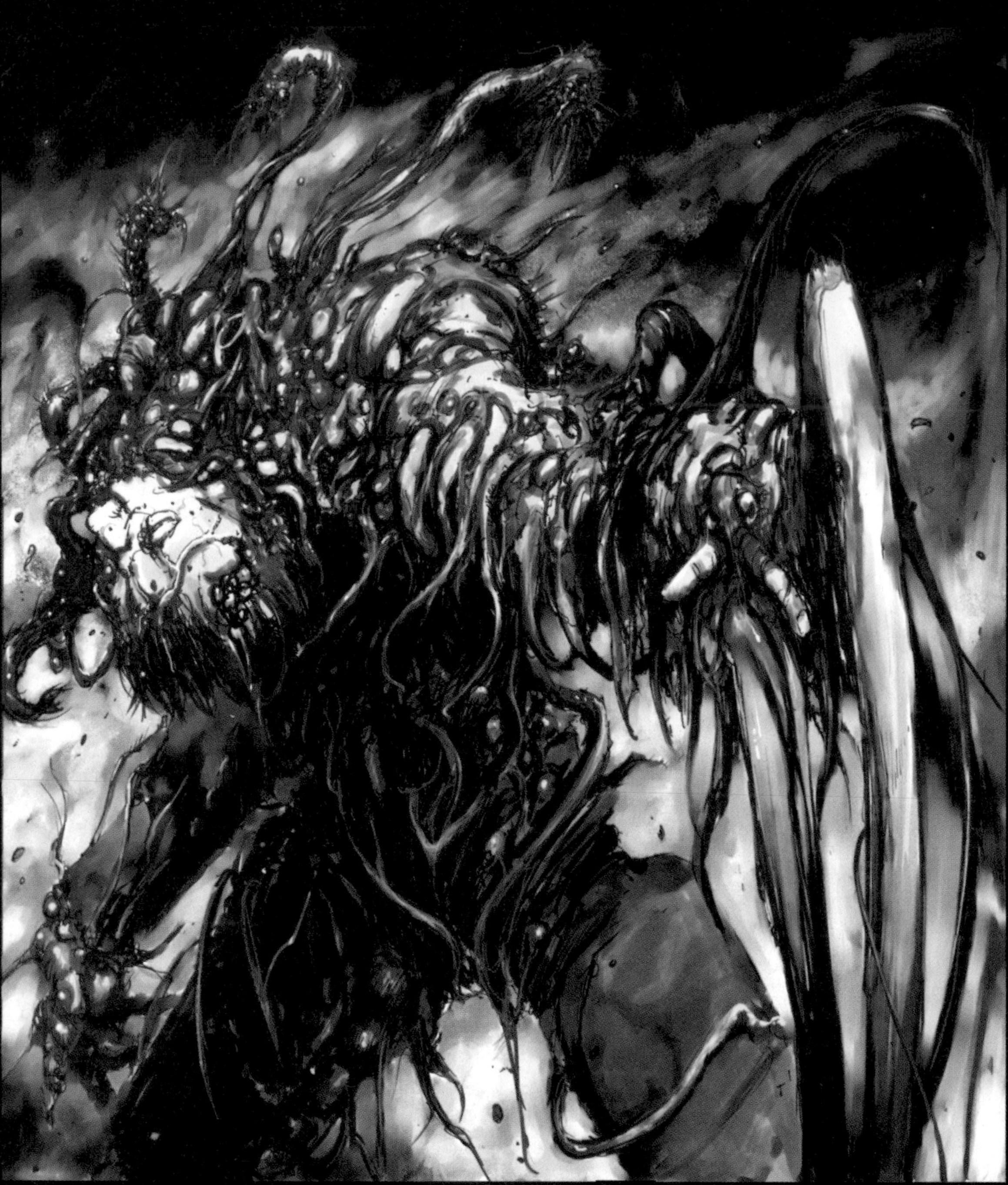

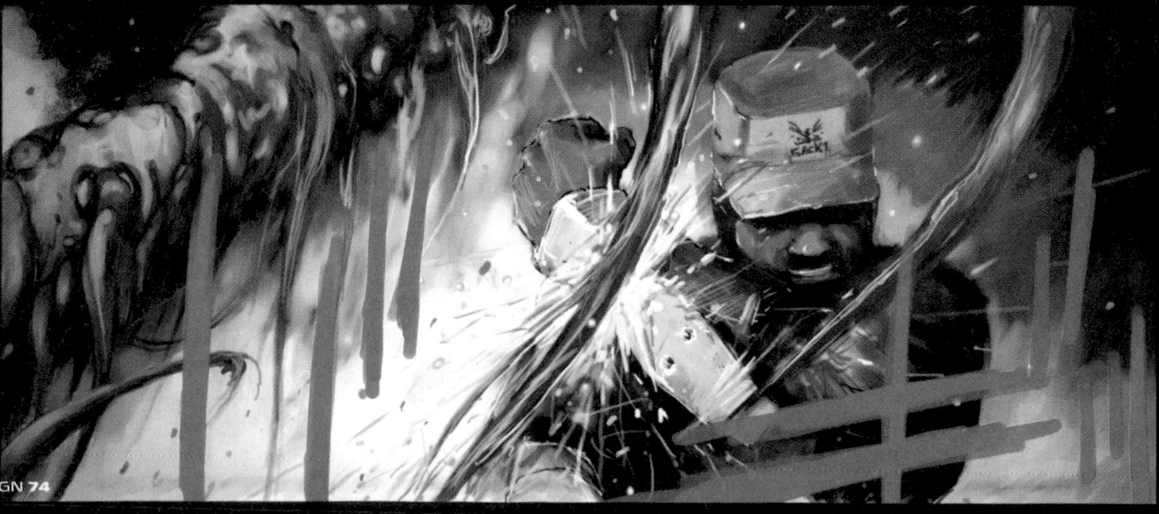

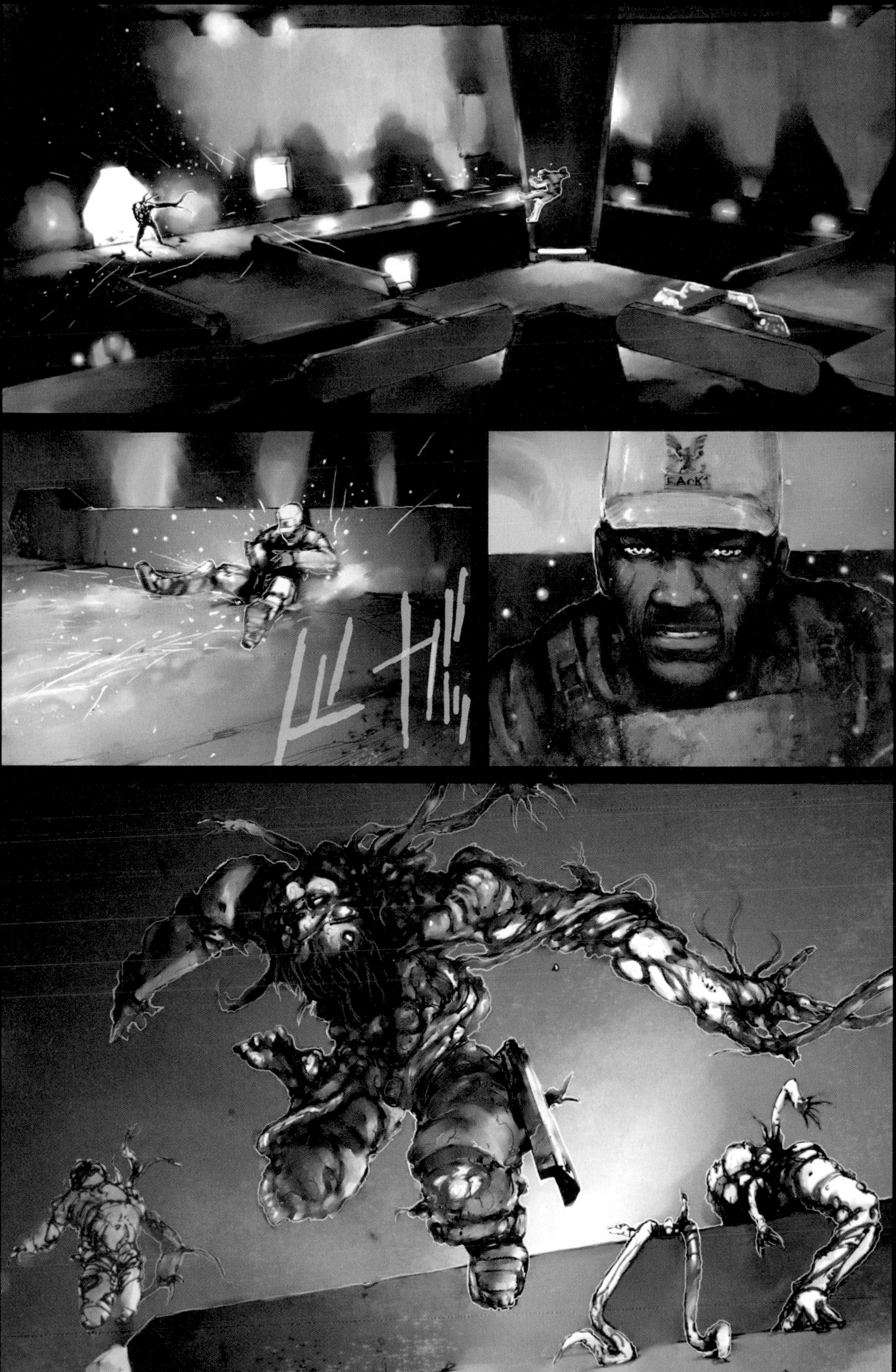

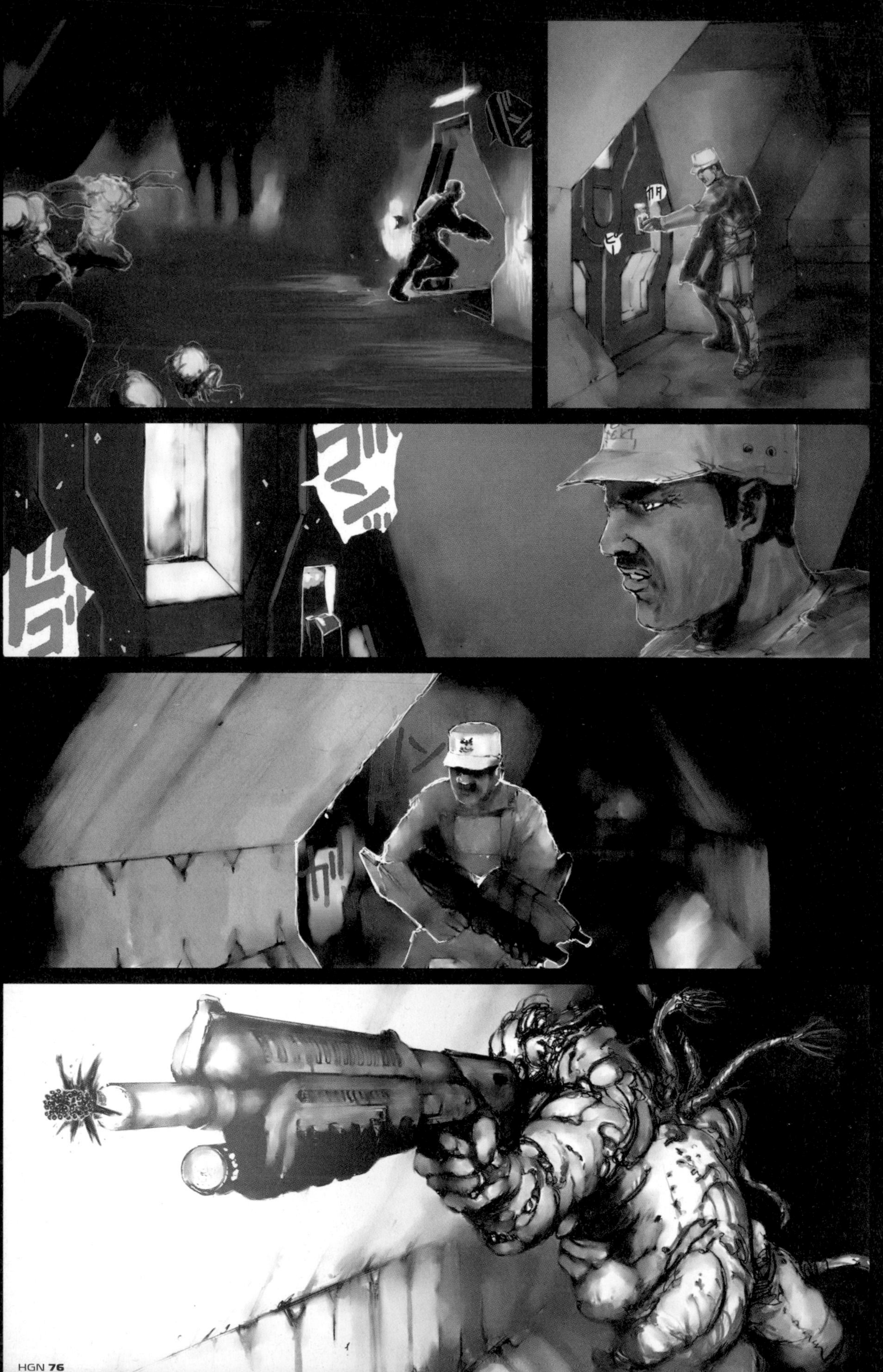

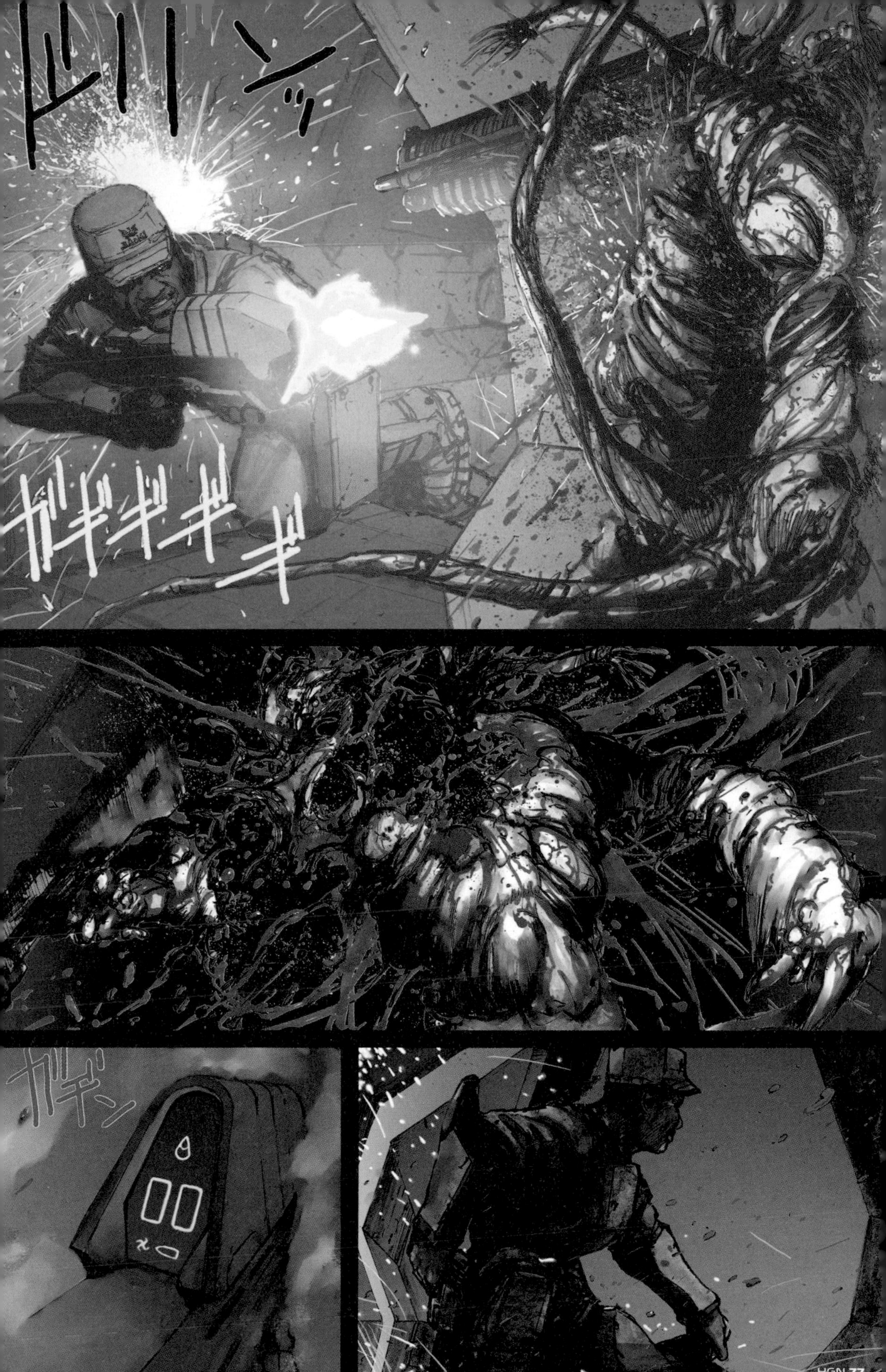
ドリーンッ
ガギギギギ
ガギン

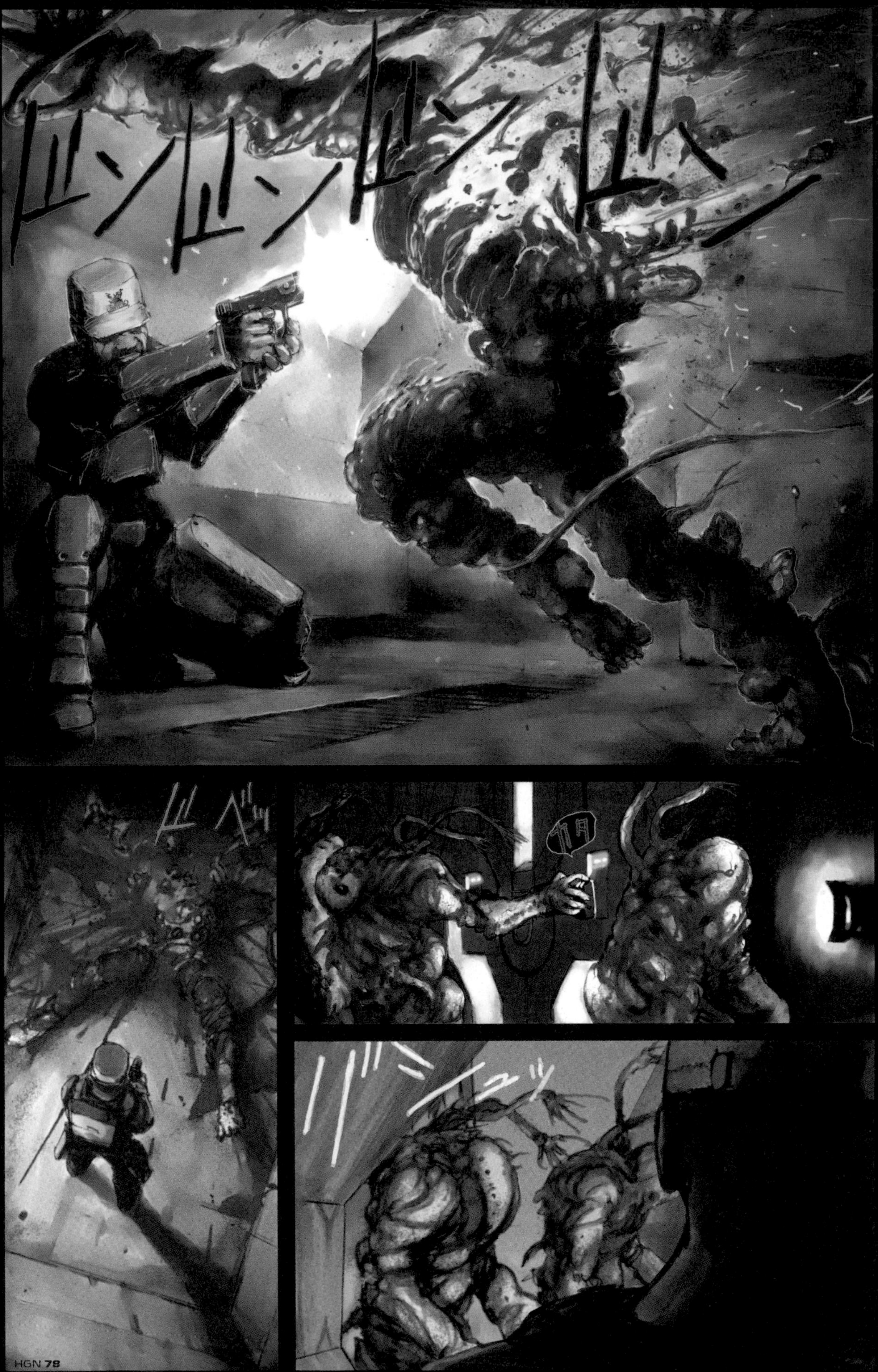

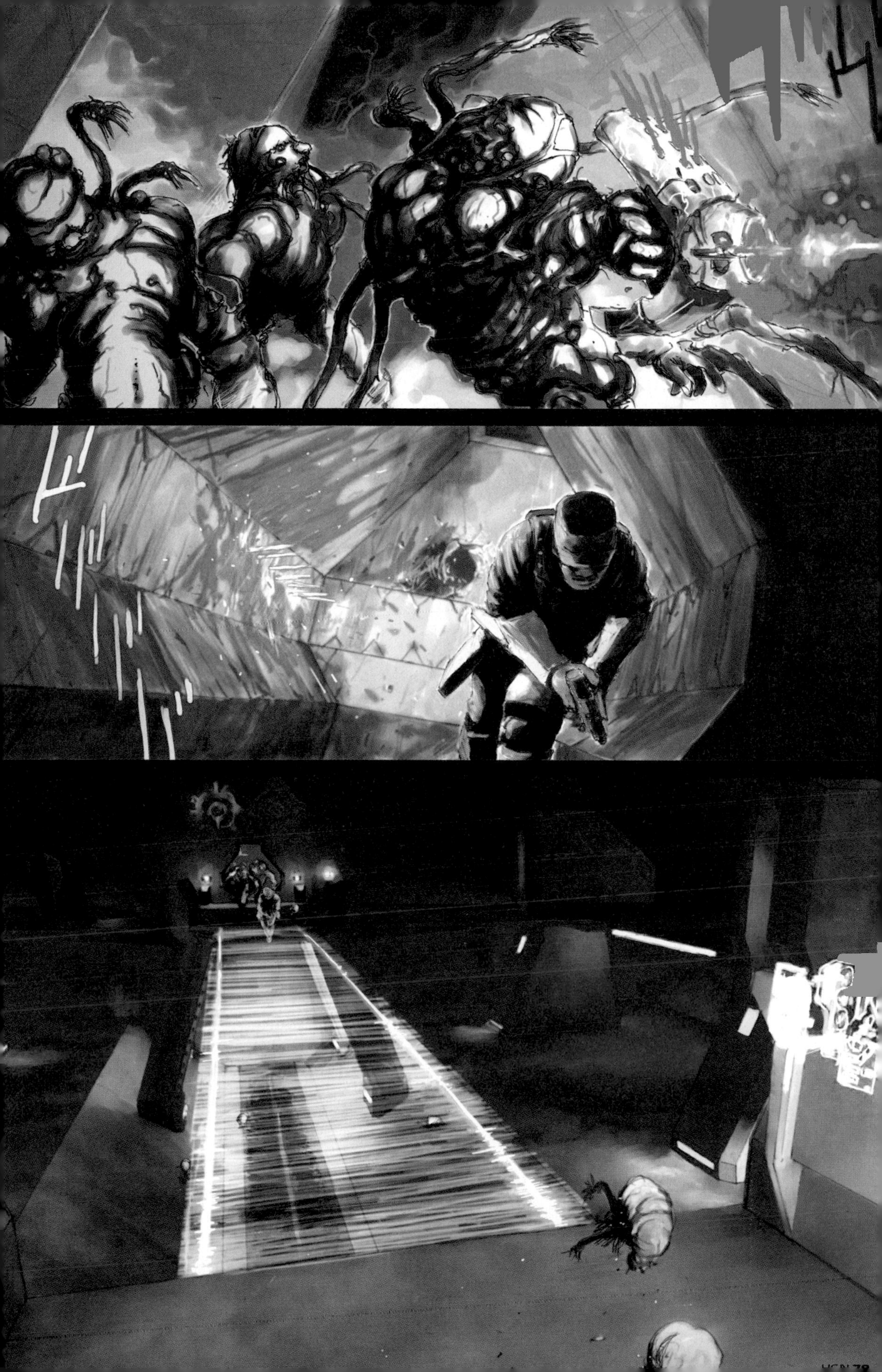

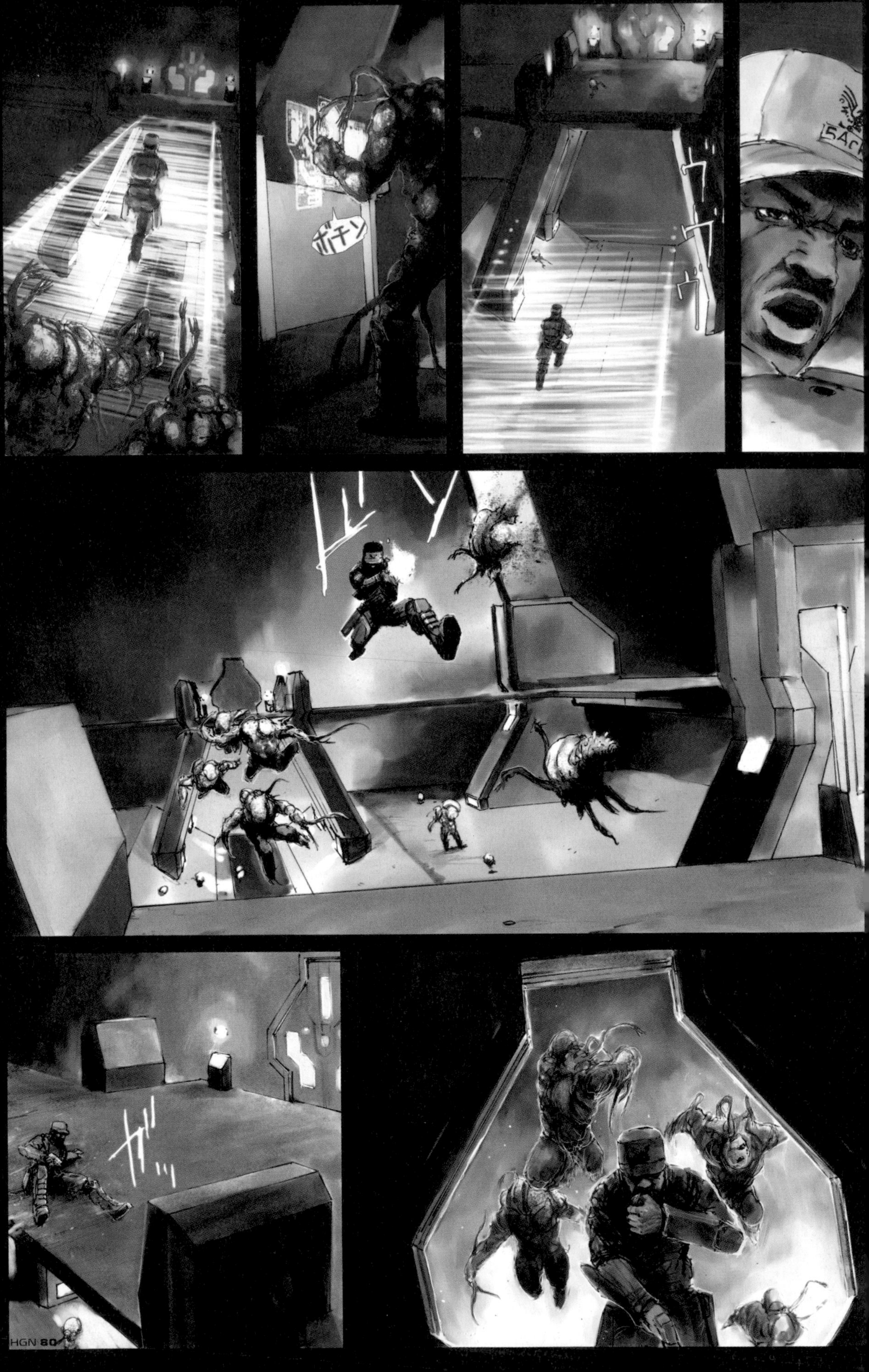
ボキン
ヴヴヴ
ドン
ガッ

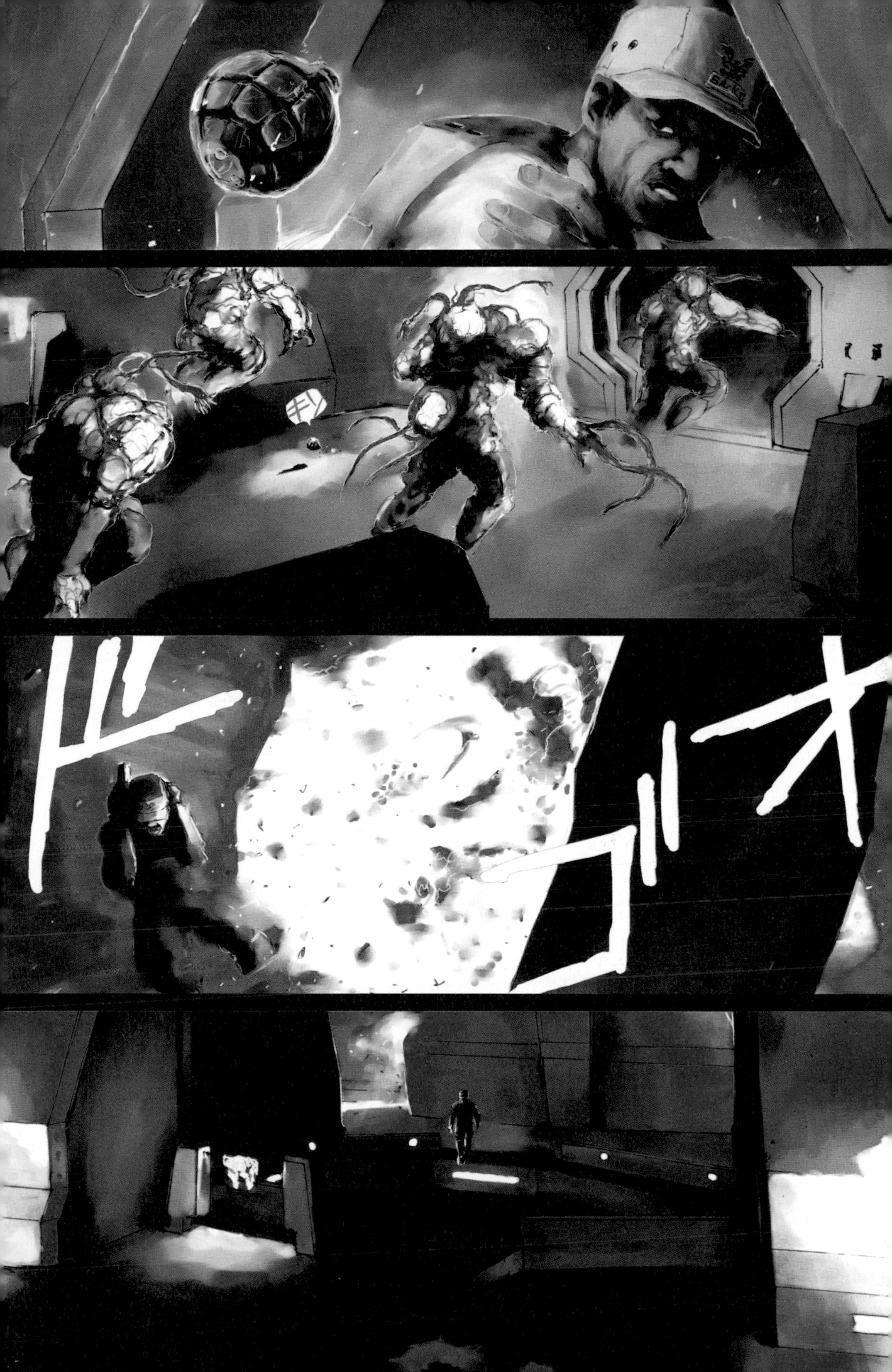

キン
ドゴオ

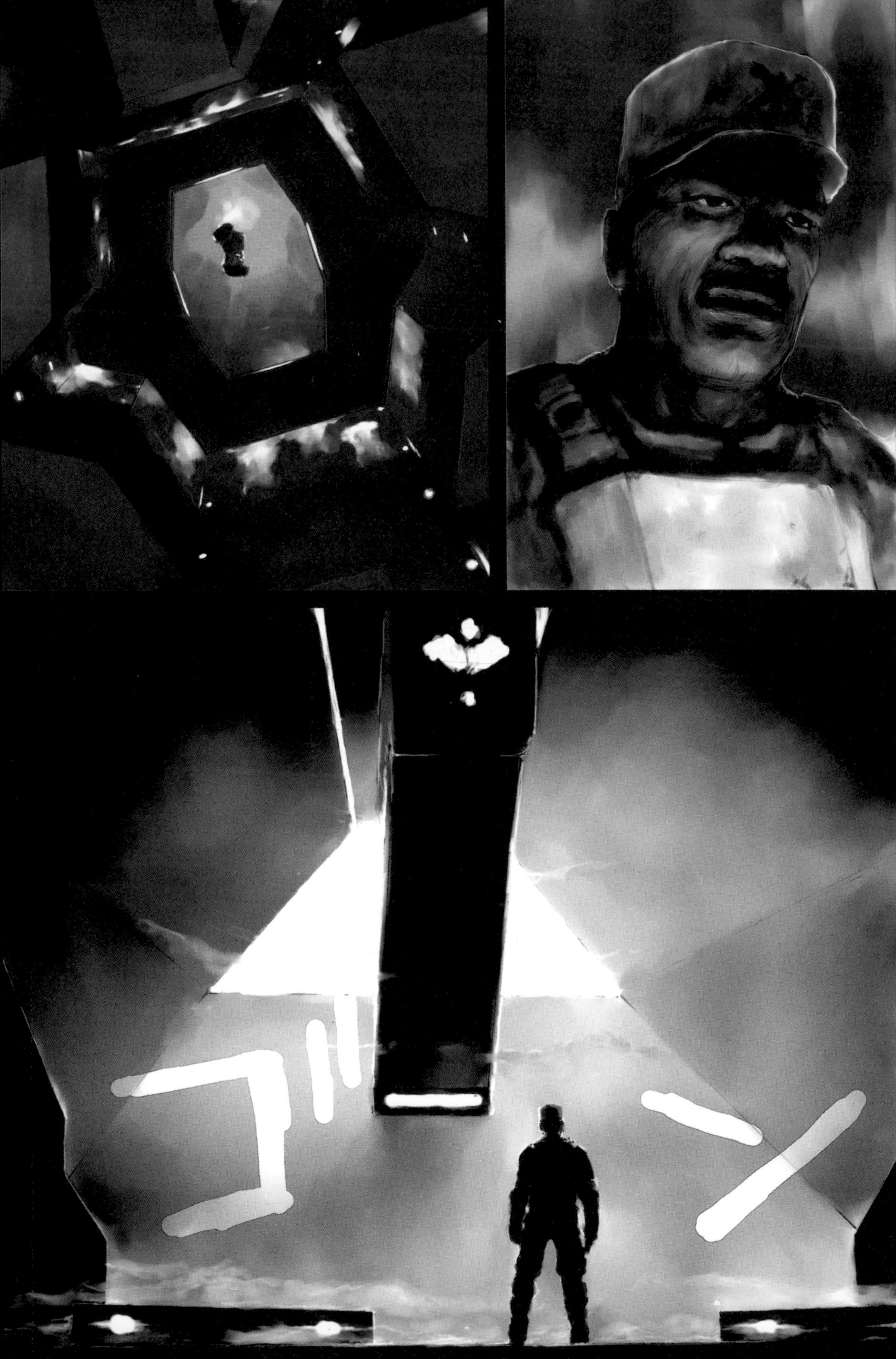
ゴーン

I was so excited to hear the news about the HALO comic, and it's an honor for me as an artist to be asked to participate in this project. When I first bought my XBOX, I purchased HALO at the same time and I would spend countless hours playing it, often playing all night through to morning with my friends. HALO 2 is even more amazing, allowing me to play with people from all over the world. As a huge fan, there was no way I could say no to this opportunity.

I originally wanted to write my own story, but Bungie soon asked me to illustrate their own story, *"Sgt. Johnson Gets the Heck Out of Flood Central."* This was the first time I've drawn a comic based on someone else's script. I was little nervous at first because all the characters, buildings and other designs had been already established. While I was working on the pages, I kept the game on and used the inner structure as part of the reference materials for my illustrations. I'm still wondering if I accurately maintained consistency with the game.

The first time I drew the scene in which Flood shoots the shotgun, I drew tons of bullets coming from the muzzle, but Bungie gave me specific reference and asked me to add more shells. That reference was very helpful in helping keep my drawing more realistic. I've drawn many shooting scenes in my manga but Japanese editors have never pointed out something like this. I'm very impressed by American editors and, unlike Japan, I think America is more of a gun-friendly society.

Some of my favorite artists are also participating in this book. *I can't wait to see it!*

– Tsutomu Nihei
(Translated by Mutsumi Masuda)

SECOND SUNRISE OVER NEW MOMBASA

BRETT LEWIS AND MOEBIUS

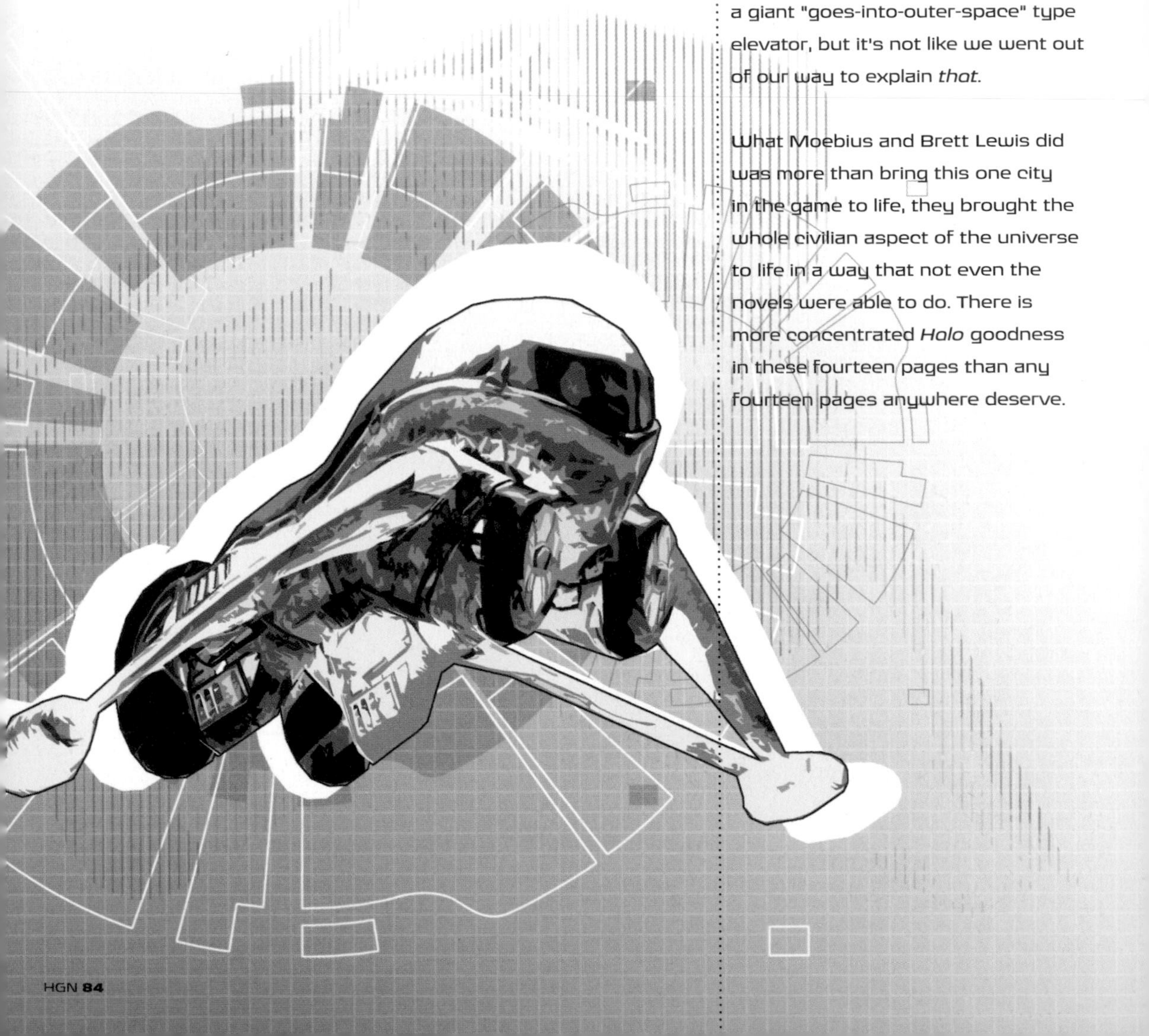

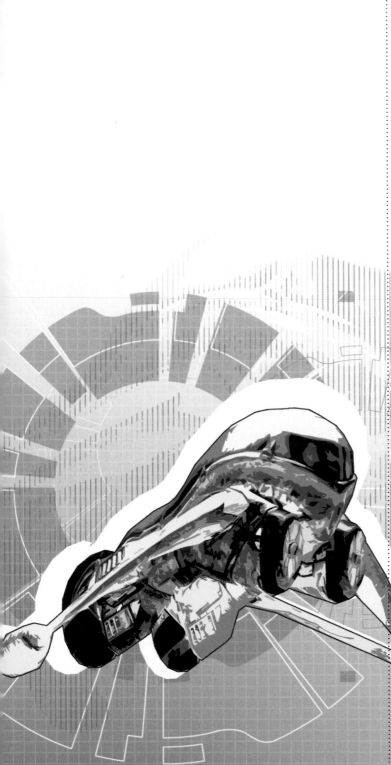

New Mombasa, by the time you got there as Master Chief Petty Officer "John" SPARTAN-117, was a ghost town. And I don't think I'm overstating it when I say that the post-invasion New and Old Mombasa you were defending in the game were *bereft* of life. This story began merely as a way to show that the city wasn't always like that. You can say what you want about the size and accessibility of public disaster shelters and evacuation protocols of a city with a giant "goes-into-outer-space" type elevator, but it's not like we went out of our way to explain *that*.

What Moebius and Brett Lewis did was more than bring this one city in the game to life, they brought the whole civilian aspect of the universe to life in a way that not even the novels were able to do. There is more concentrated *Halo* goodness in these fourteen pages than any fourteen pages anywhere deserve.

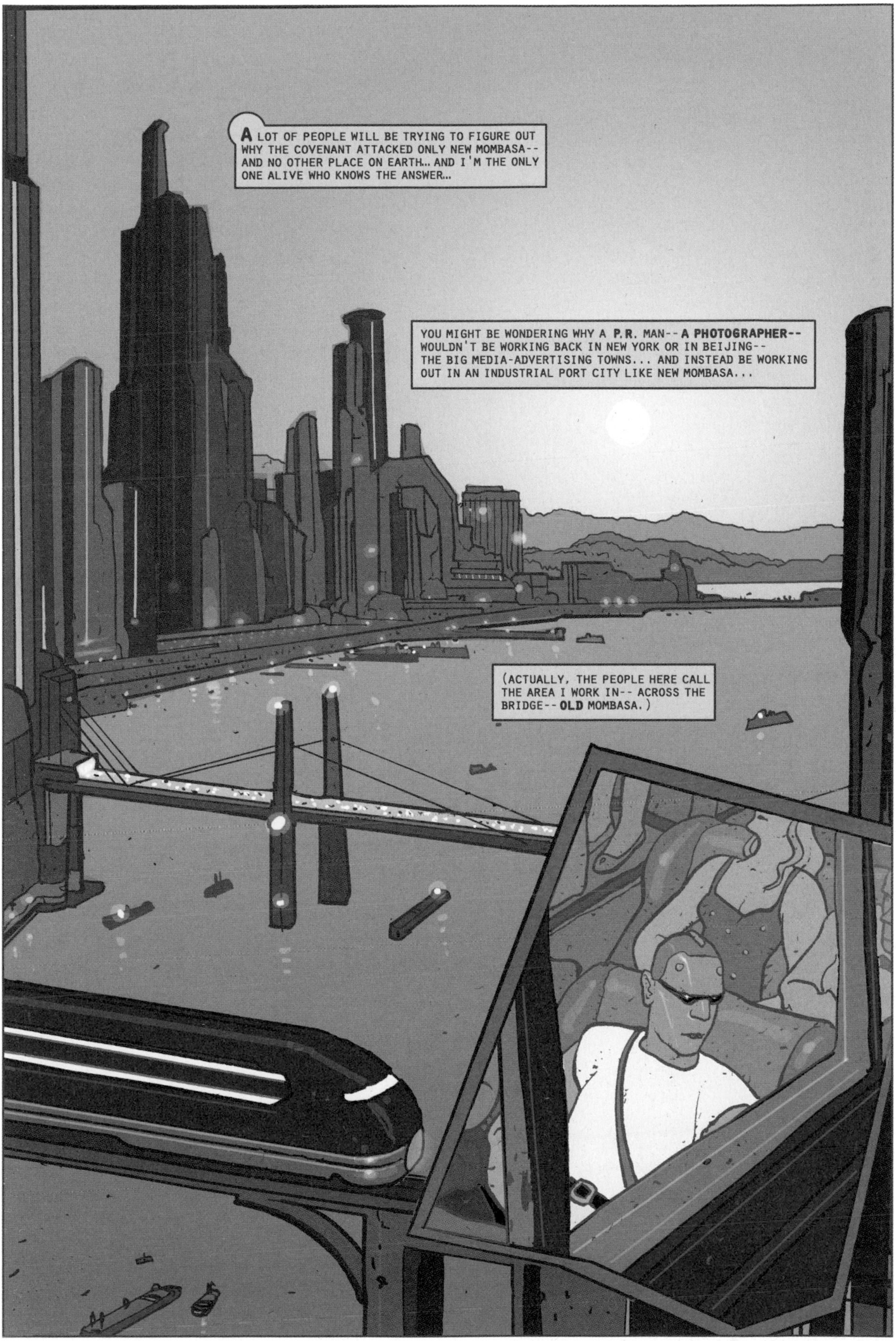
A LOT OF PEOPLE WILL BE TRYING TO FIGURE OUT WHY THE COVENANT ATTACKED ONLY NEW MOMBASA-- AND NO OTHER PLACE ON EARTH.. AND I'M THE ONLY ONE ALIVE WHO KNOWS THE ANSWER..
YOU MIGHT BE WONDERING WHY A **P.R.** MAN-- **A PHOTOGRAPHER--** WOULDN'T BE WORKING BACK IN NEW YORK OR IN BEIJING-- THE BIG MEDIA-ADVERTISING TOWNS... AND INSTEAD BE WORKING OUT IN AN INDUSTRIAL PORT CITY LIKE NEW MOMBASA...
(ACTUALLY, THE PEOPLE HERE CALL THE AREA I WORK IN-- ACROSS THE BRIDGE-- **OLD** MOMBASA.)

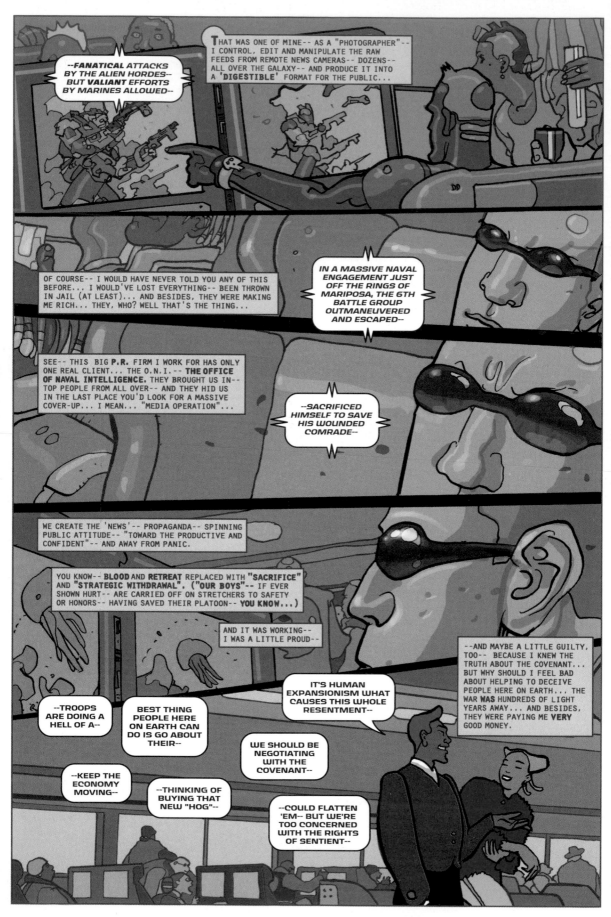

--FANATICAL *ATTACKS* BY THE ALIEN HORDES-- BUT *VALIANT* EFFORTS BY MARINES ALLOWED--

THAT WAS ONE OF MINE-- AS A "PHOTOGRAPHER"-- I CONTROL, EDIT AND MANIPULATE THE RAW FEEDS FROM REMOTE NEWS CAMERAS-- DOZENS-- ALL OVER THE GALAXY-- AND PRODUCE IT INTO A *'DIGESTIBLE'* FORMAT FOR THE PUBLIC...

OF COURSE-- I WOULD HAVE NEVER TOLD YOU ANY OF THIS BEFORE... I WOULD'VE LOST EVERYTHING-- BEEN THROWN IN JAIL (AT LEAST)... AND BESIDES, THEY WERE MAKING ME RICH... THEY, WHO? WELL THAT'S THE THING...

IN A MASSIVE NAVAL ENGAGEMENT JUST OFF THE RINGS OF MARIPOSA, THE 6TH BATTLE GROUP OUTMANEUVERED AND ESCAPED--

SEE-- THIS BIG *P.R.* FIRM I WORK FOR HAS ONLY ONE REAL CLIENT... THE O.N.I.-- *THE OFFICE OF NAVAL INTELLIGENCE.* THEY BROUGHT US IN-- TOP PEOPLE FROM ALL OVER-- AND THEY HID US IN THE LAST PLACE YOU'D LOOK FOR A MASSIVE COVER-UP... I MEAN... "MEDIA OPERATION"...

--SACRIFICED HIMSELF TO SAVE HIS WOUNDED COMRADE--

WE CREATE THE 'NEWS'-- PROPAGANDA-- SPINNING PUBLIC ATTITUDE-- "TOWARD THE PRODUCTIVE AND CONFIDENT"-- AND AWAY FROM PANIC.

YOU KNOW-- *BLOOD* AND *RETREAT* REPLACED WITH "SACRIFICE" AND "STRATEGIC WITHDRAWAL". ("OUR BOYS"-- IF EVER SHOWN HURT-- ARE CARRIED OFF ON STRETCHERS TO SAFETY OR HONORS-- HAVING SAVED THEIR PLATOON-- *YOU KNOW*...)

AND IT WAS WORKING-- I WAS A LITTLE PROUD--

--AND MAYBE A LITTLE GUILTY, TOO-- BECAUSE I KNEW THE TRUTH ABOUT THE COVENANT... BUT WHY SHOULD I FEEL BAD ABOUT HELPING TO DECEIVE PEOPLE HERE ON EARTH... THE WAR *WAS* HUNDREDS OF LIGHT YEARS AWAY... AND BESIDES, THEY WERE PAYING ME *VERY* GOOD MONEY.

IT'S HUMAN EXPANSIONISM WHAT CAUSES THIS WHOLE RESENTMENT--

--TROOPS ARE DOING A HELL OF A--

BEST THING PEOPLE HERE ON EARTH CAN DO IS GO ABOUT THEIR--

WE SHOULD BE NEGOTIATING WITH THE COVENANT--

--KEEP THE ECONOMY MOVING--

--THINKING OF BUYING THAT NEW "HOG"--

--COULD FLATTEN 'EM-- BUT WE'RE TOO CONCERNED WITH THE RIGHTS OF SENTIENT--

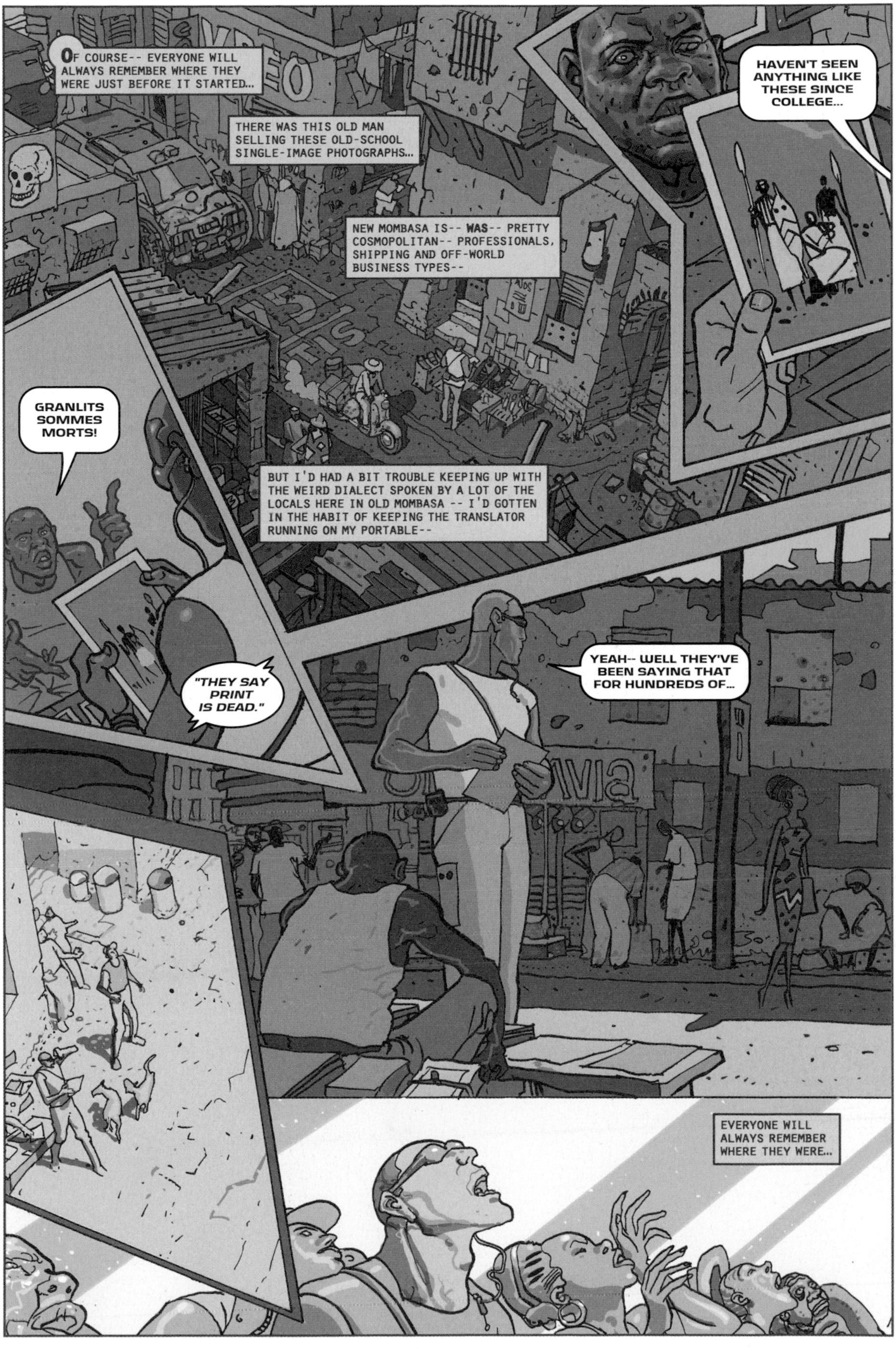
OF COURSE-- EVERYONE WILL ALWAYS REMEMBER WHERE THEY WERE JUST BEFORE IT STARTED...
THERE WAS THIS OLD MAN SELLING THESE OLD-SCHOOL SINGLE-IMAGE PHOTOGRAPHS...
HAVEN'T SEEN ANYTHING LIKE THESE SINCE COLLEGE...
NEW MOMBASA IS-- WAS-- PRETTY COSMOPOLITAN-- PROFESSIONALS, SHIPPING AND OFF-WORLD BUSINESS TYPES--
GRANLITS SOMMES MORTS!
BUT I'D HAD A BIT TROUBLE KEEPING UP WITH THE WEIRD DIALECT SPOKEN BY A LOT OF THE LOCALS HERE IN OLD MOMBASA -- I'D GOTTEN IN THE HABIT OF KEEPING THE TRANSLATOR RUNNING ON MY PORTABLE--
"THEY SAY PRINT IS DEAD."
YEAH-- WELL THEY'VE BEEN SAYING THAT FOR HUNDREDS OF...
EVERYONE WILL ALWAYS REMEMBER WHERE THEY WERE...

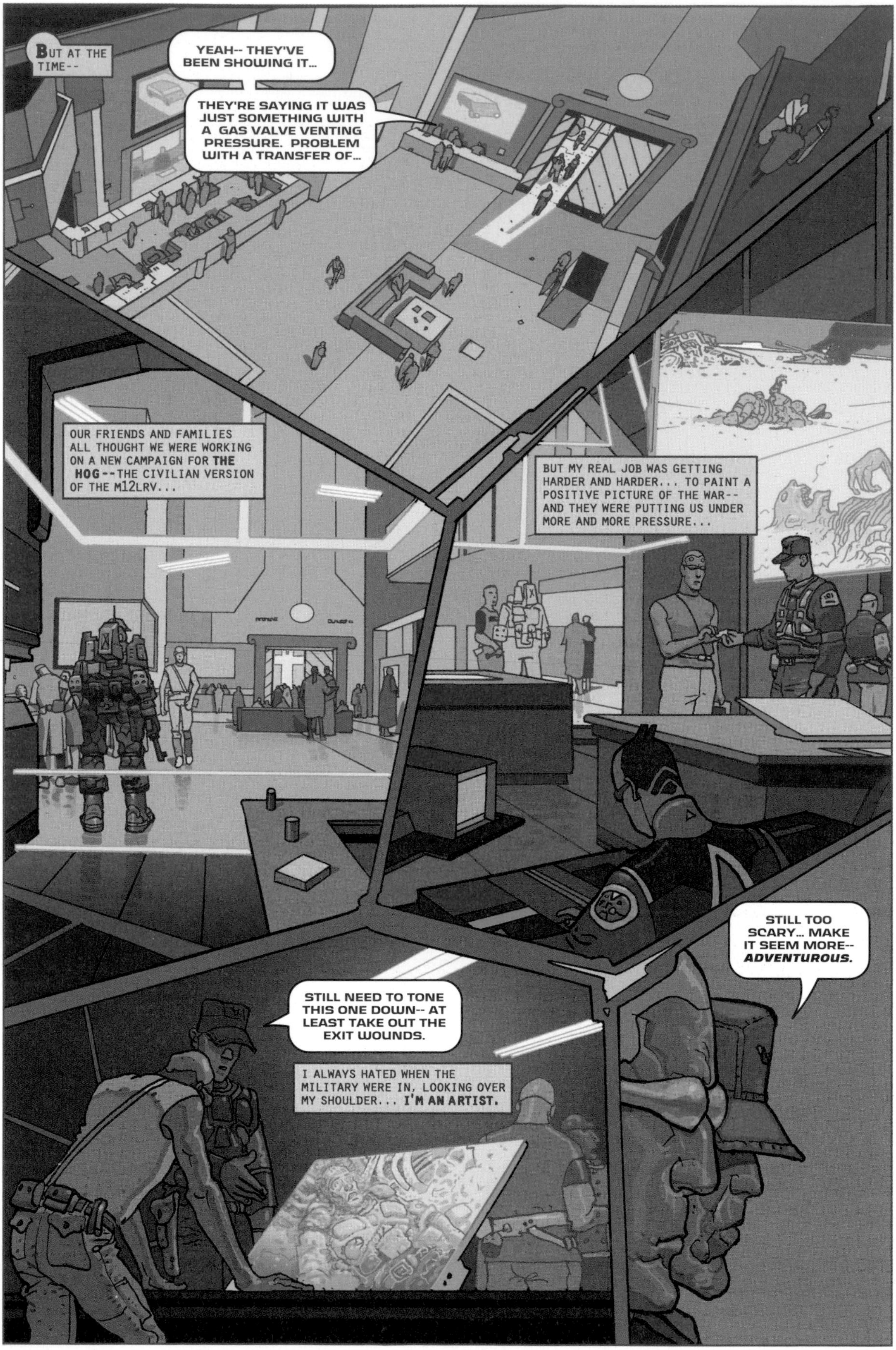
BUT AT THE TIME--
YEAH-- THEY'VE BEEN SHOWING IT...
THEY'RE SAYING IT WAS JUST SOMETHING WITH A GAS VALVE VENTING PRESSURE. PROBLEM WITH A TRANSFER OF...
OUR FRIENDS AND FAMILIES ALL THOUGHT WE WERE WORKING ON A NEW CAMPAIGN FOR **THE HOG**--THE CIVILIAN VERSION OF THE M12LRV...
BUT MY REAL JOB WAS GETTING HARDER AND HARDER... TO PAINT A POSITIVE PICTURE OF THE WAR-- AND THEY WERE PUTTING US UNDER MORE AND MORE PRESSURE...
STILL TOO SCARY... MAKE IT SEEM MORE-- ***ADVENTUROUS.***
STILL NEED TO TONE THIS ONE DOWN-- AT LEAST TAKE OUT THE EXIT WOUNDS.
I ALWAYS HATED WHEN THE MILITARY WERE IN, LOOKING OVER MY SHOULDER... **I'M AN ARTIST.**

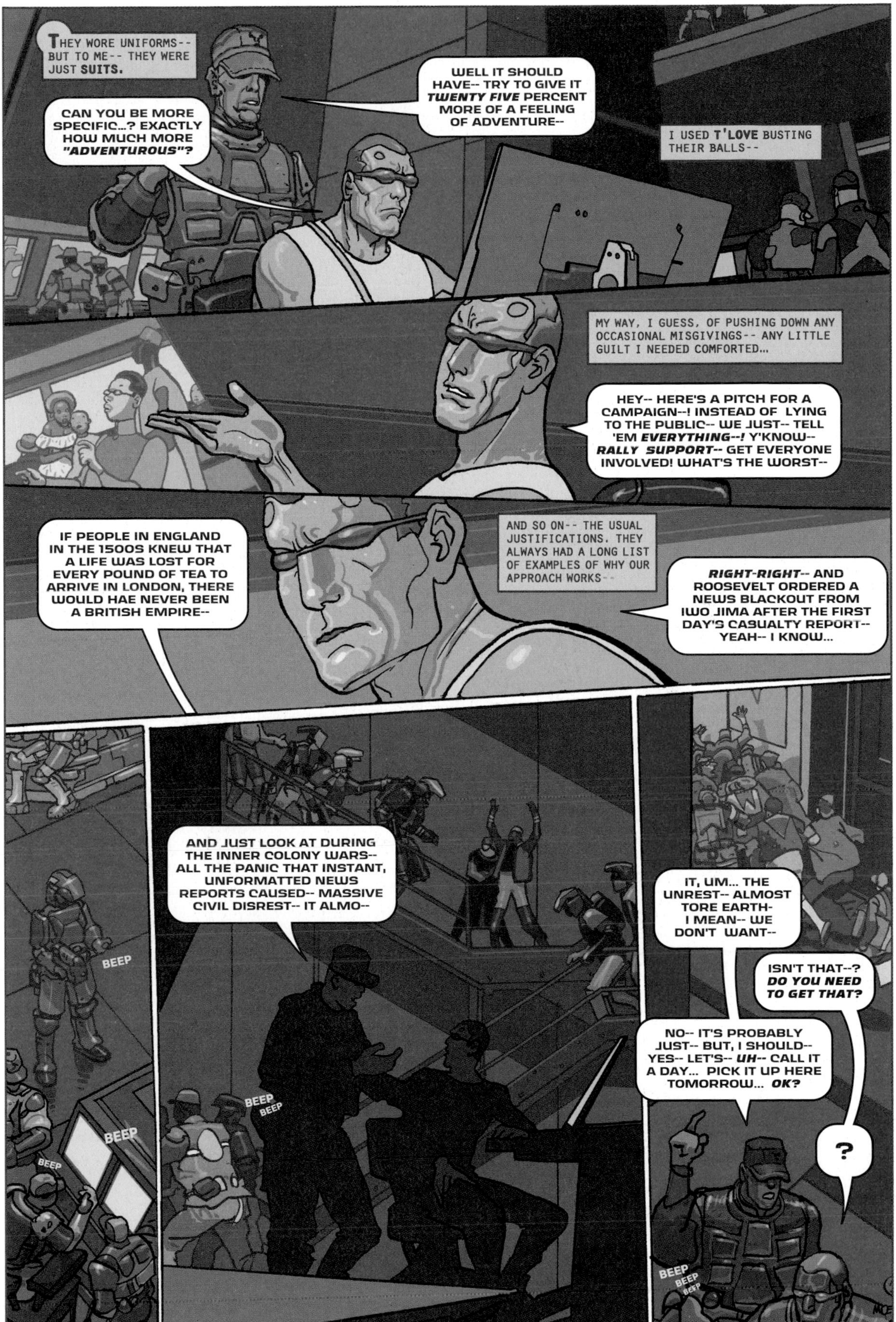

THEY WORE UNIFORMS-- BUT TO ME-- THEY WERE JUST SUITS.
WELL IT SHOULD HAVE-- TRY TO GIVE IT TWENTY FIVE PERCENT MORE OF A FEELING OF ADVENTURE--
CAN YOU BE MORE SPECIFIC...? EXACTLY HOW MUCH MORE "ADVENTUROUS"?
I USED T'LOVE BUSTING THEIR BALLS--
MY WAY, I GUESS, OF PUSHING DOWN ANY OCCASIONAL MISGIVINGS-- ANY LITTLE GUILT I NEEDED COMFORTED...
HEY-- HERE'S A PITCH FOR A CAMPAIGN--! INSTEAD OF LYING TO THE PUBLIC-- WE JUST-- TELL 'EM EVERYTHING--! Y'KNOW-- RALLY SUPPORT-- GET EVERYONE INVOLVED! WHAT'S THE WORST--
IF PEOPLE IN ENGLAND IN THE 1500S KNEW THAT A LIFE WAS LOST FOR EVERY POUND OF TEA TO ARRIVE IN LONDON, THERE WOULD HAE NEVER BEEN A BRITISH EMPIRE--
AND SO ON-- THE USUAL JUSTIFICATIONS. THEY ALWAYS HAD A LONG LIST OF EXAMPLES OF WHY OUR APPROACH WORKS--
RIGHT-RIGHT-- AND ROOSEVELT ORDERED A NEWS BLACKOUT FROM IWO JIMA AFTER THE FIRST DAY'S CASUALTY REPORT-- YEAH-- I KNOW...
BEEP
AND JUST LOOK AT DURING THE INNER COLONY WARS-- ALL THE PANIC THAT INSTANT, UNFORMATTED NEWS REPORTS CAUSED-- MASSIVE CIVIL DISREST-- IT ALMO--
BEEP BEEP
BEEP
BEEP
IT, UM... THE UNREST-- ALMOST TORE EARTH- I MEAN-- WE DON'T WANT--
ISN'T THAT--? DO YOU NEED TO GET THAT?
NO-- IT'S PROBABLY JUST-- BUT, I SHOULD-- YES-- LET'S-- UH-- CALL IT A DAY... PICK IT UP HERE TOMORROW... OK?
?
BEEP BEEP BEEP

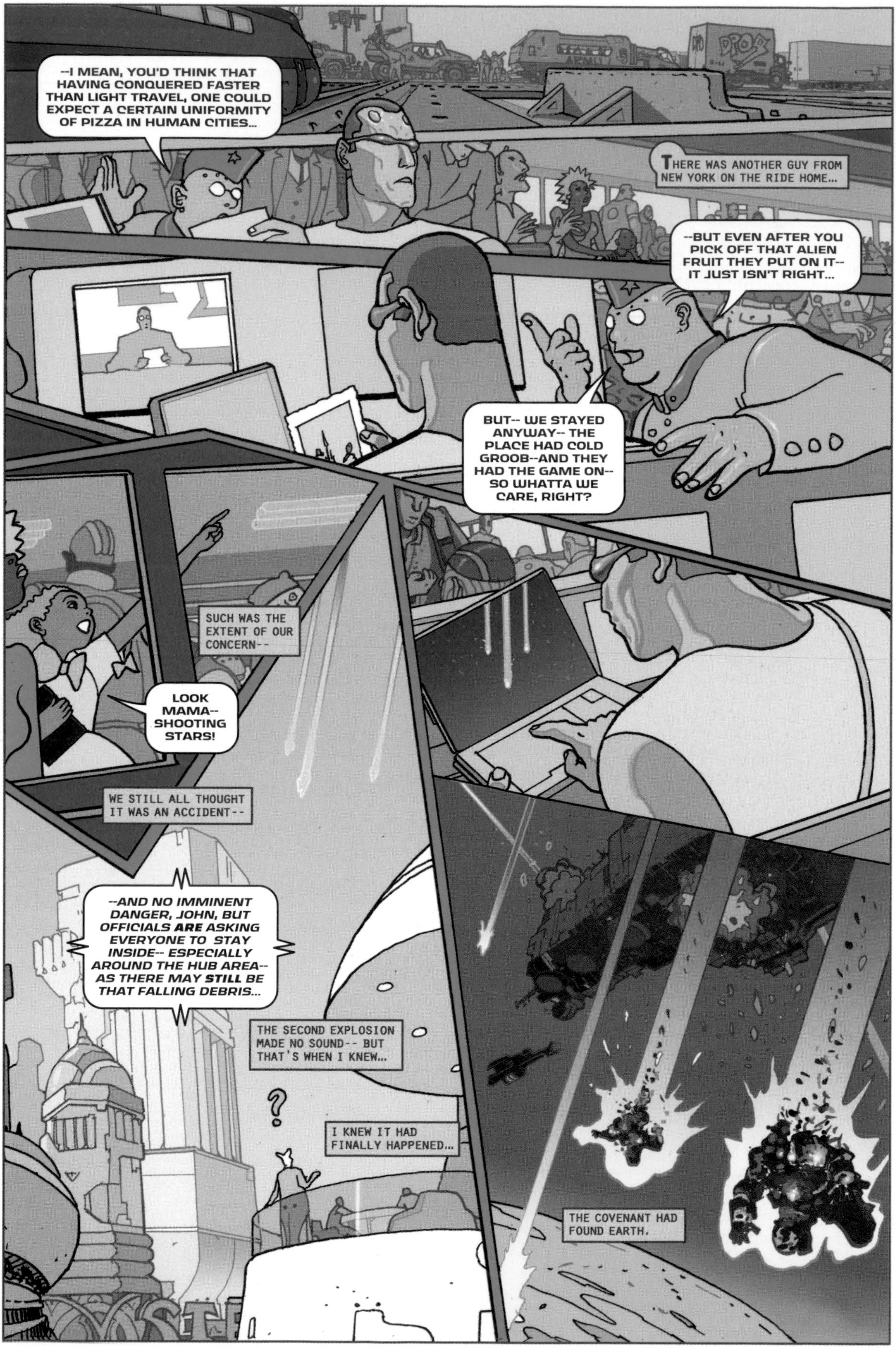
--I MEAN, YOU'D THINK THAT HAVING CONQUERED FASTER THAN LIGHT TRAVEL, ONE COULD EXPECT A CERTAIN UNIFORMITY OF PIZZA IN HUMAN CITIES...
THERE WAS ANOTHER GUY FROM NEW YORK ON THE RIDE HOME...
--BUT EVEN AFTER YOU PICK OFF THAT ALIEN FRUIT THEY PUT ON IT-- IT JUST ISN'T RIGHT...
BUT-- WE STAYED ANYWAY-- THE PLACE HAD COLD GROOB--AND THEY HAD THE GAME ON-- SO WHATTA WE CARE, RIGHT?
SUCH WAS THE EXTENT OF OUR CONCERN--
LOOK MAMA-- SHOOTING STARS!
WE STILL ALL THOUGHT IT WAS AN ACCIDENT--
--AND NO IMMINENT DANGER, JOHN, BUT OFFICIALS ARE ASKING EVERYONE TO STAY INSIDE-- ESPECIALLY AROUND THE HUB AREA-- AS THERE MAY STILL BE THAT FALLING DEBRIS...
THE SECOND EXPLOSION MADE NO SOUND-- BUT THAT'S WHEN I KNEW...
?
I KNEW IT HAD FINALLY HAPPENED...
THE COVENANT HAD FOUND EARTH.

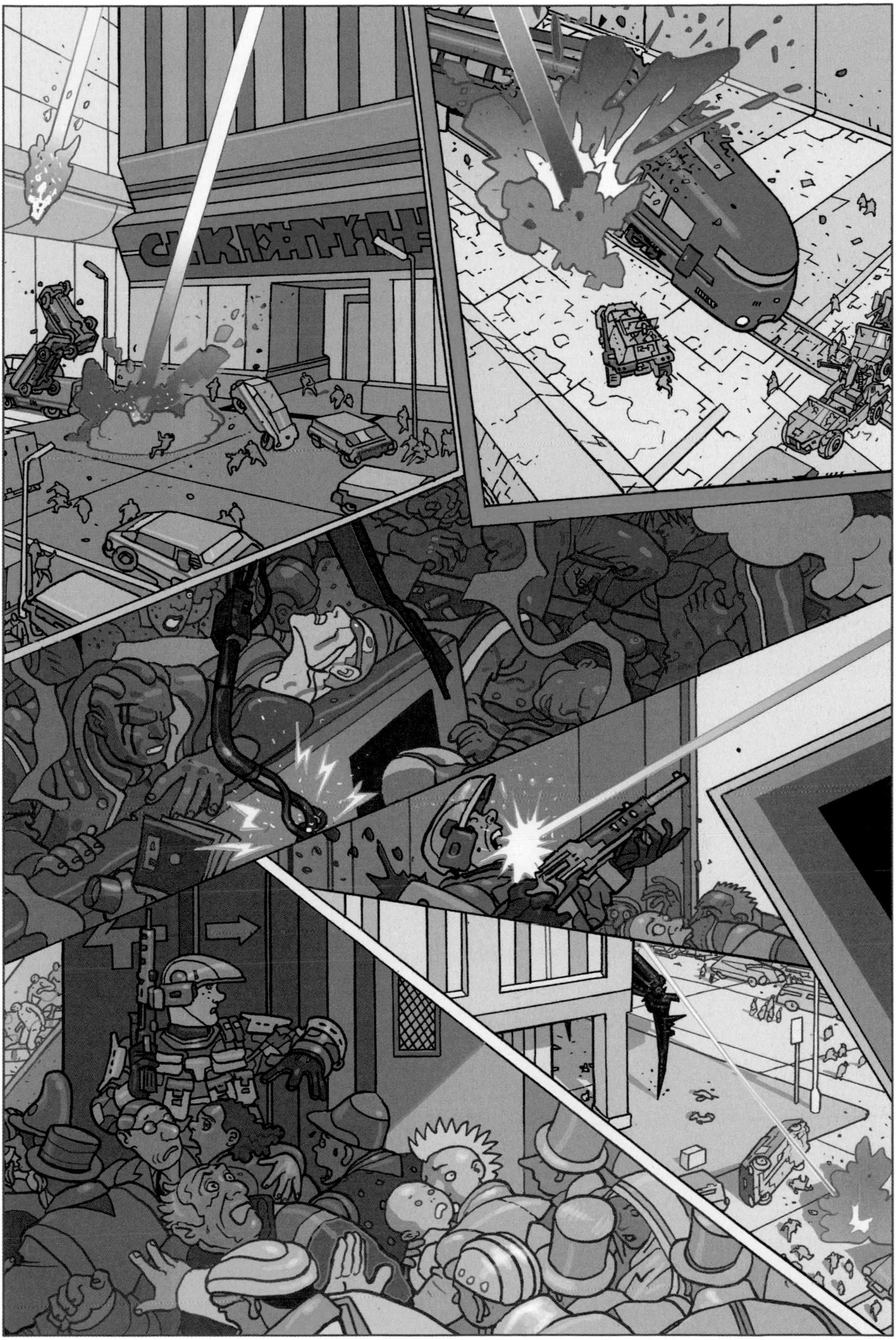

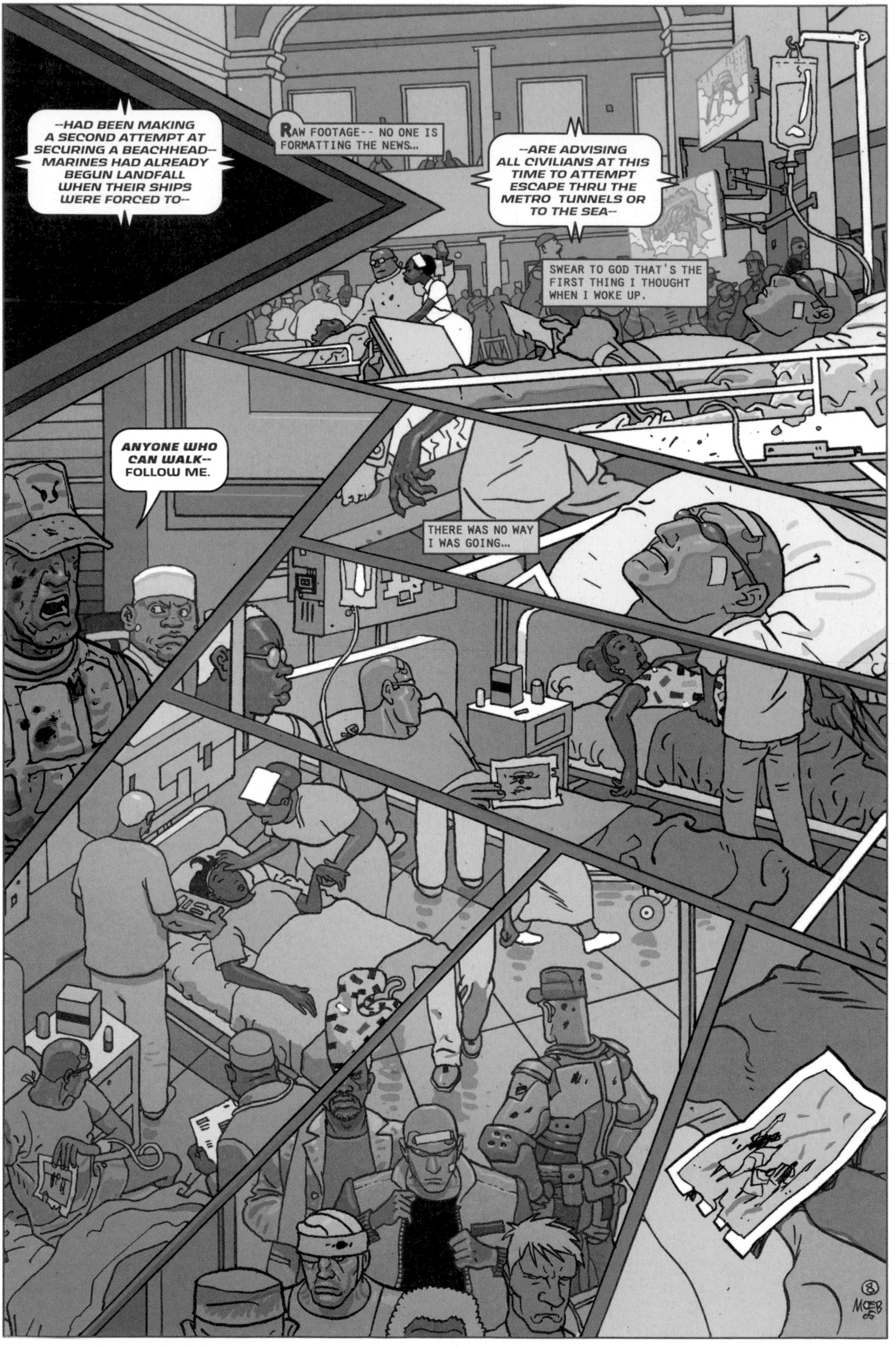
--HAD BEEN MAKING A SECOND ATTEMPT AT SECURING A BEACHHEAD-- MARINES HAD ALREADY BEGUN LANDFALL WHEN THEIR SHIPS WERE FORCED TO--
RAW FOOTAGE-- NO ONE IS FORMATTING THE NEWS...
--ARE ADVISING ALL CIVILIANS AT THIS TIME TO ATTEMPT ESCAPE THRU THE METRO TUNNELS OR TO THE SEA--
SWEAR TO GOD THAT'S THE FIRST THING I THOUGHT WHEN I WOKE UP.
ANYONE WHO CAN WALK-- FOLLOW ME.
THERE WAS NO WAY I WAS GOING...
8
MOEB

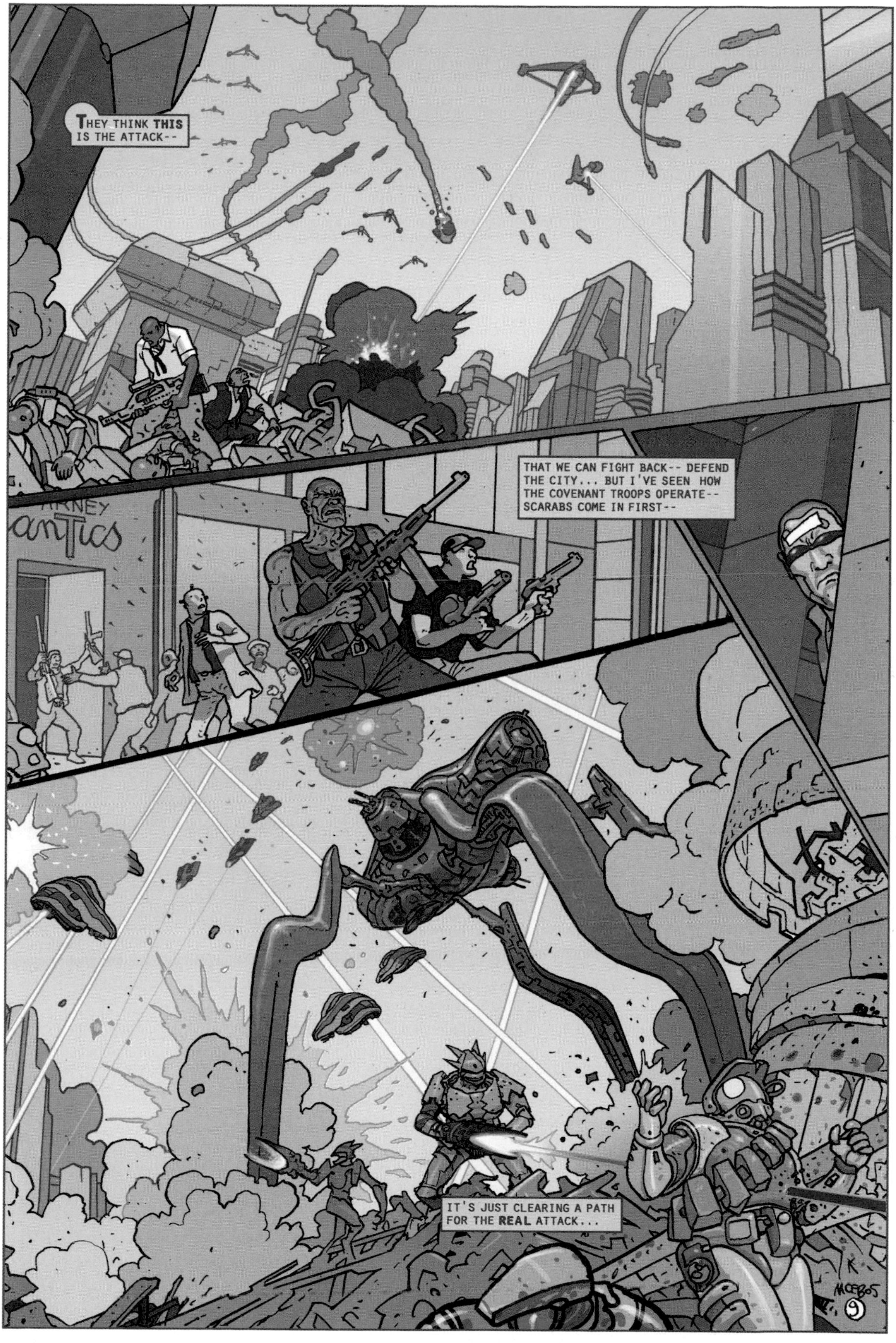
THEY THINK THIS IS THE ATTACK--
THAT WE CAN FIGHT BACK-- DEFEND THE CITY... BUT I'VE SEEN HOW THE COVENANT TROOPS OPERATE-- SCARABS COME IN FIRST--
IT'S JUST CLEARING A PATH FOR THE REAL ATTACK...
9

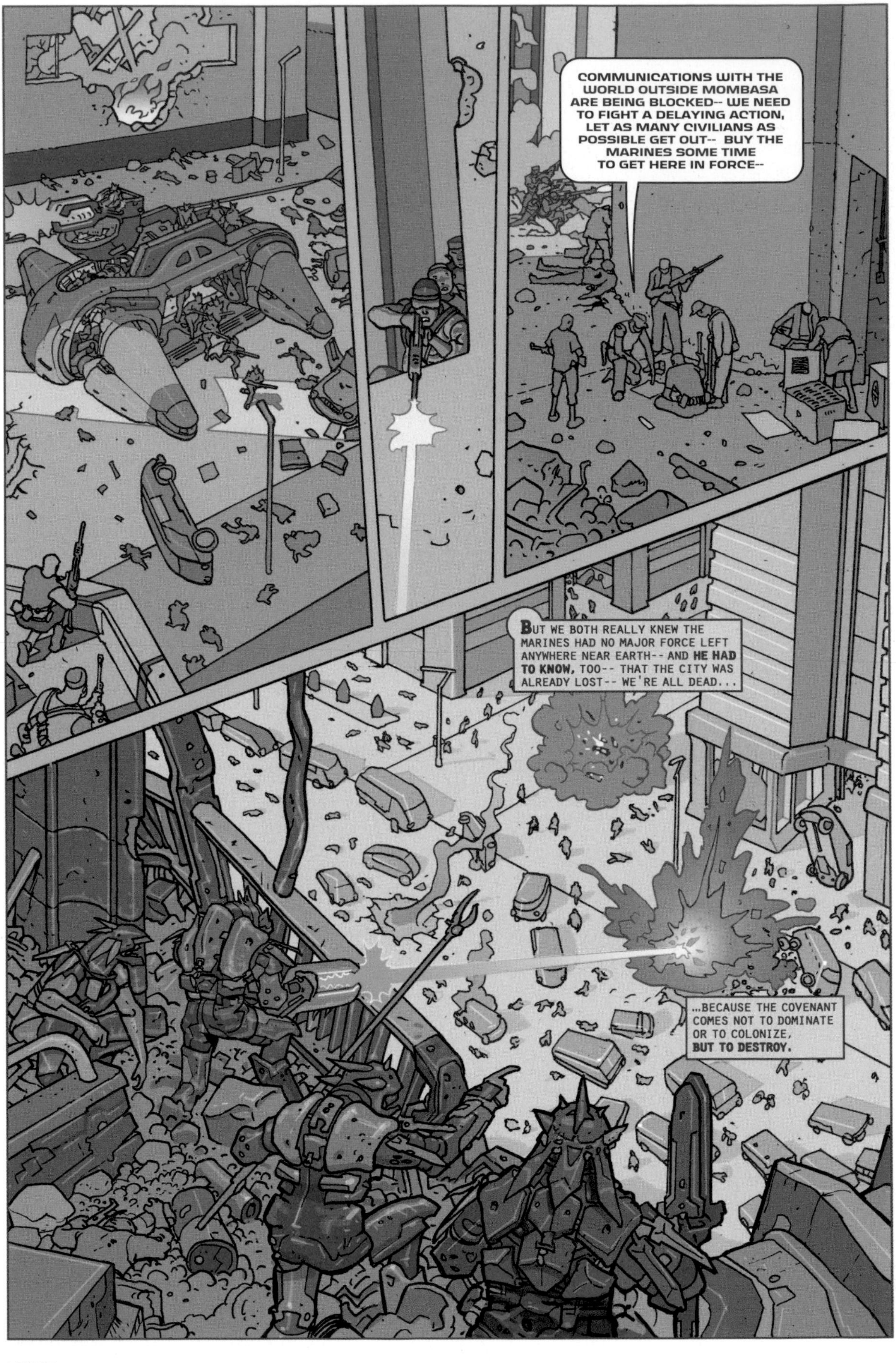
COMMUNICATIONS WITH THE WORLD OUTSIDE MOMBASA ARE BEING BLOCKED-- WE NEED TO FIGHT A DELAYING ACTION, LET AS MANY CIVILIANS AS POSSIBLE GET OUT-- BUY THE MARINES SOME TIME TO GET HERE IN FORCE--
BUT WE BOTH REALLY KNEW THE MARINES HAD NO MAJOR FORCE LEFT ANYWHERE NEAR EARTH-- AND HE HAD TO KNOW, TOO-- THAT THE CITY WAS ALREADY LOST-- WE'RE ALL DEAD...
...BECAUSE THE COVENANT COMES NOT TO DOMINATE OR TO COLONIZE, BUT TO DESTROY.

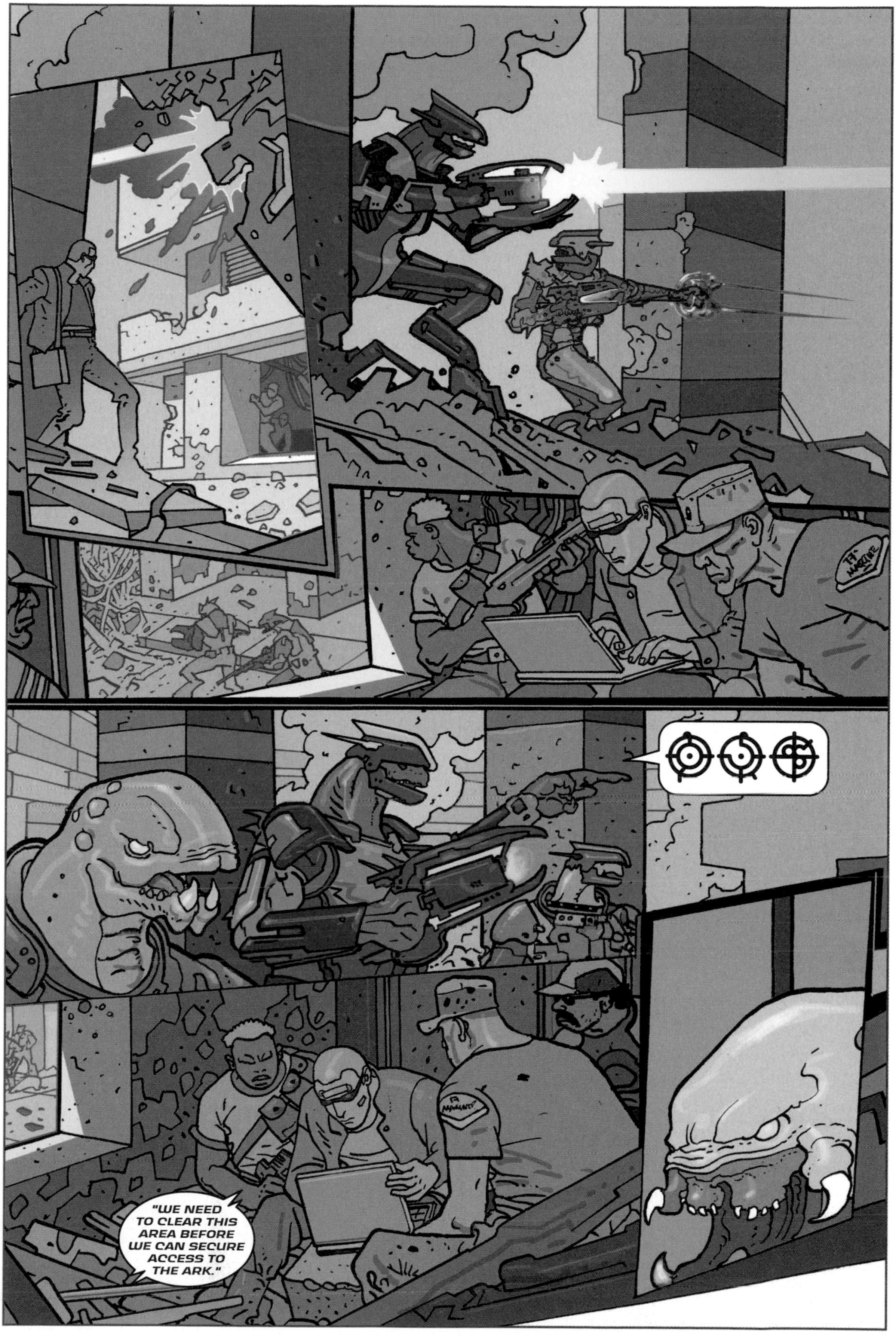
"WE NEED TO CLEAR THIS AREA BEFORE WE CAN SECURE ACCESS TO THE ARK."

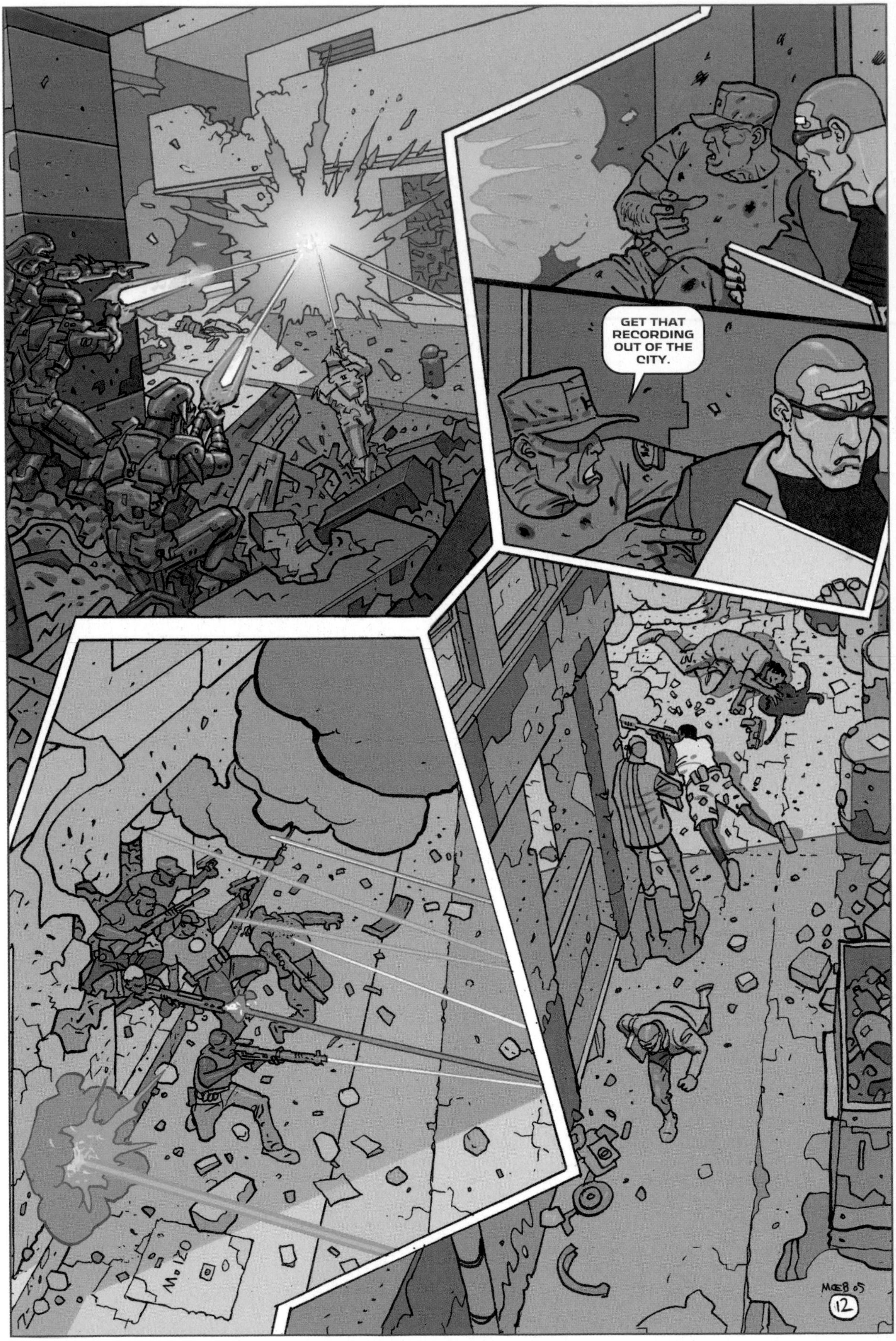
GET THAT RECORDING OUT OF THE CITY.
MŒB 05
12

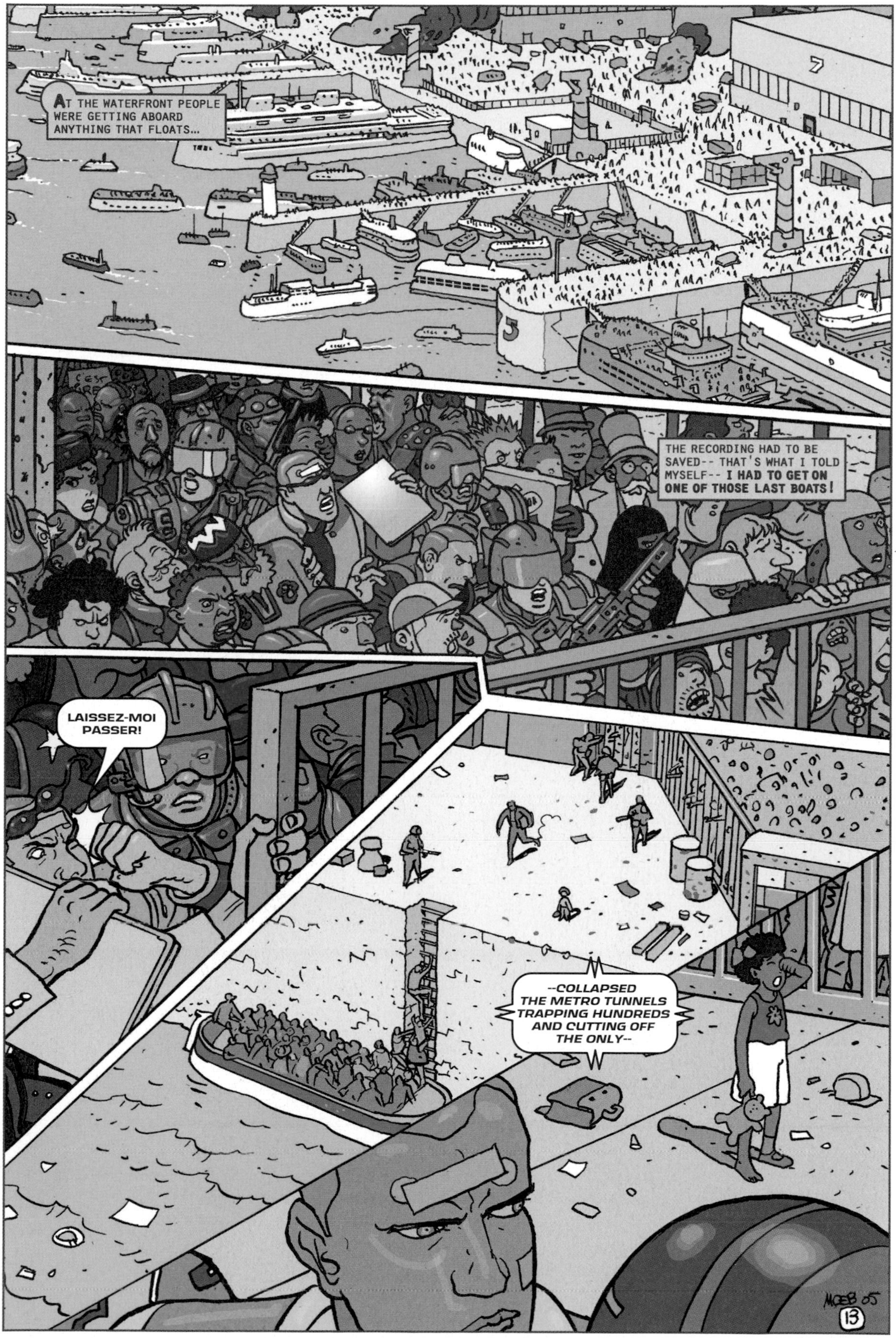
AT THE WATERFRONT PEOPLE WERE GETTING ABOARD ANYTHING THAT FLOATS...
THE RECORDING HAD TO BE SAVED-- THAT'S WHAT I TOLD MYSELF-- **I HAD TO GET ON ONE OF THOSE LAST BOATS!**
LAISSEZ-MOI PASSER!
--COLLAPSED THE METRO TUNNELS TRAPPING HUNDREDS AND CUTTING OFF THE ONLY--
13

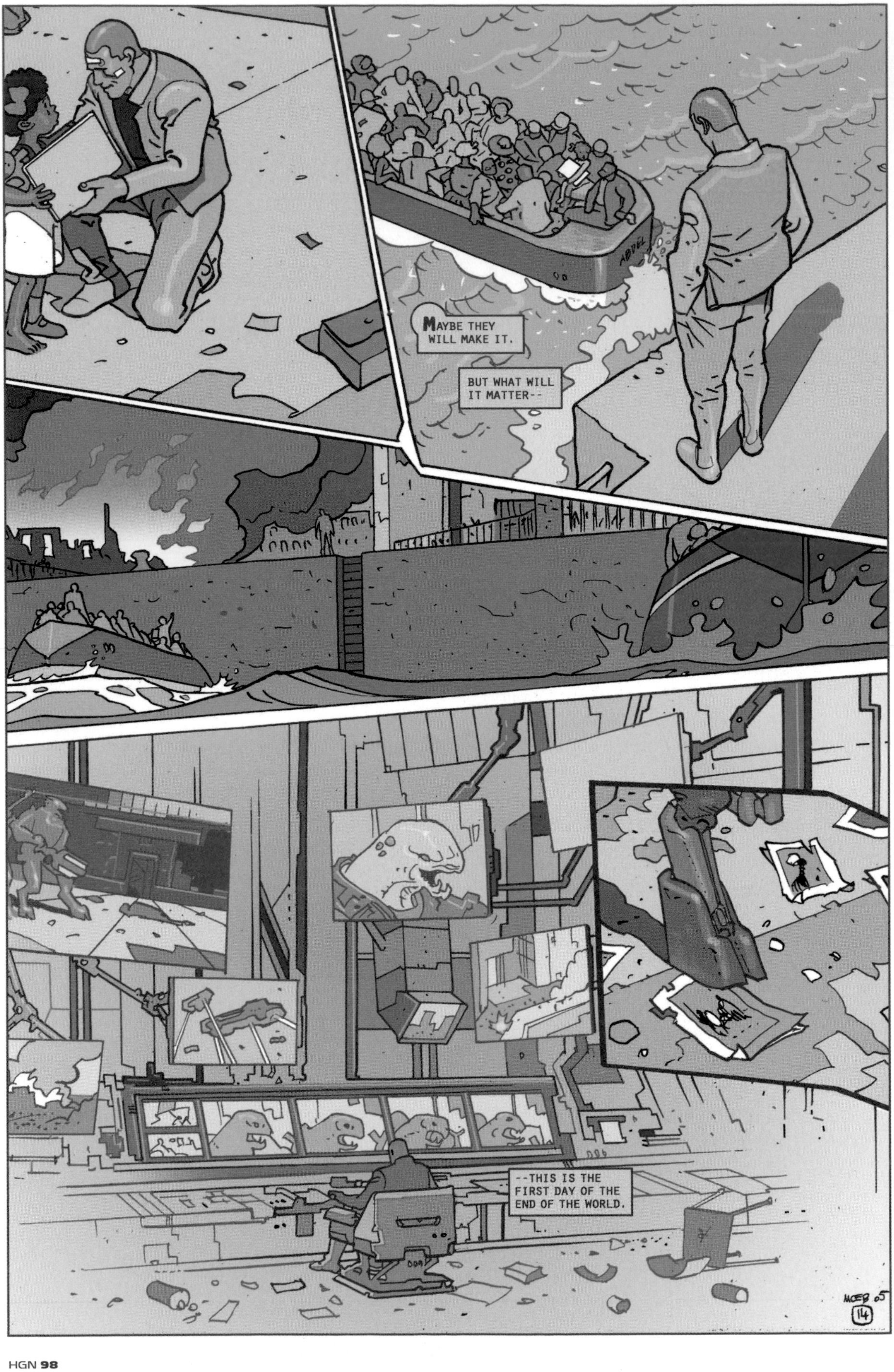
ABDEL
MAYBE THEY WILL MAKE IT.
BUT WHAT WILL IT MATTER--
--THIS IS THE FIRST DAY OF THE END OF THE WORLD.
MOEB 05
14

It was Febuary of 2005 when I had dinner with Maria at the Hôtel Costes on Rue St. Honoré in Paris. My exhibition with Hayao Miyazaki was finally underway, making it an opportune moment to begin another project. My son Raphael plays the HALO videogame, so I was familiar with how it looks, and the idea of a HALO graphic novel intrigued me. It had also been a while since I'd worked with an American publisher, and this provided me with just such a chance.

I enjoyed working on this book, and was amazed at the collection of artists involved with it. However, when Maria asked me to turn in my biography in one or two paragraphs, I replied that it might be quite a task, considering the problems of condensing over 50 years' worth of work onto half a page. So I told her to just have them look me up on the Web instead — now that's futuristic!

– Jean "Moebius" Giraud

Brett Lewis was a little apprehensive when first approached with the HALO project. He doesn't drive, has problems with computers, owns no television and doesn't play many games. However, his work experience in such industries as movies, music, video games, sports entertainment and, of course, comics has turned him into a versatile writer who can tackle any assignment through meticulous study and research. For the HALO graphic novel, Lewis managed to read through all of the published HALO books, and he became quite involved with them. Finding the New Mombasa theme to be his favorite, he submitted a story proposal so poignant that it almost made Bungie's Lorraine McLees want to cry. As a result, he was teamed up with legendary French comics artist Moebius, and together they concocted a stunning visual and visceral experience for hardcore HALO fans.

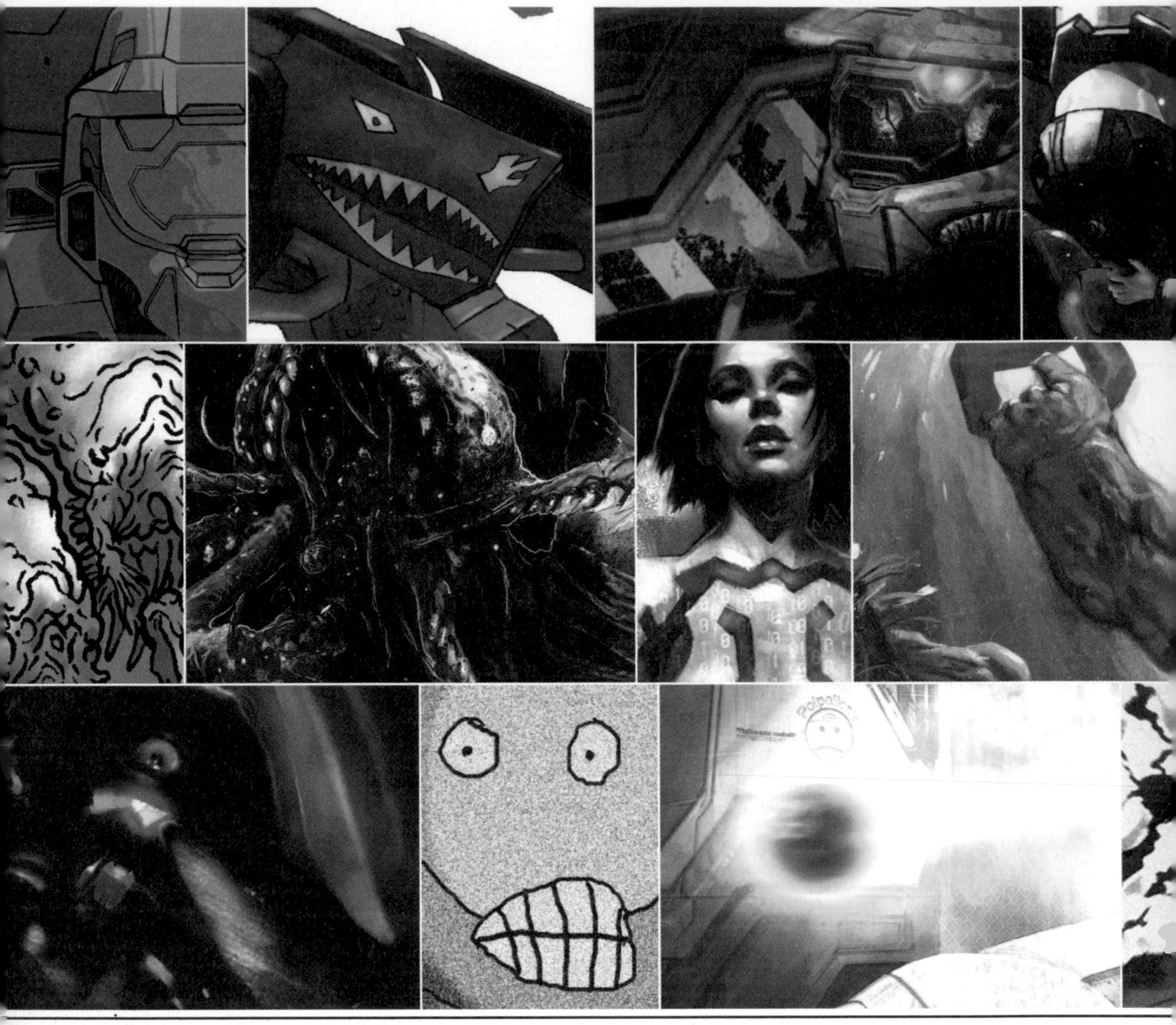

GALLERY

In the process of assembling the artists for the preceding stories, we found ourselves with a grim dilemma. We'd gone to enormous effort, and made contact with these incredibly talented artists, and we wouldn't be able to use them all in just four stories. Well, we didn't want to waste what was effectively a providential opportunity. So we did what we always do: we made it work. We assigned every artist who'd agree to submit a gallery piece, their own unique interpretation of a moment from the Halo universe.

Each contributor, from the pantheon of contemporary artists to the dusty halls of Bungie itself, created a new vision of what their vision of Halo is.

And here they are. Enjoy them. We did.

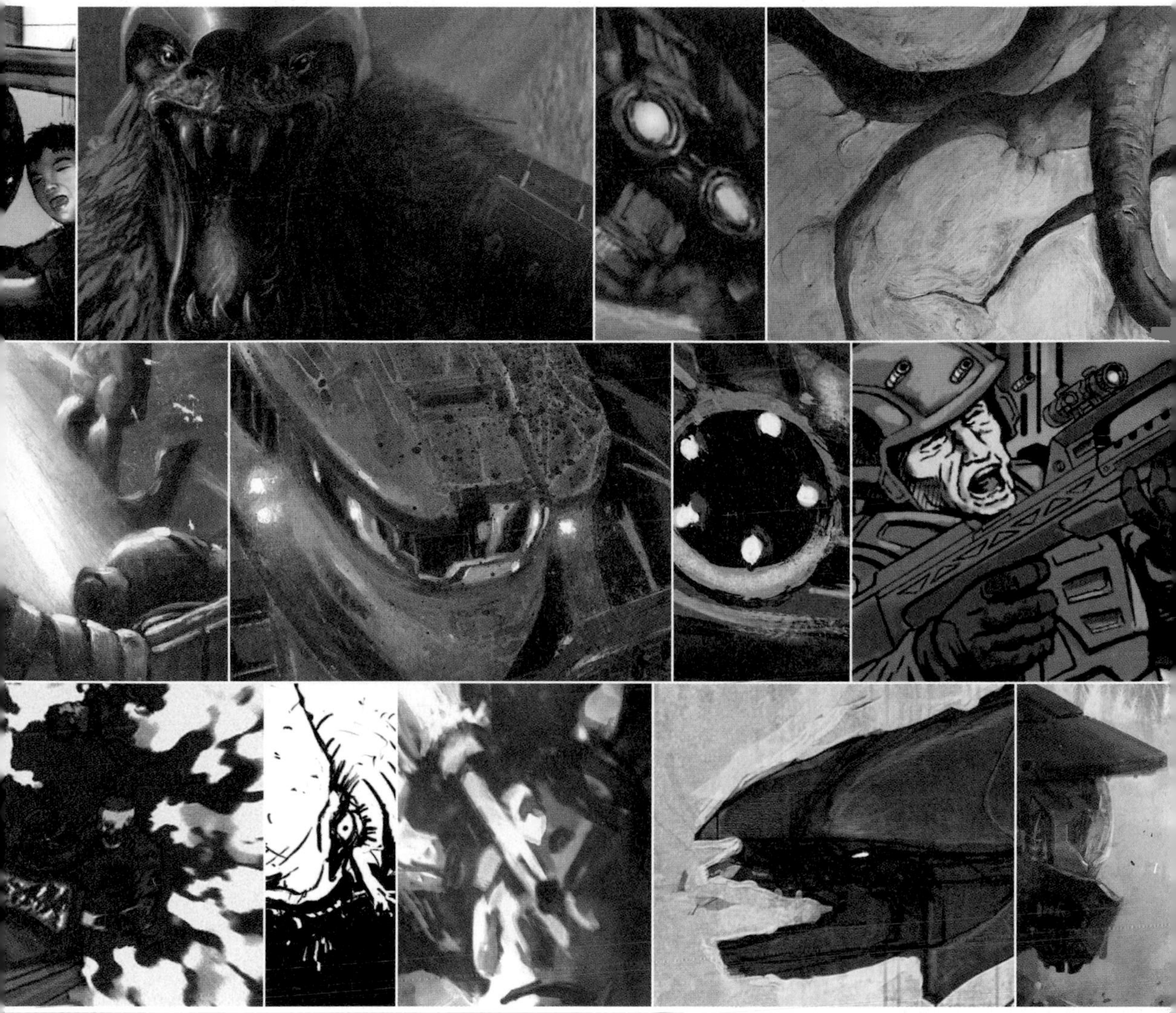

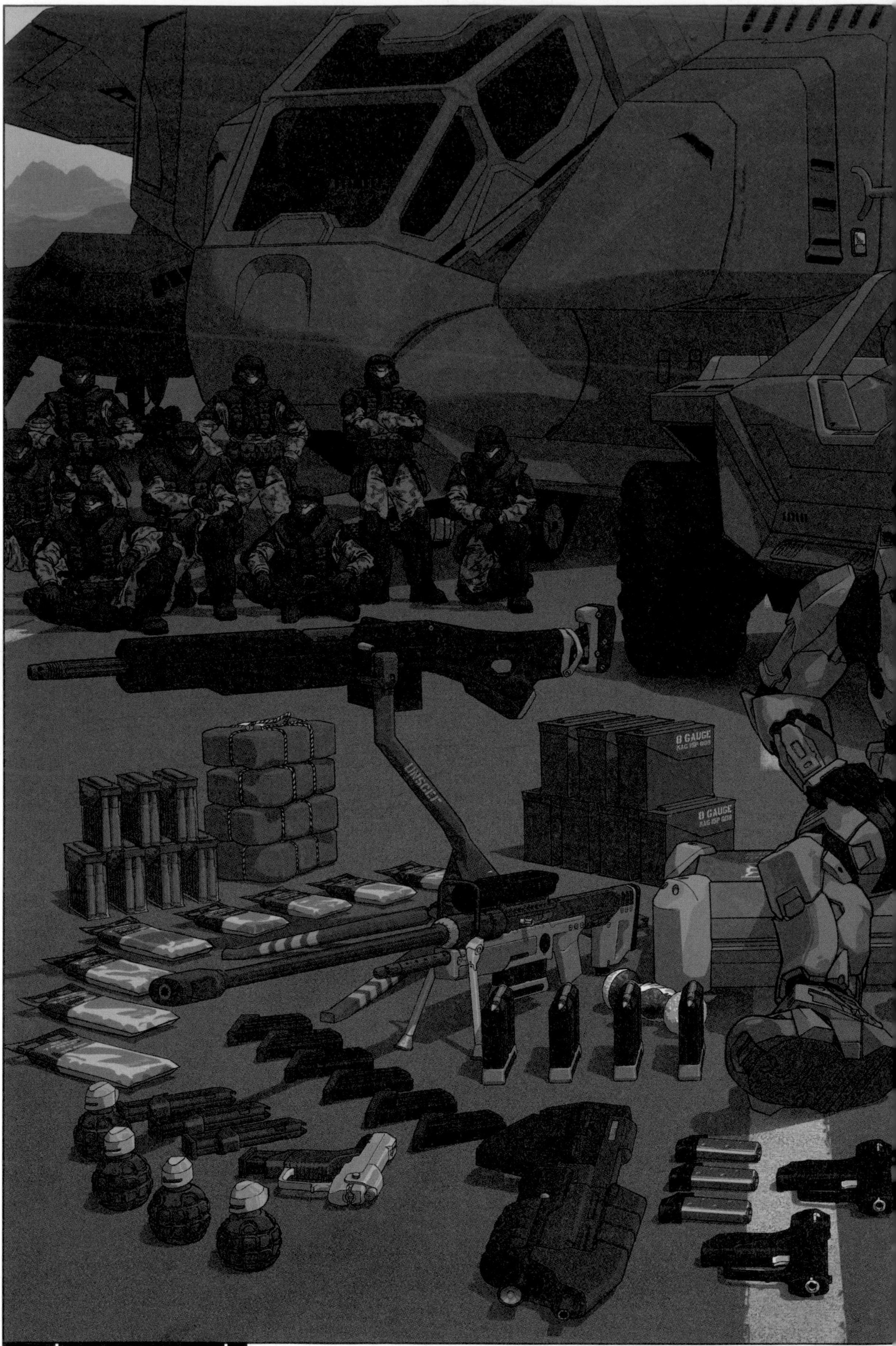
8 GAUGE
8 GAUGE

Lorraine McLees

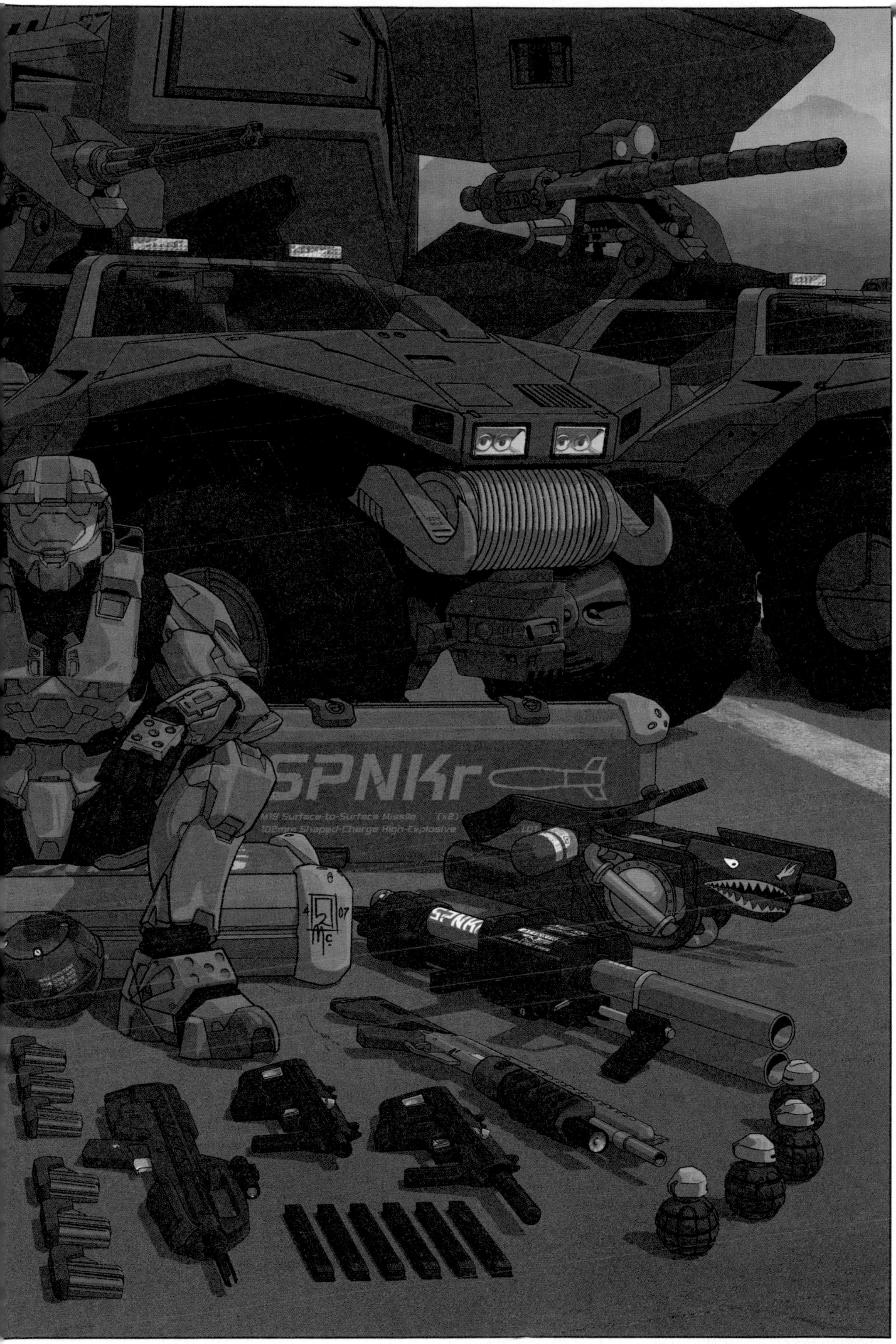
SPNKr
M19 Surface-to-Surface Missile (x2)
102mm Shaped-Charge High-Explosive

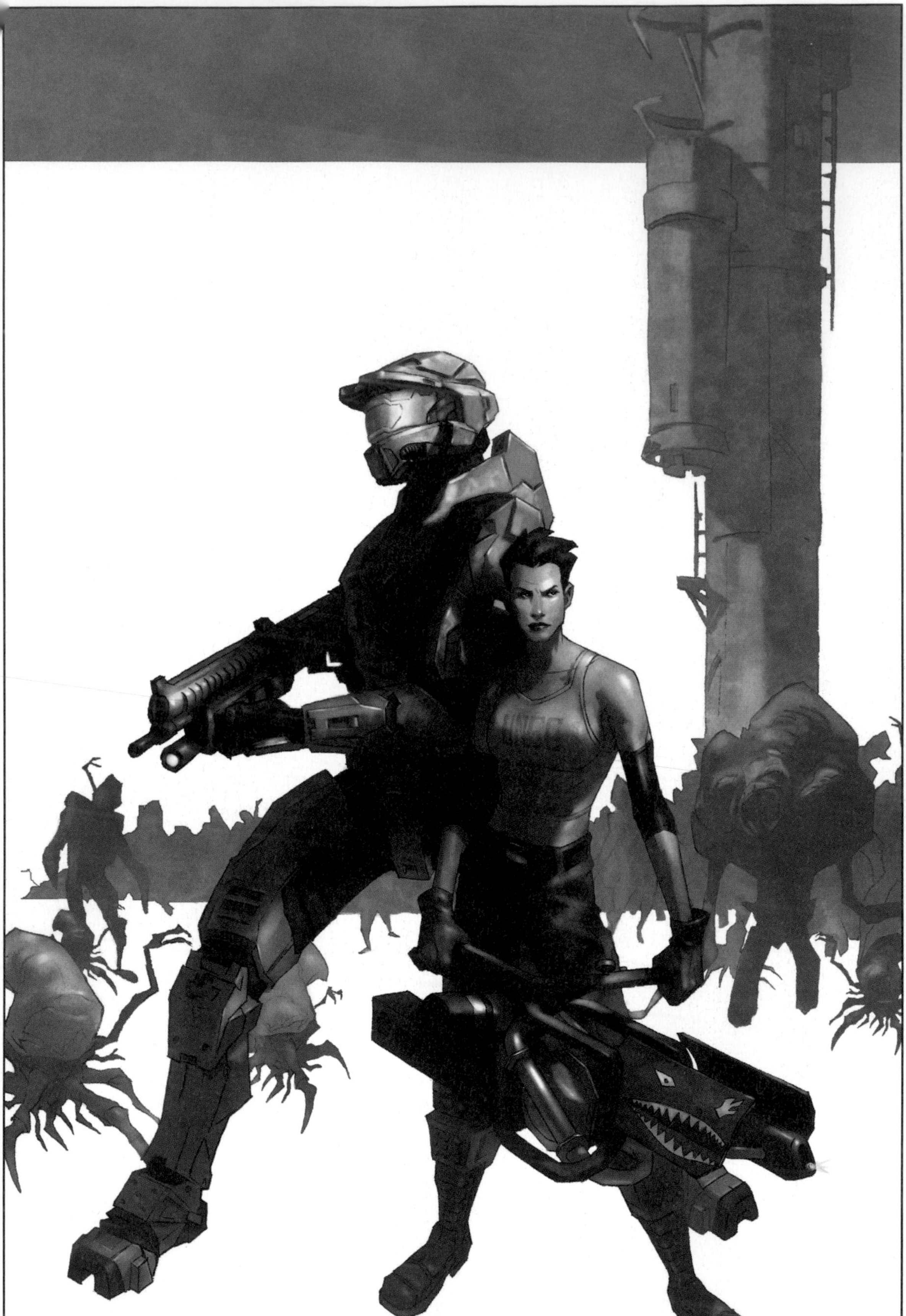
UNSC

Doug Alexander

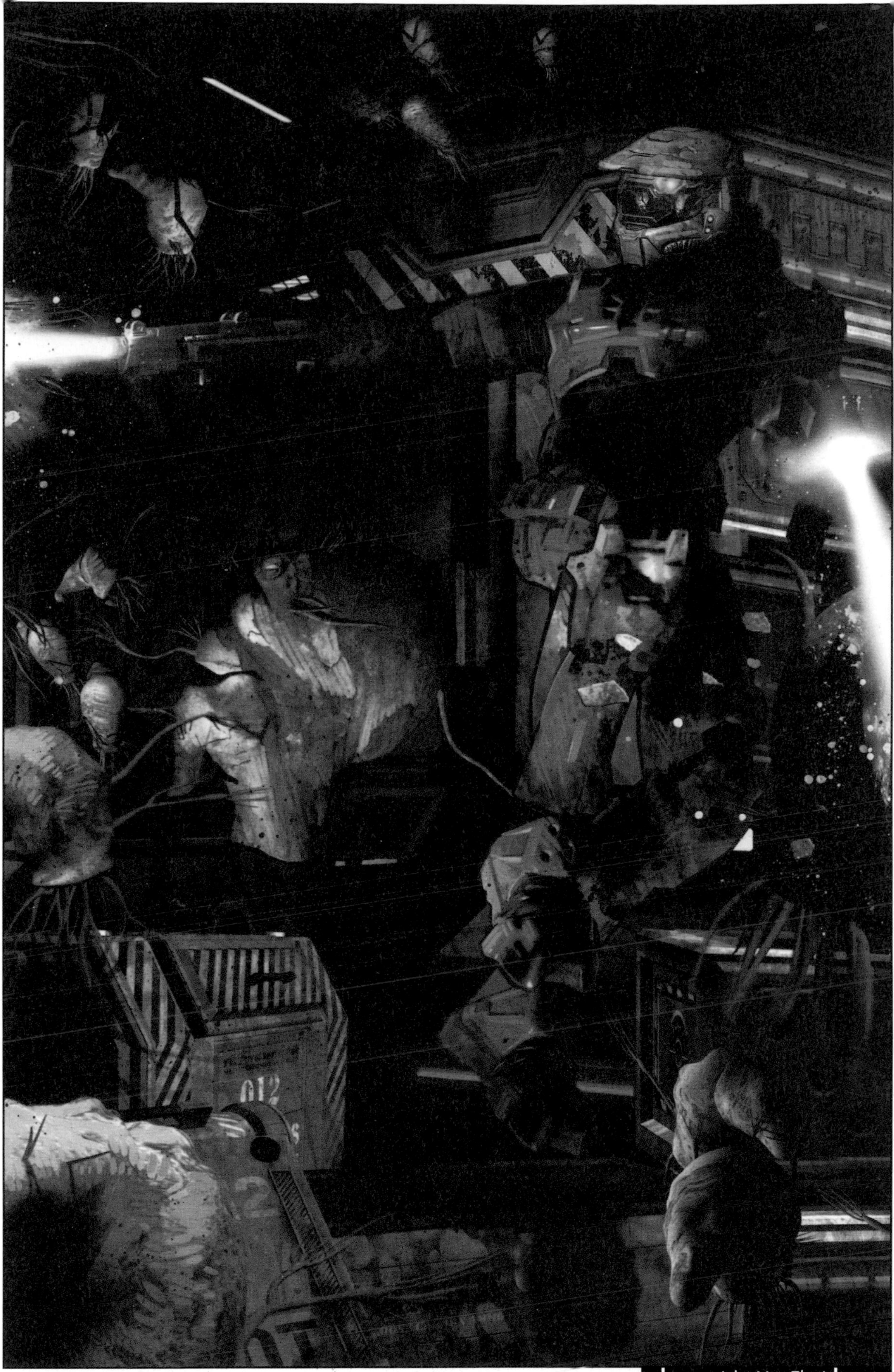
012

John Van Fleet

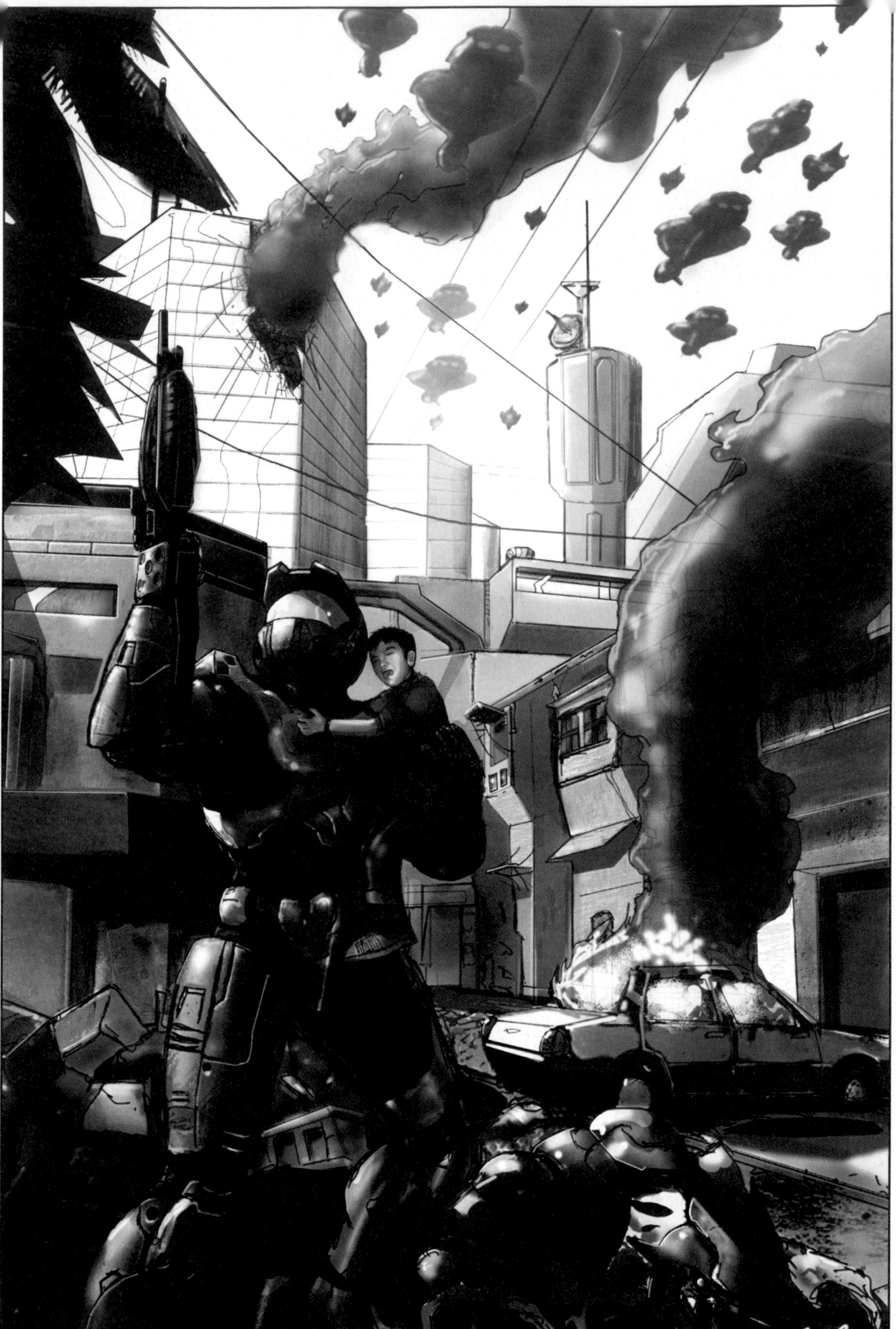

Tom Doyle

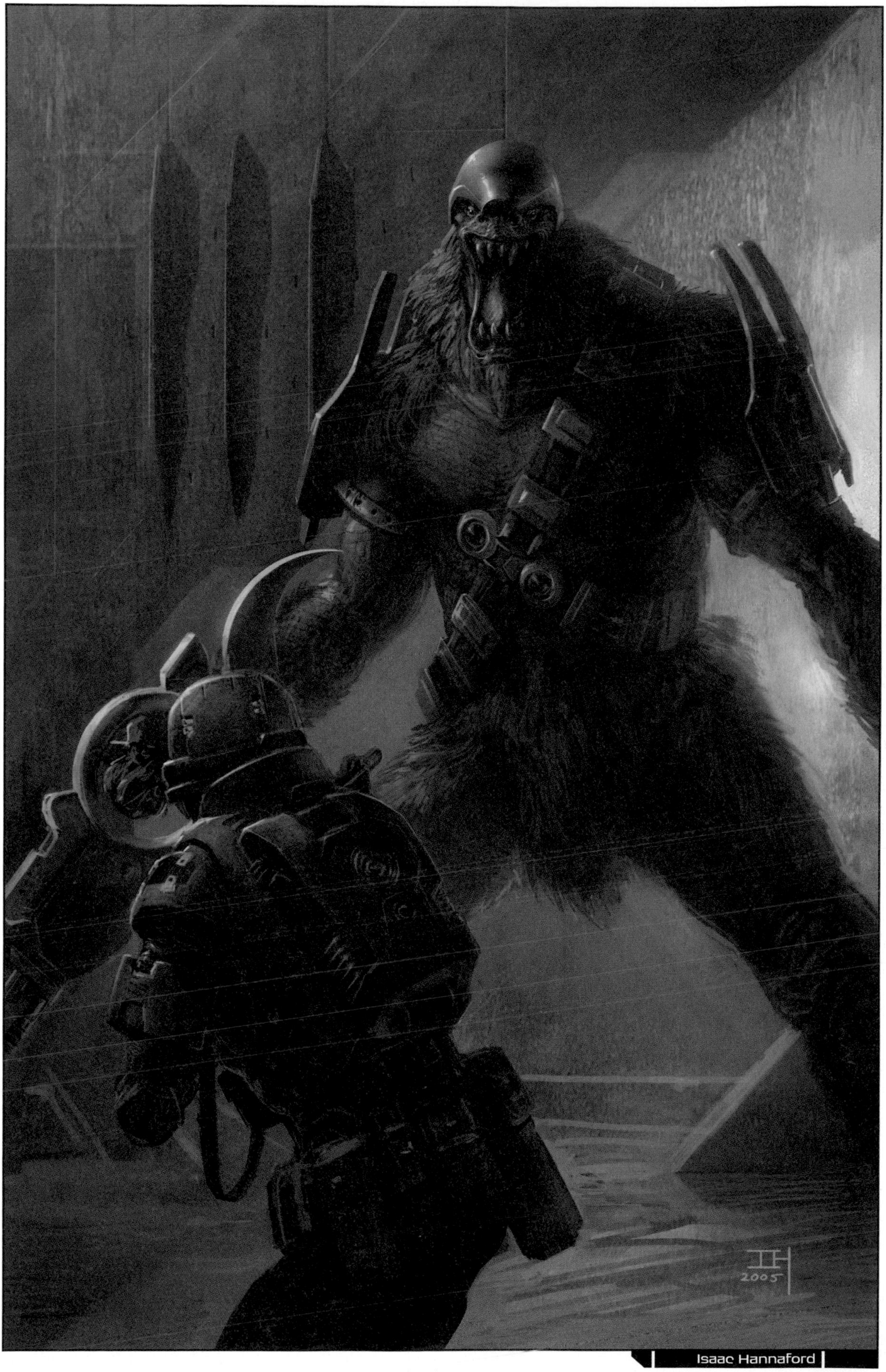
IH
2005

Isaac Hannaford

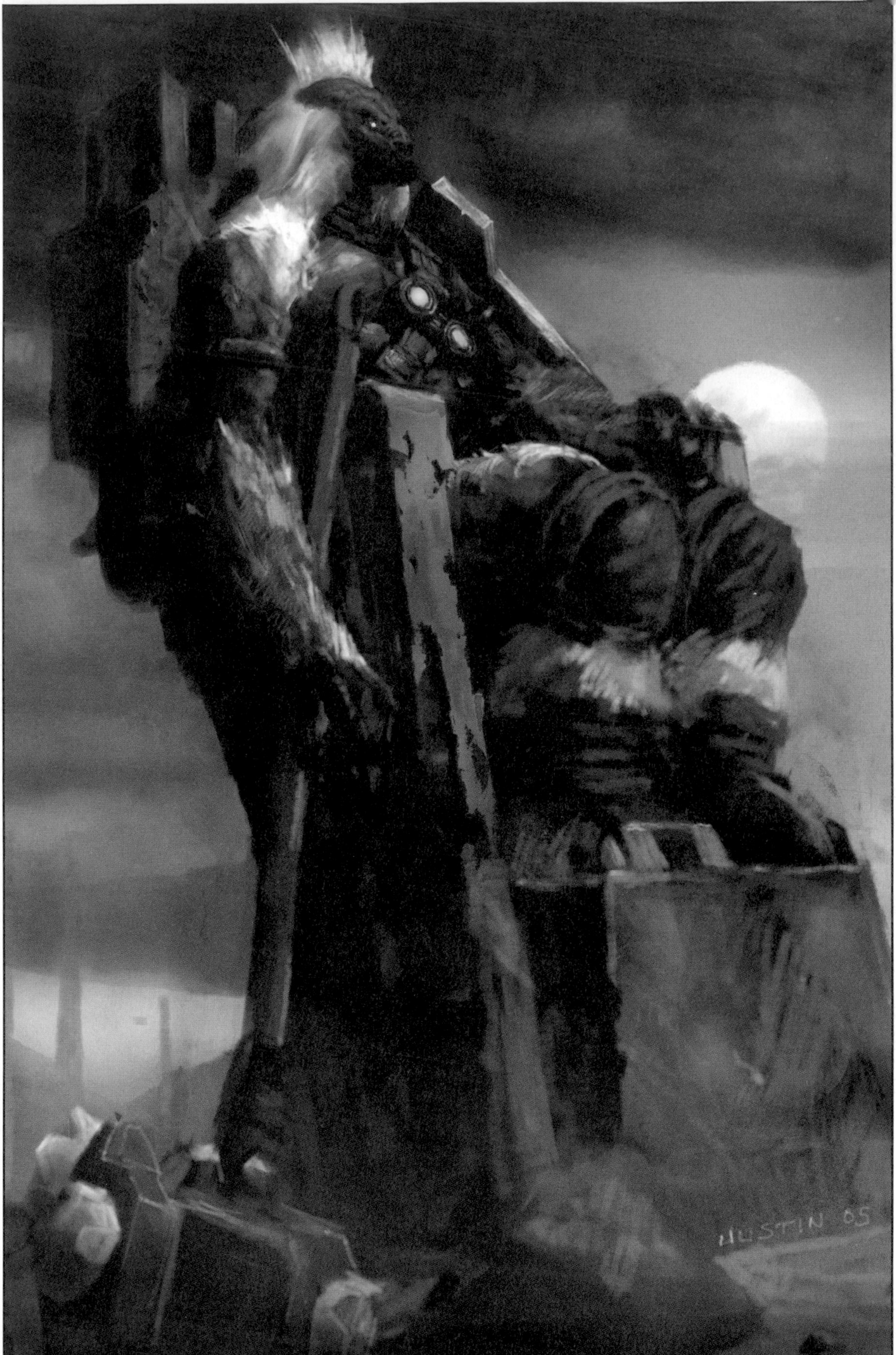
JUSTIN 05

Justin Sweet

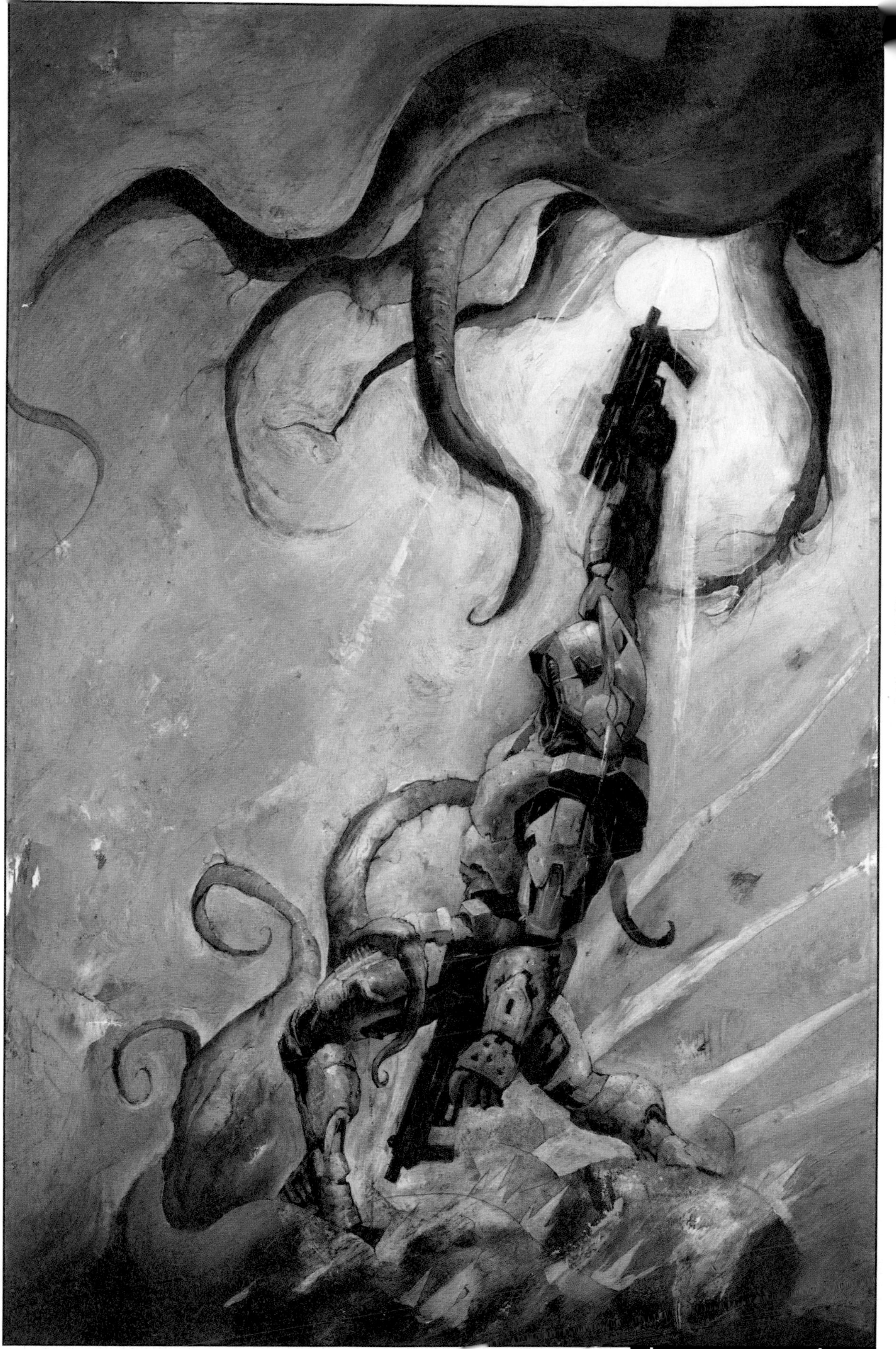
Kent Williams

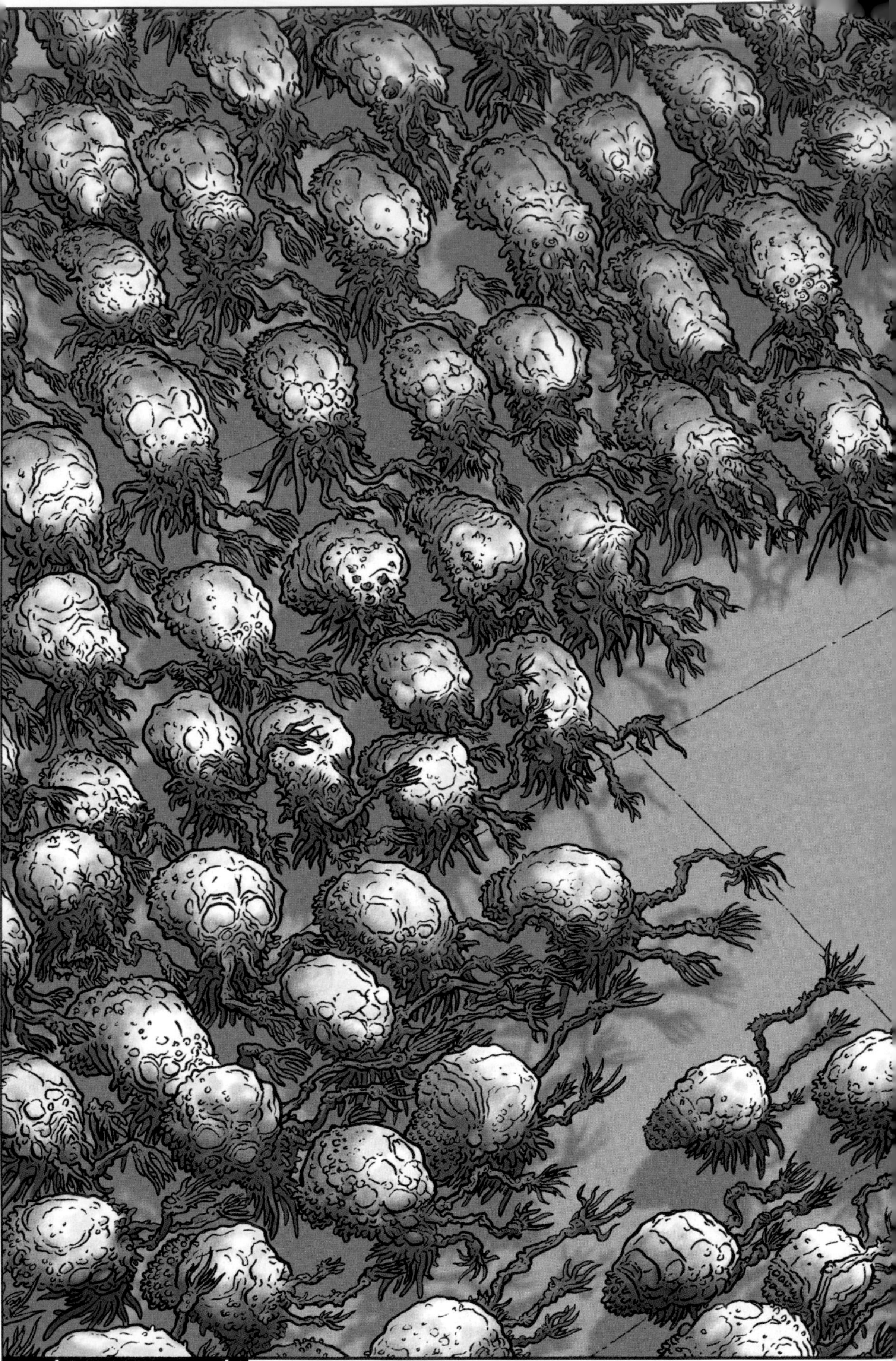

Geof Darrow

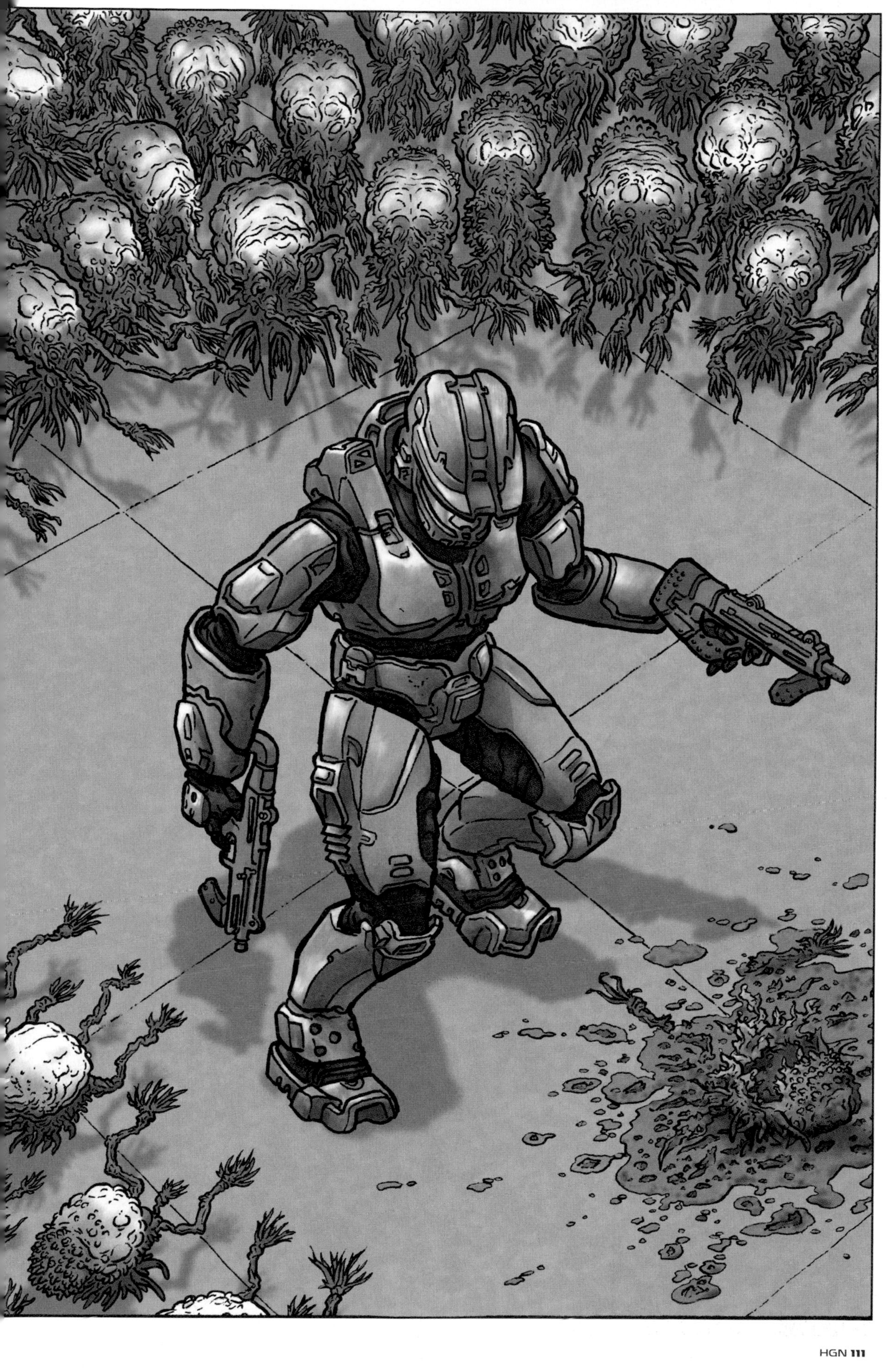

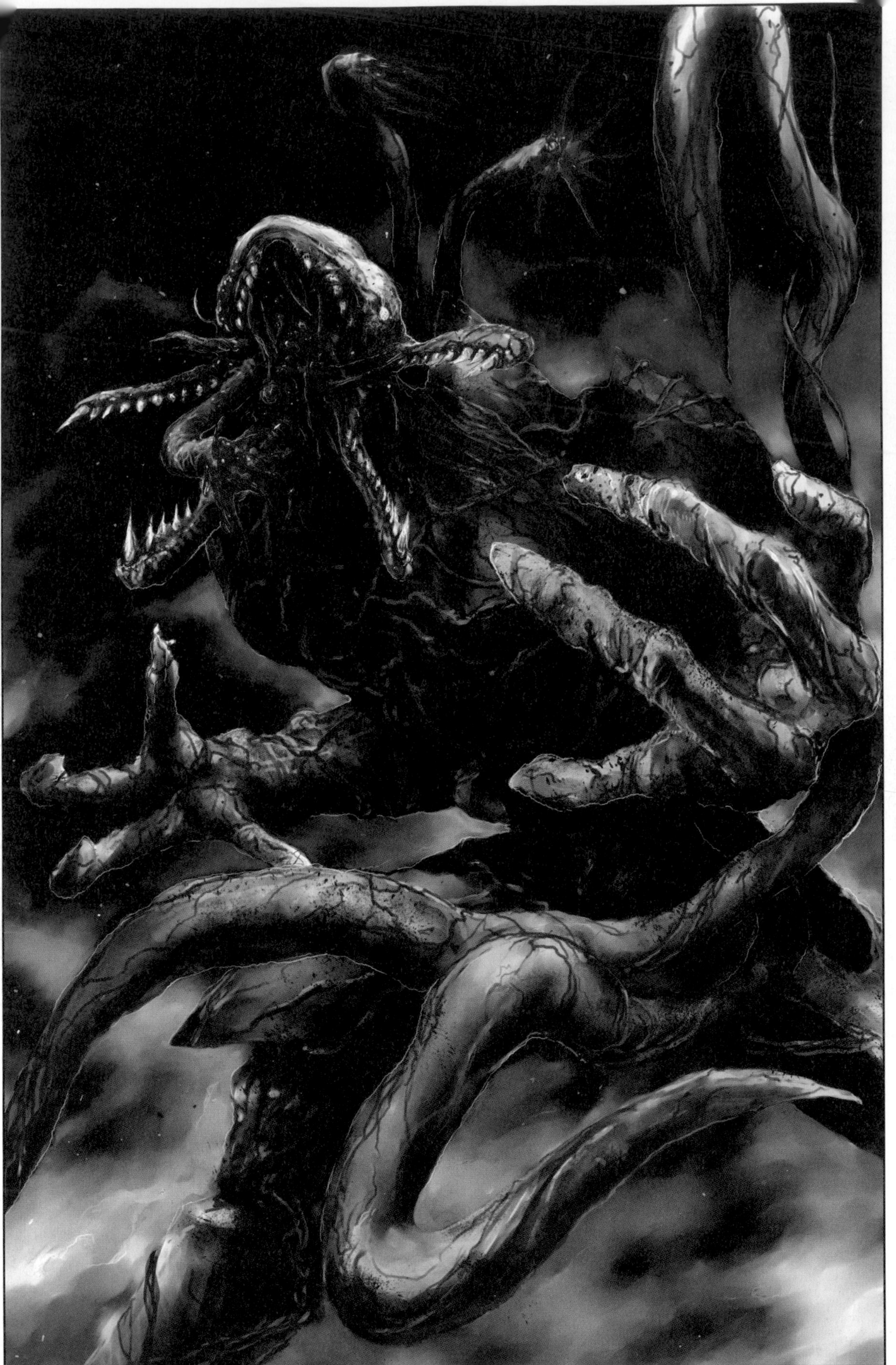

Tsutomu Nihei

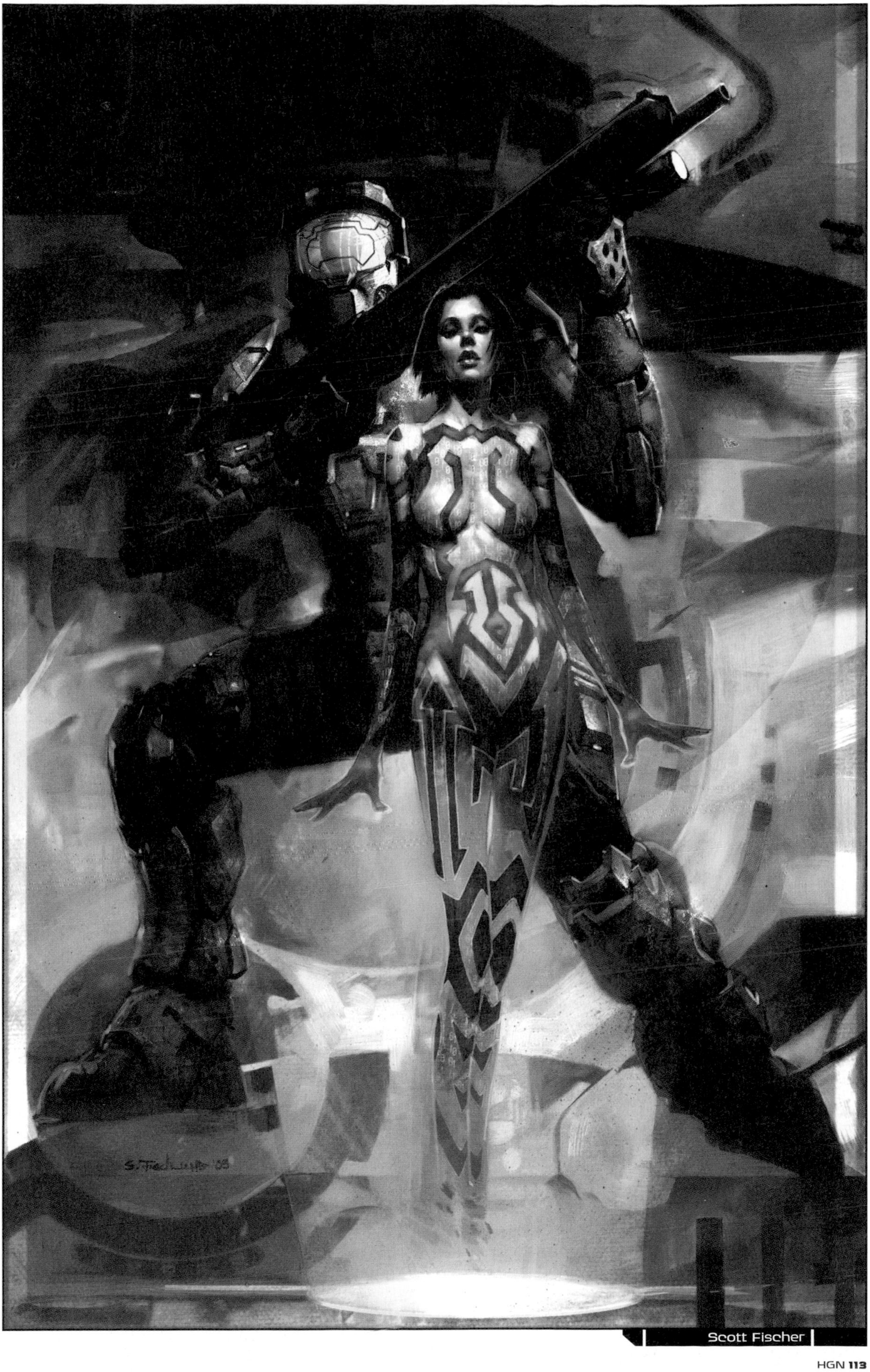
S. Fischer '08
Scott Fischer

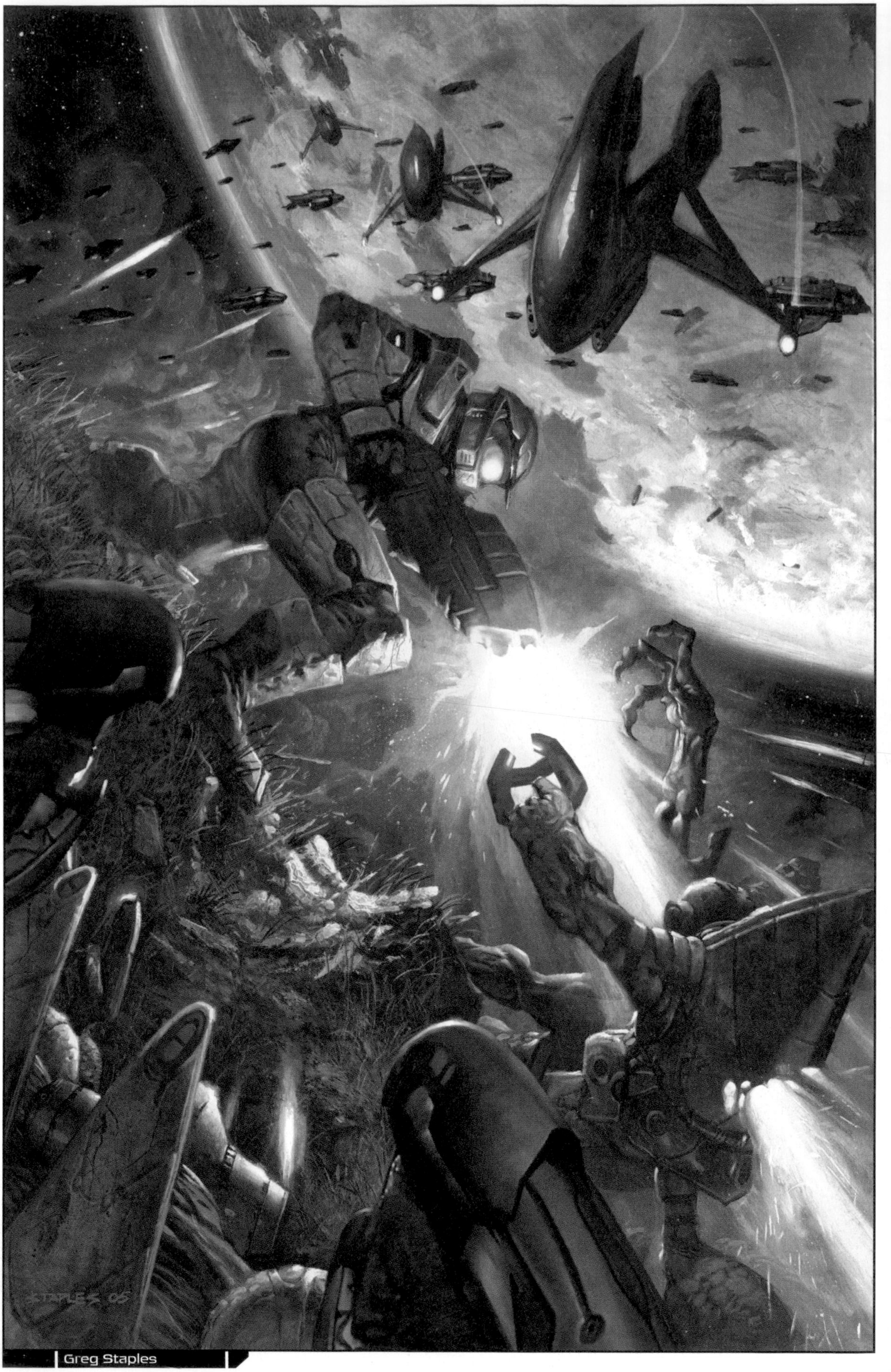
STAPLES 05

Greg Staples

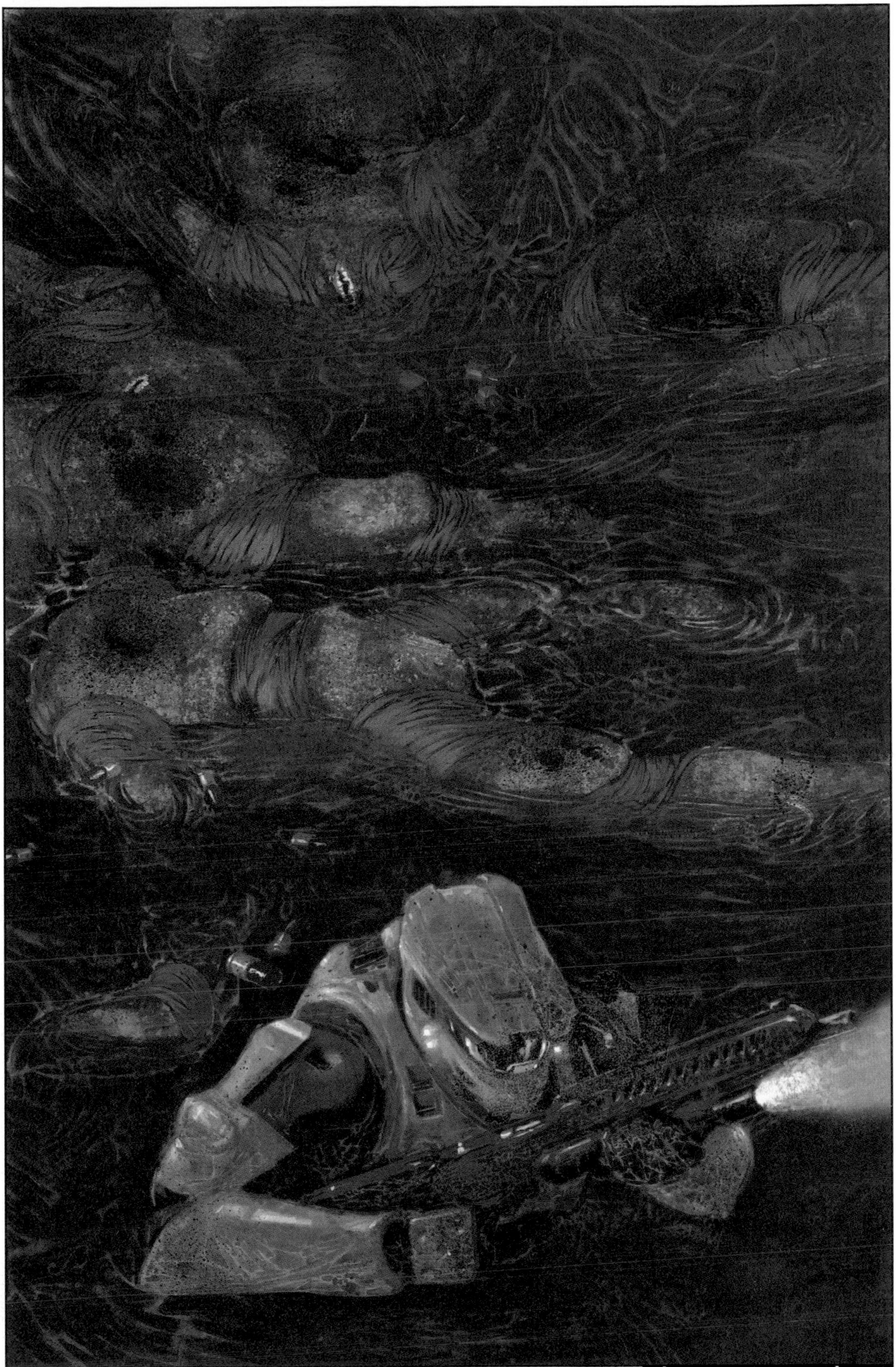

Sterling Hundley

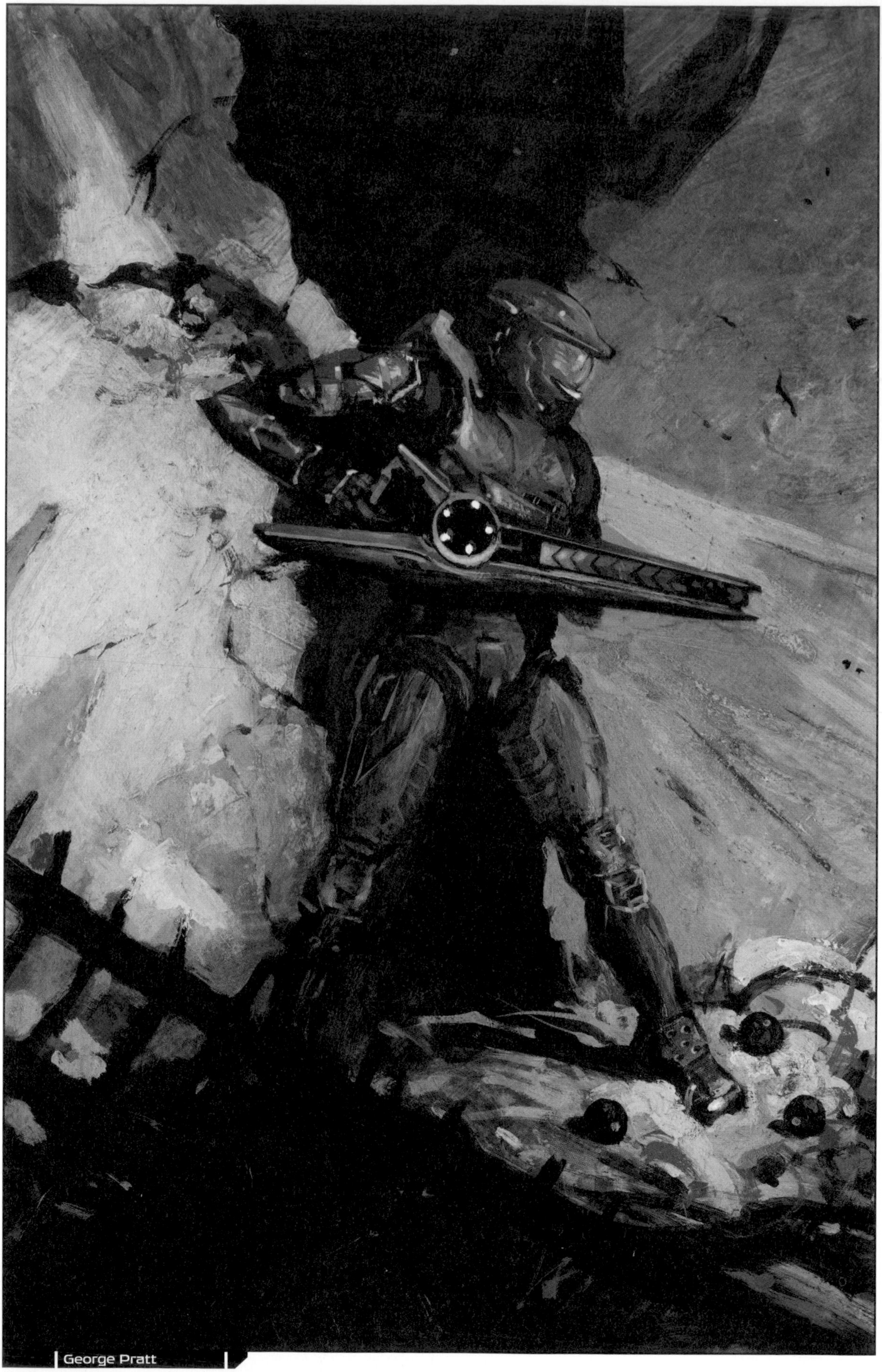

George Pratt

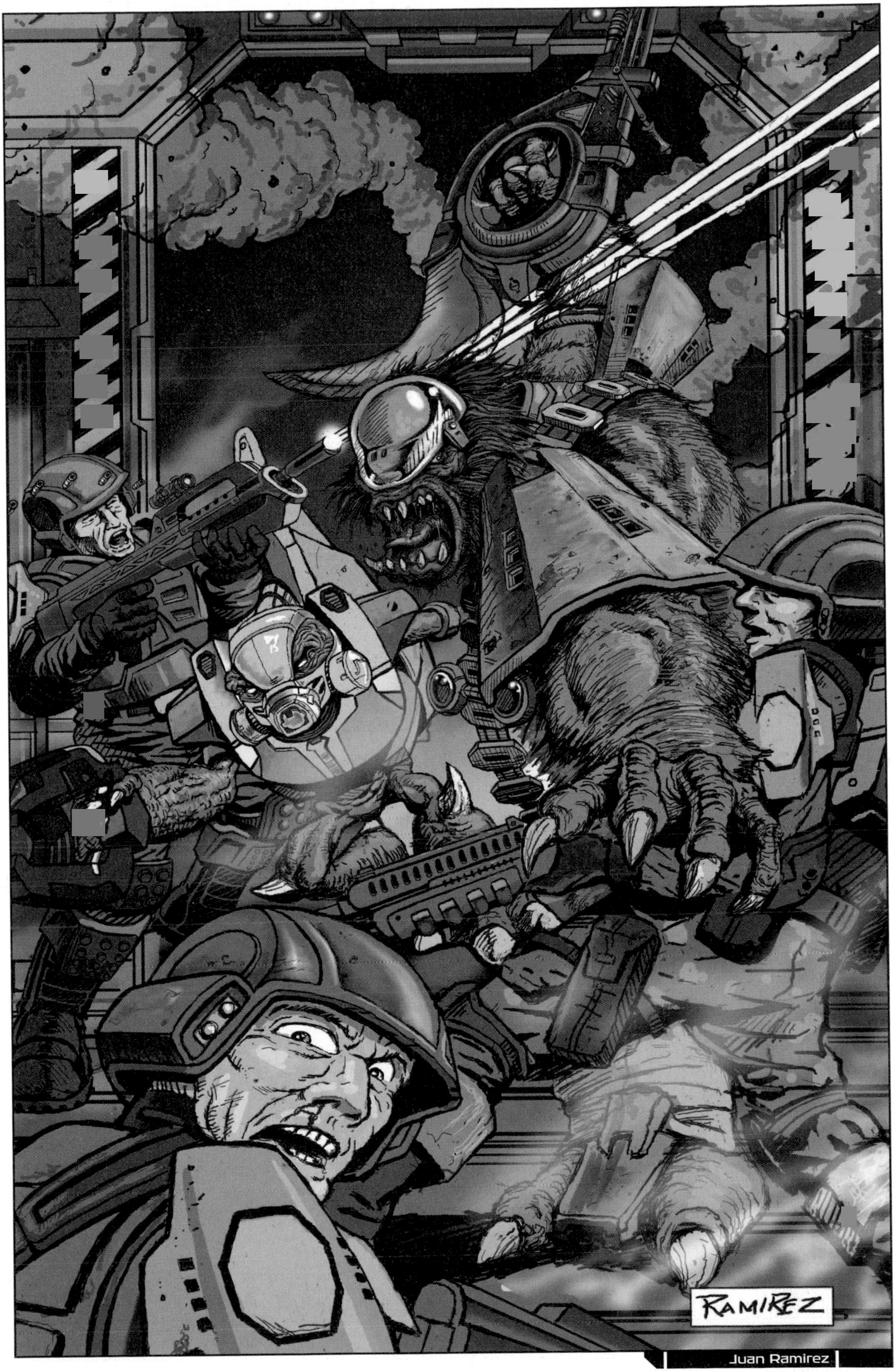
RAMIREZ

Juan Ramirez

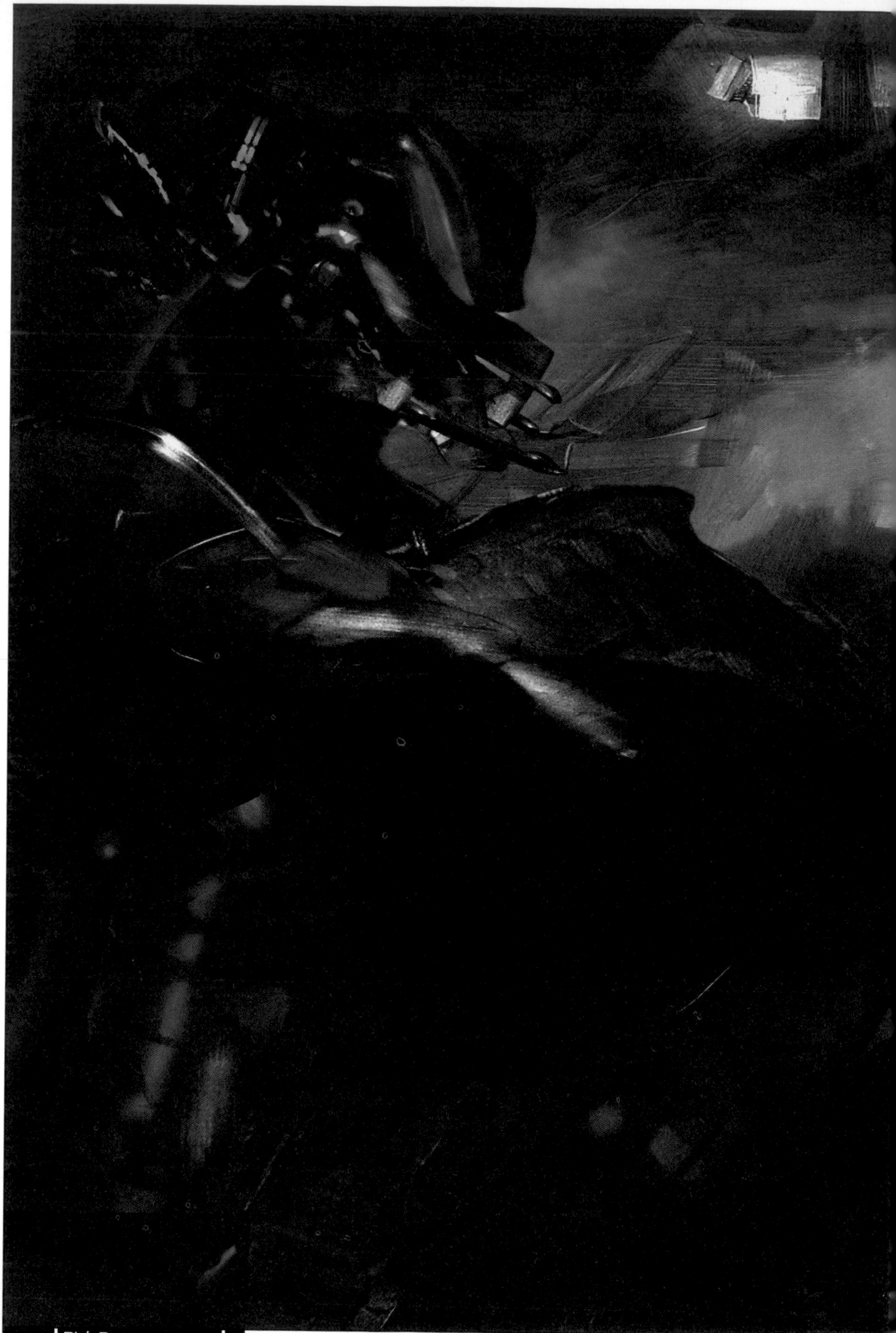

Rick Berry

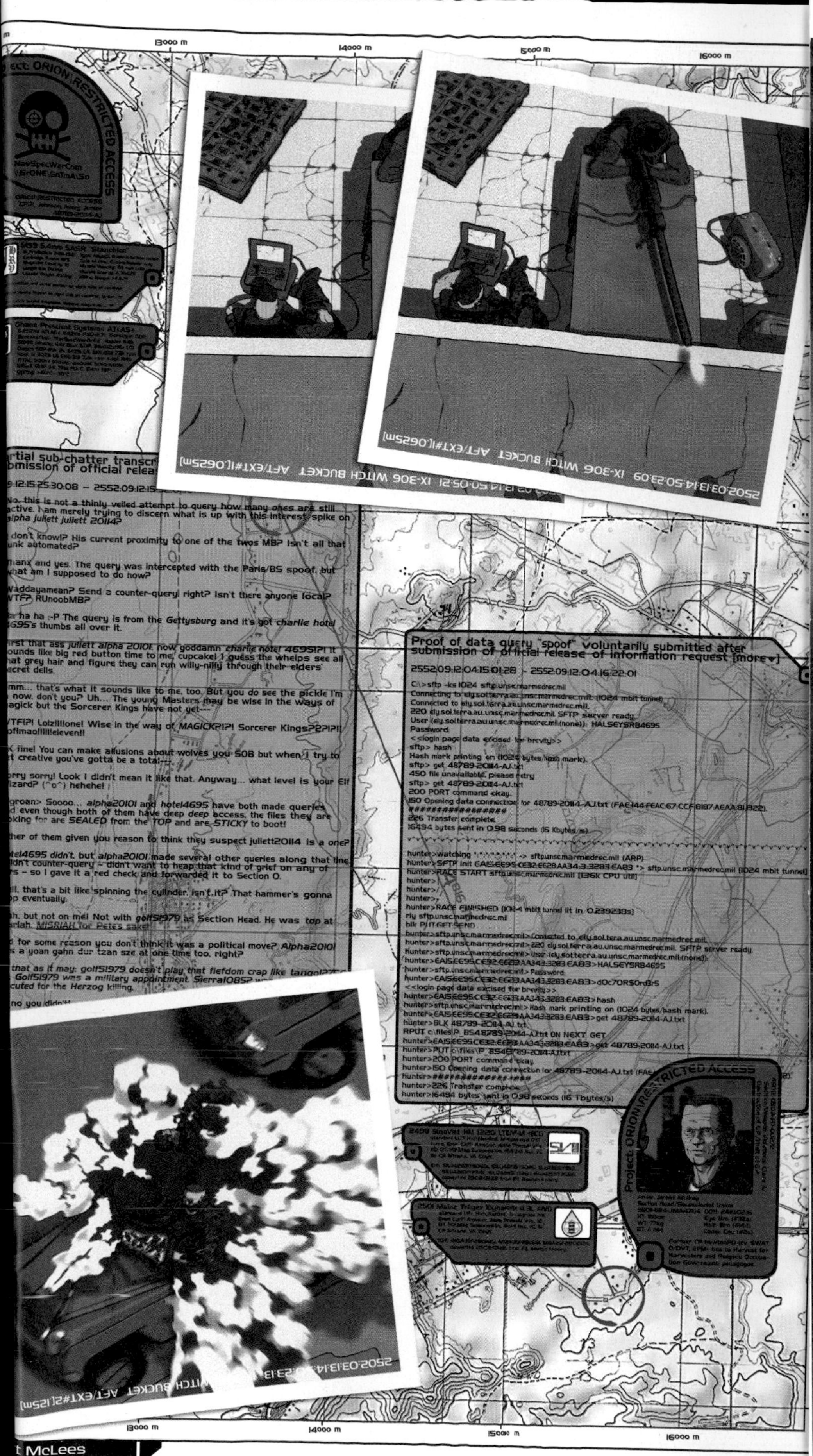
13000 m
14000 m
15000 m
16000 m
ect: ORION\RESTRICTED ACCESS
2552.03.13.14.50.23.09 IX-306 WITCH BUCKET AFT/EXT#1[.0625m]
IX-306 WITCH BUCKET AFT/EXT#1[.0625m]
rtial sub-chatter transcr
bmission of official relea
9:12:15:25:30:08 ~ 2552:09:12:15
No, this is not a thinly veiled attempt to query how many ones are still active. I am merely trying to discern what is up with this interest spike on alpha juliett juliett 20114?
don't know!? His current proximity to one of the twos MB? Isn't all that unk automated?
Thanx and yes. The query was intercepted with the Paris/BS spoof, but what am I supposed to do now?
Waddayamean? Send a counter-query, right? Isn't there anyone local? WTF? RUnoobMB?
ha ha ha :-P The query is from the Gettysburg and it's got charlie hotel 4695's thumbs all over it.
irst that ass juliett alpha 20101, now goddamn charlie hotel 4695!?! It ounds like big red button time to me, cupcake! I guess the whelps see all hat grey hair and figure they can run willy-nilly through their elders' ecret dells.
mm... that's what it sounds like to me, too. But you do see the pickle I'm now, don't you? Uh... The young Masters may be wise in the ways of agick but the Sorcerer Kings have not yet---
TF!?! Lolzlllllone! Wise in the way of MAGICK?!?! Sorcerer Kings??!?!! ofimaolllllleleven!!
K fine! You can make allusions about wolves you SOB but when I try to t creative you've gotta be a total---.
orry sorry! Look I didn't mean it like that. Anyway... what level is your Elf izard? (^o^) hehehe!
groan> Soooo... alpha20101 and hotel4695 have both made queries d even though both of them have deep deep access, the files they are oking for are SEALED from the TOP and are STICKY to boot!
ther of them given you reason to think they suspect juliett20114 is a one?
tel4695 didn't, but alpha20101 made several other queries along that line. idn't counter-query – didn't want to heap that kind of grief on any of rs – so I gave it a red check and forwarded it to Section O.
ll, that's a bit like spinning the cylinder, isn't it? That hammer's gonna p eventually.
h, but not on me! Not with golf51979 as Section Head. He was top at riah. MISRIAH for Pete's sake!
d for some reason you don't think it was a political move? Alpha20101 s a yoan gahn dur tzan sze at one time too, right?
that as it may: golf51979 doesn't play that fiefdom crap like tango Golf51979 was a military appointment. Sierra10852 cuted for the Herzog killing.
no you didn't
Proof of data query "spoof" voluntarily submitted after submission of official release of information request [more▾]
2552:09:12:04:15:01:28 ~ 2552:09:12:04:16:22:01
C:\>sftp -ks 1024 sftp.unsc.marmedrec.mil
Connecting to ely.sol.terra.au.unsc.marmedrec.mil: (1024 mbit tunnel)
Connected to ely.sol.terra.au.unsc.marmedrec.mil.
220 ely.sol.terra.au.unsc.marmedrec.mil. SFTP server ready.
User (ely.sol.terra.au.unsc.marmedrec.mil:(none)): HALSEYSRB4695
Password:
<<login page data excised for brevity>>
sftp> hash
Hash mark printing on (1024 bytes/hash mark).
sftp> get 48789-20114-AJ.txt
450 file unavailable, please retry
sftp> get 48789-20114-AJ.txt
200 PORT command okay.
150 Opening data connection for 48789-20114-AJ.txt (FAE144:FEAC:67:CCF:8187:AEAA:81:B22).
#################
226 Transfer complete.
16494 bytes sent in 0.98 seconds (16 Kbytes/s).
hunter>watching *.*.*.*.*.*.*.* -> sftp.unsc.marmedrec.mil (ARP)
hunter>SFTP init EA15:EE95:CE32:EE28:AA34:3:3283:EA83 *> sftp.unsc.marmedrec.mil [1024 mbit tunnel]
hunter>RACE START sftp.unsc.marmedrec.mil [136k CPU util]
hunter>|
hunter>/
hunter>-
hunter>RACE FINISHED [1024 mbit tunnel lit in 0.239238s]
rly sftp.unsc.marmedrec.mil
blk PUT:GET:SEND
hunter>sftp.unsc.marmedrec.mil>Connected to ely.sol.tera.au.unsc.marmedrec.mil.
hunter>sftp.unsc.marmedrec.mil>220 ely.sol.terra.au.unsc.marmedrec.mil. SFTP server ready.
hunter>sftp.unsc.marmedrec.mil>User (ely.sol.terra.au.unsc.marmedrec.mil:(none)):
hunter>EA15:EE95:CE32:EE28:AA34:3:3283:EA83>HALSEYSRB4695
hunter>sftp.unsc.marmedrec.mil>Password:
hunter>EA15:EE95:CE32:EE28:AA34:3:3283:EA83>d0c70R$0rd3r5
<<login page data excised for brevity>>
hunter>EA15:EE95:CE32:EE28:AA34:3:3283:EA83>hash
hunter>sftp.unsc.marmedrec.mil>Hash mark printing on (1024 bytes/hash mark).
hunter>EA15:EE95:CE32:EE28:AA34:3:3283:EA83>get 48789-20114-AJ.txt
hunter>BLK 48789-20114-AJ.txt
RPUT c:\files\P_BS48789-20114-AJ.txt ON NEXT GET
hunter>EA15:EE95:CE32:EE28:AA34:3:3283:EA83>get 48789-20114-AJ.txt
hunter>PUT c:\files\P_BS48789-20114-AJ.txt
hunter>200 PORT command okay.
hunter>150 Opening data connection for 48789-20114-AJ.txt (FAE
hunter>#################
hunter>226 Transfer complete.
hunter>16494 bytes sent in 0.98 seconds (16 Tbytes/s)
Project: ORION\RESTRICTED ACCESS
2498 SinoViet HM 1220 LTBYM-BCD
2552.03.13.14.50.23.13 WITCH BUCKET AFT/EXT#2[.125m]

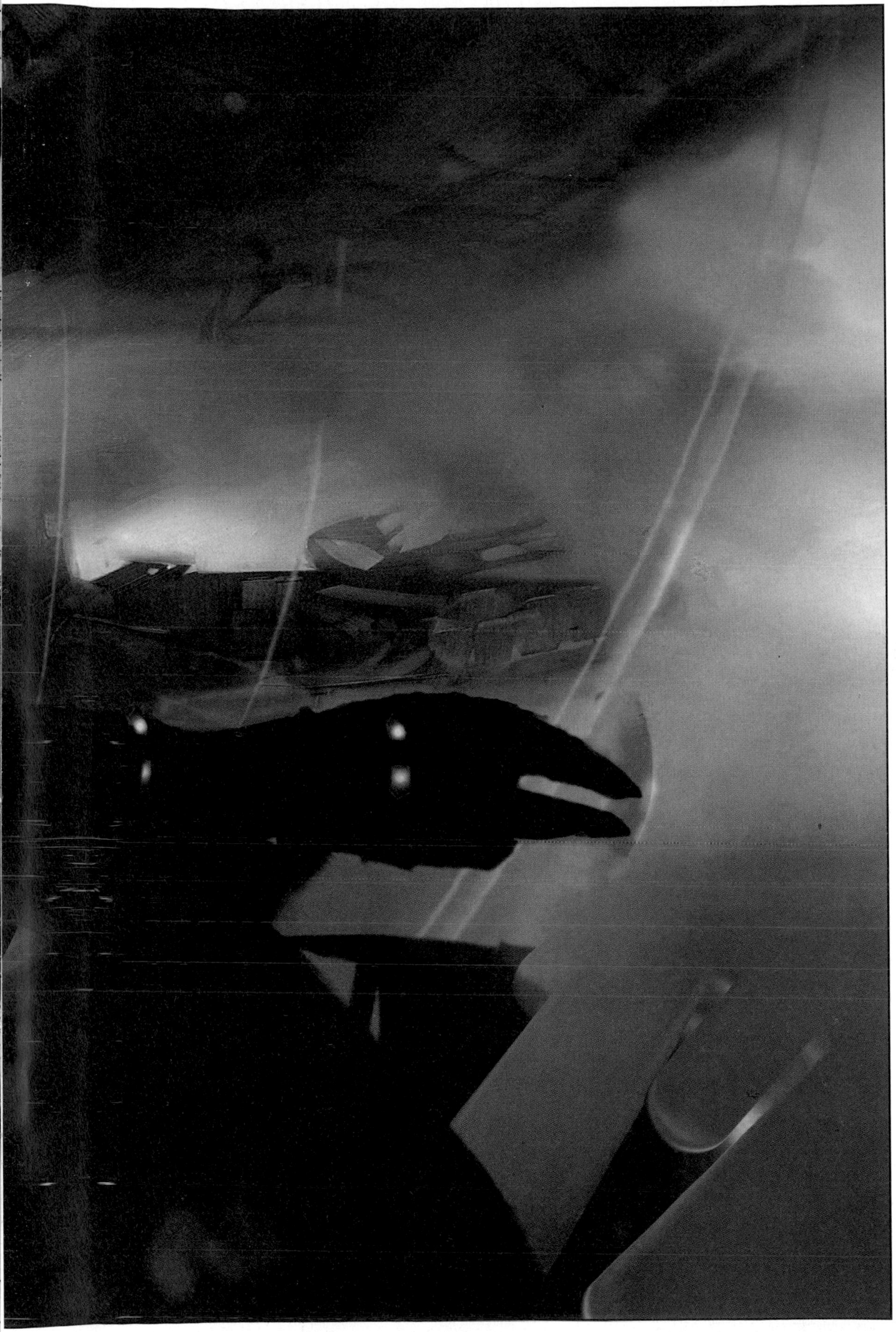

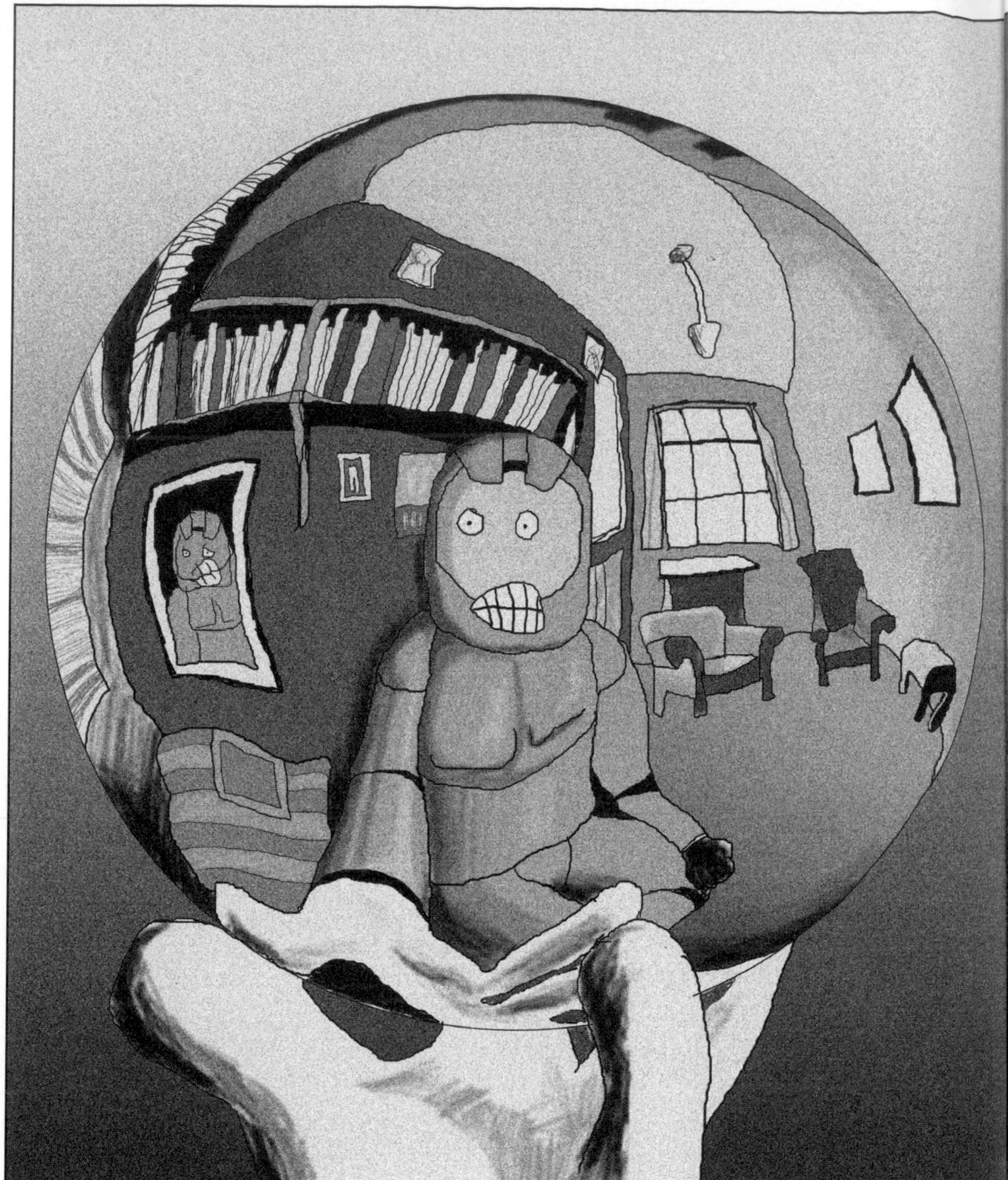

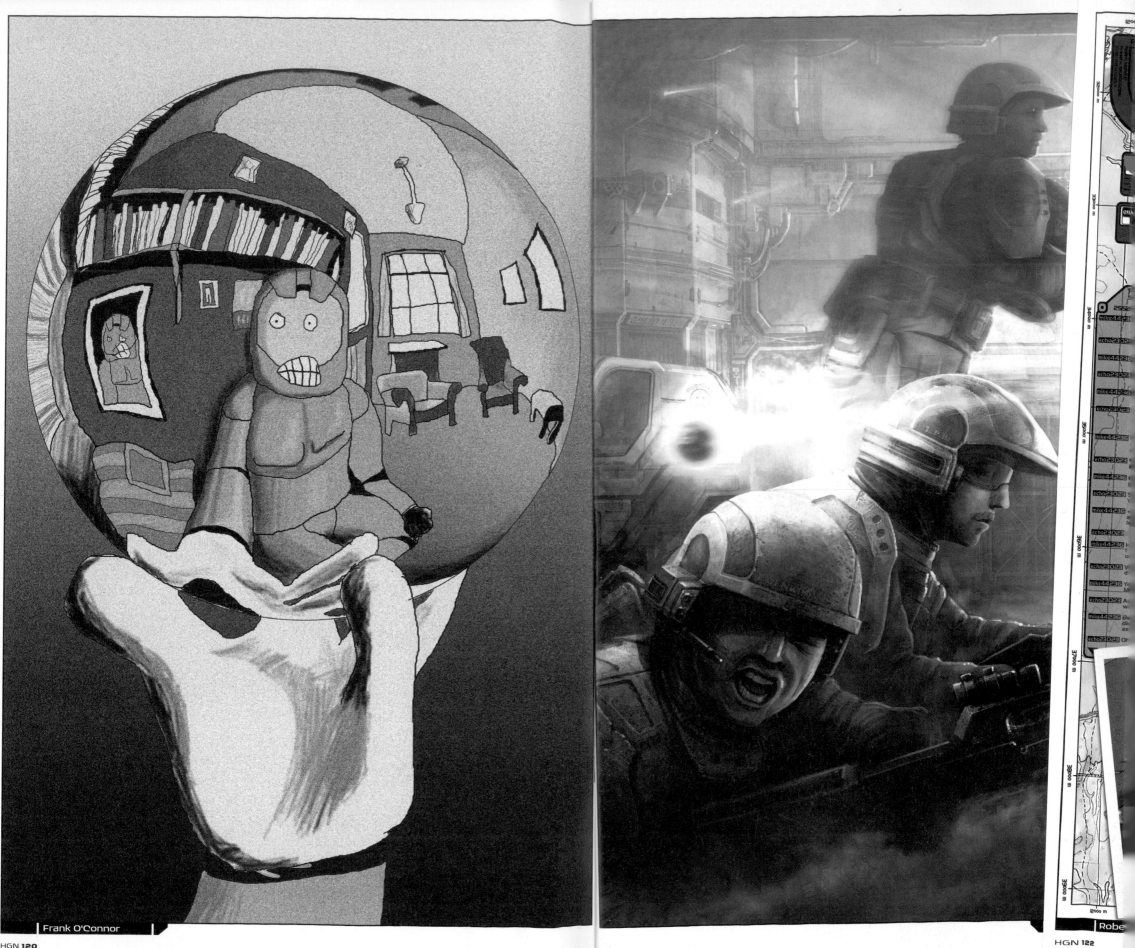

Frank O'Connor

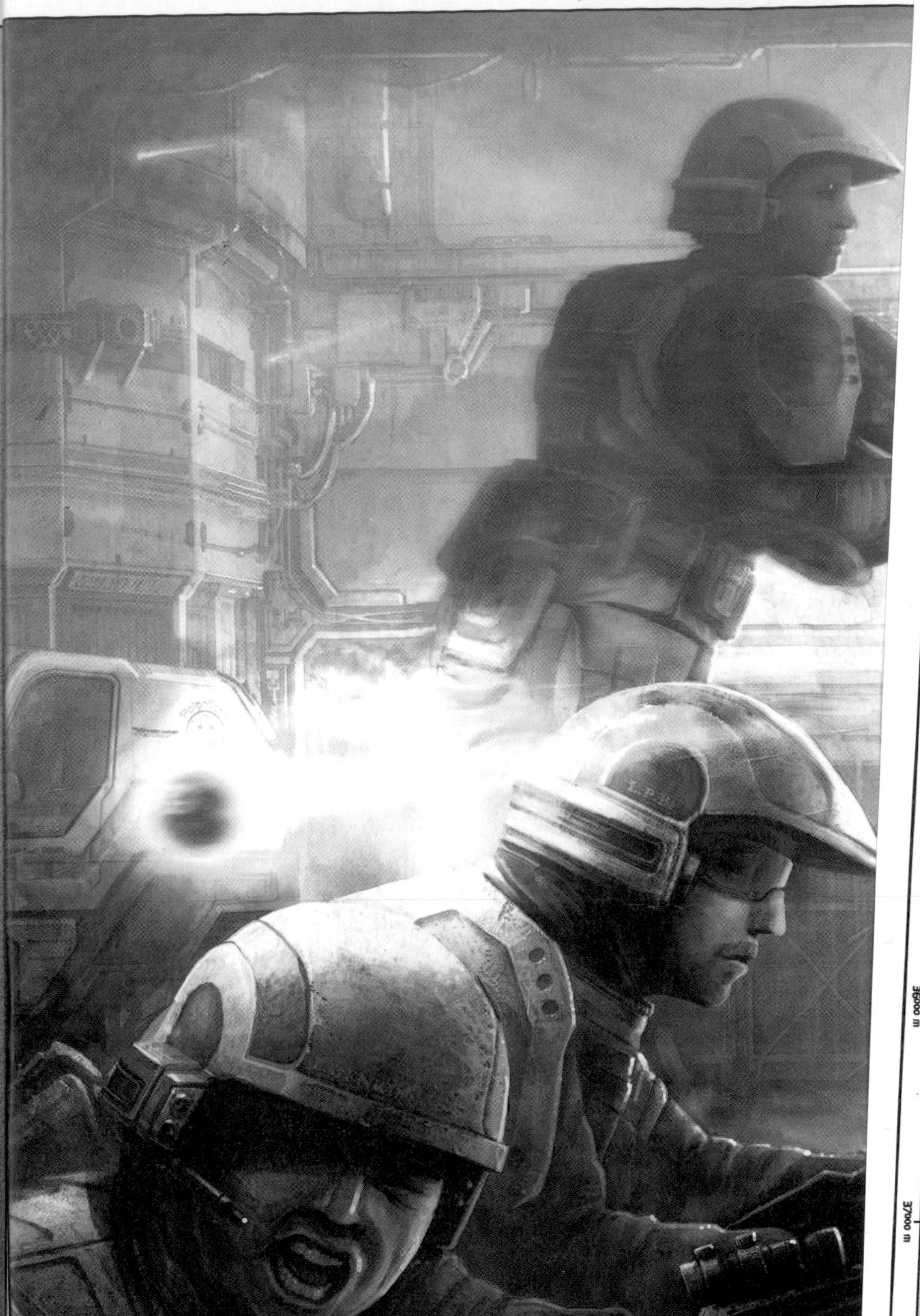

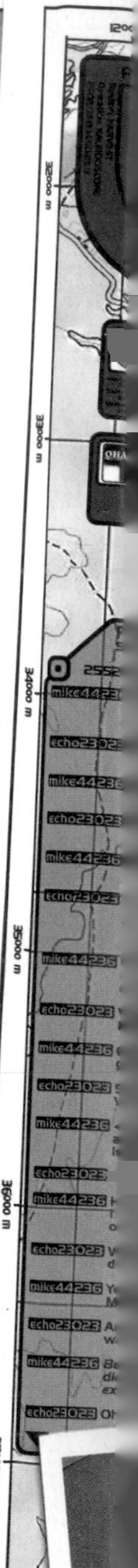

Robe

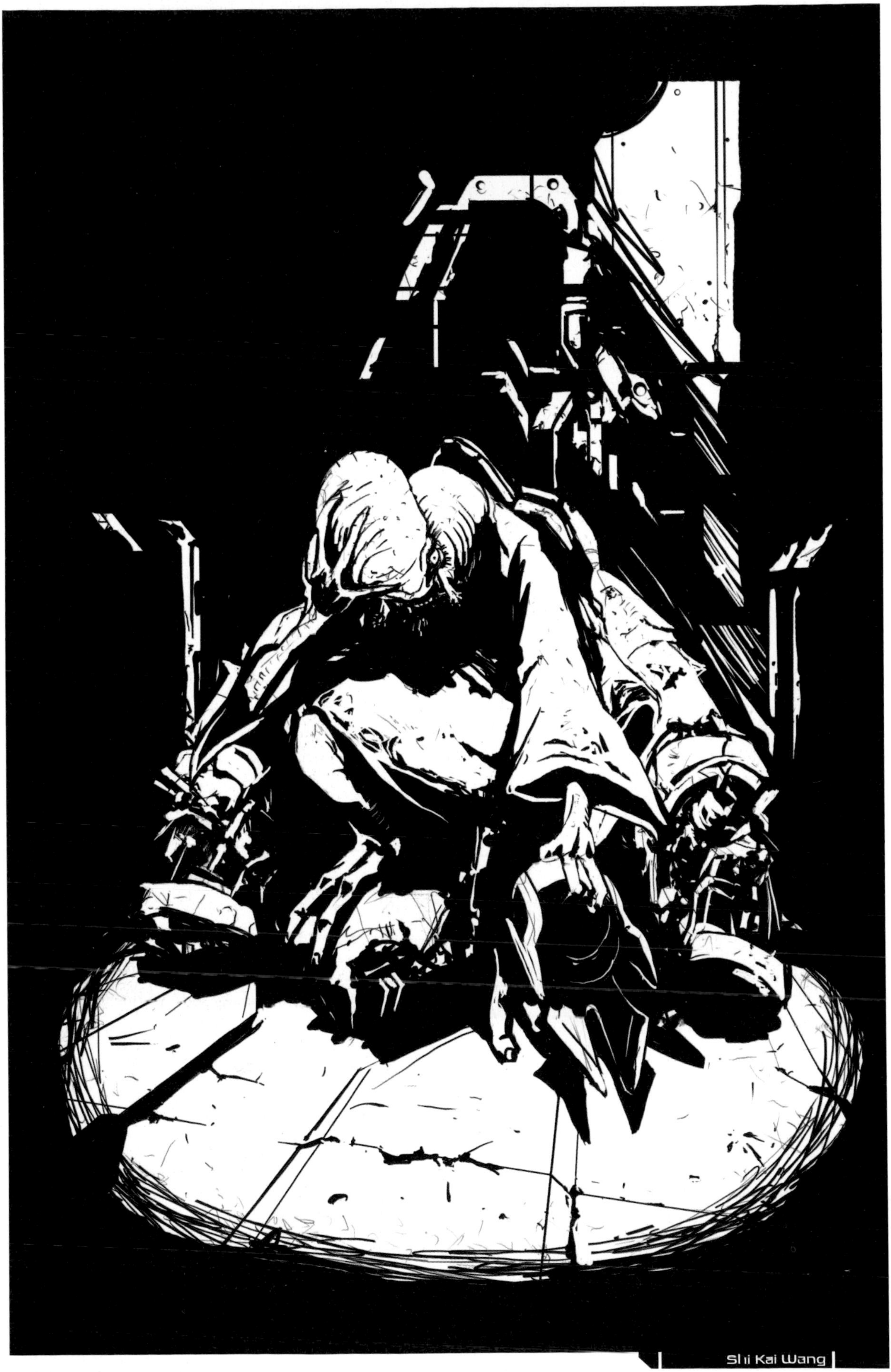

Shi Kai Wang

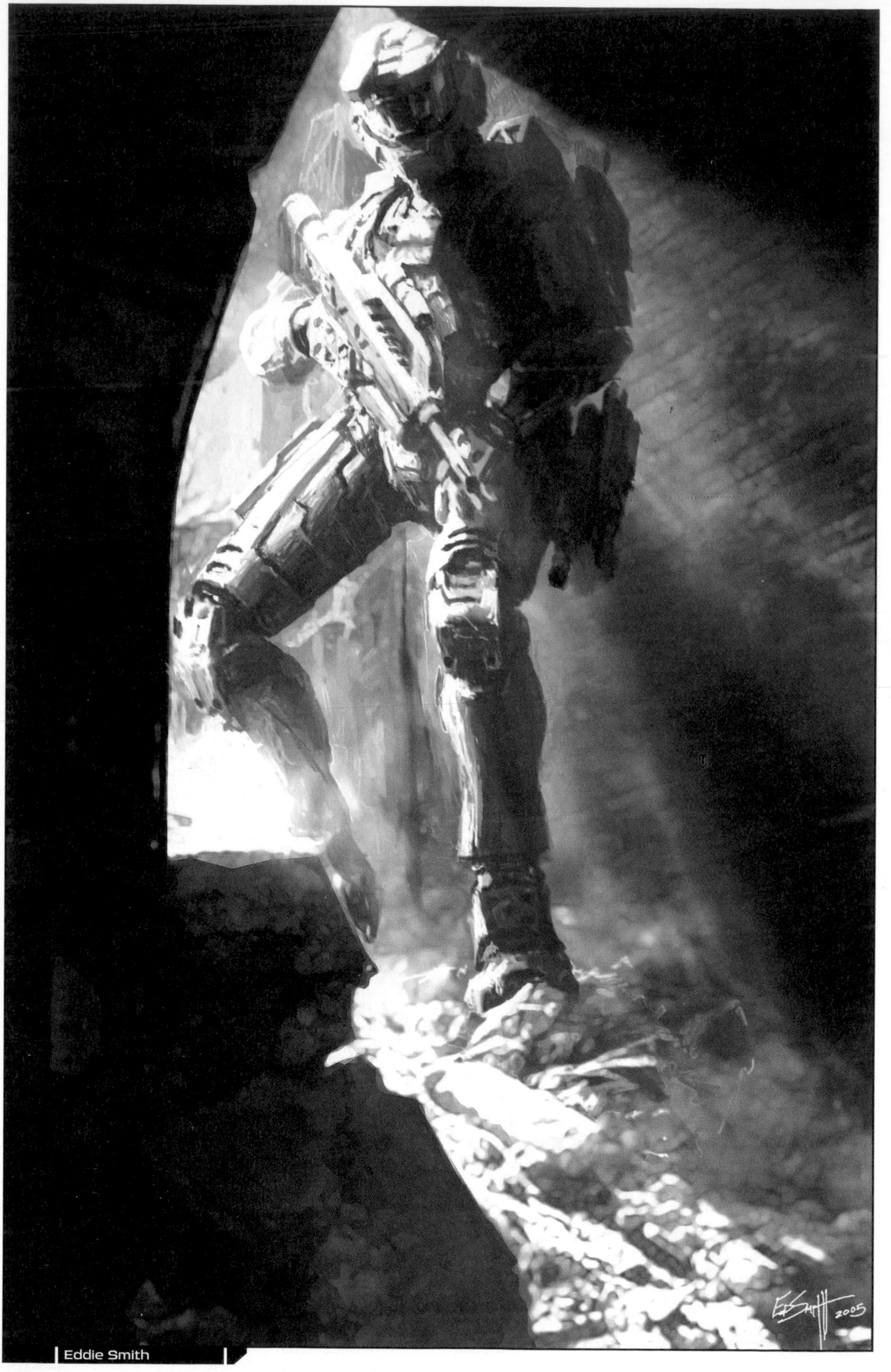

Eddie Smith

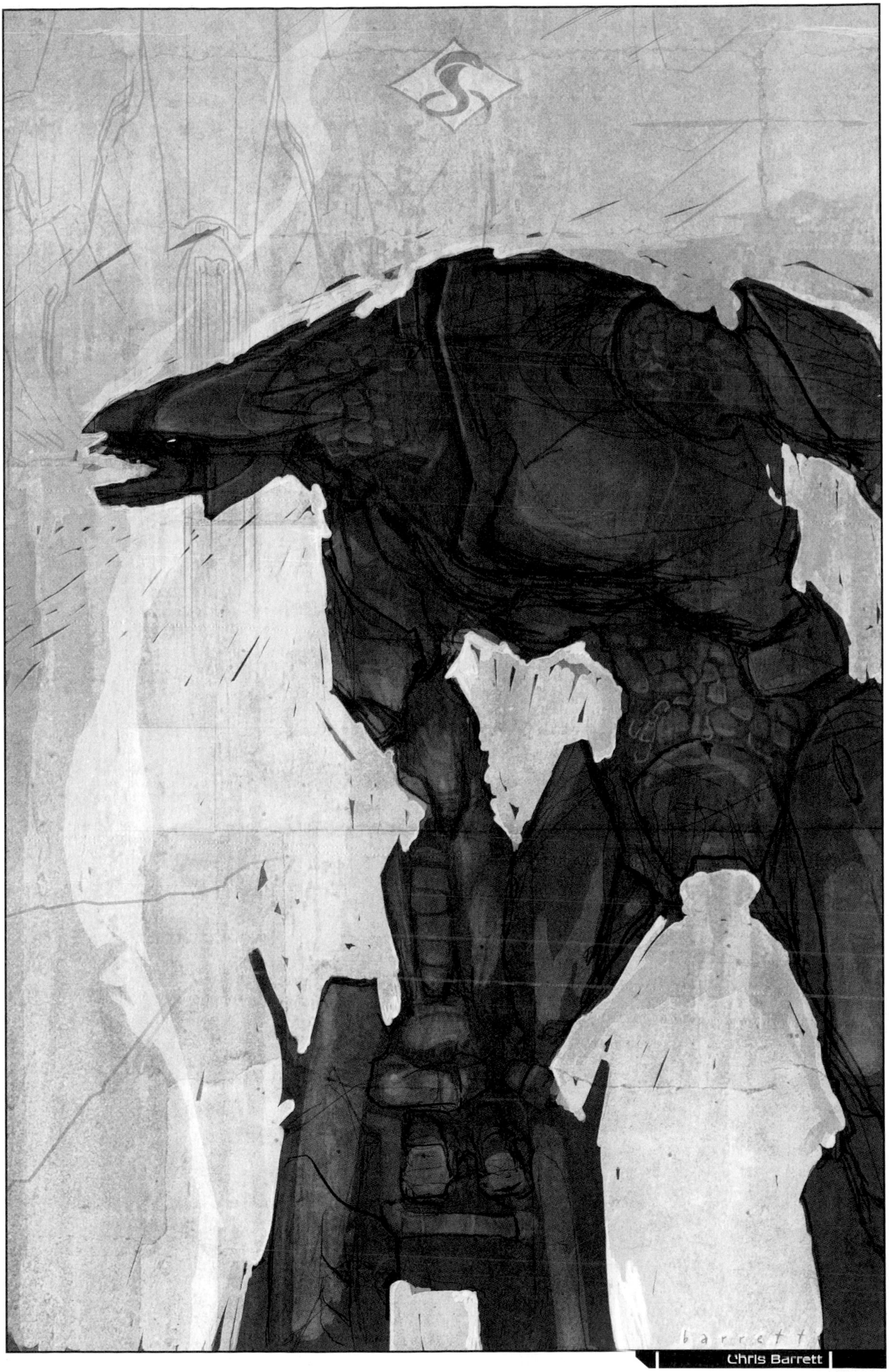
barrett

Chris Barrett

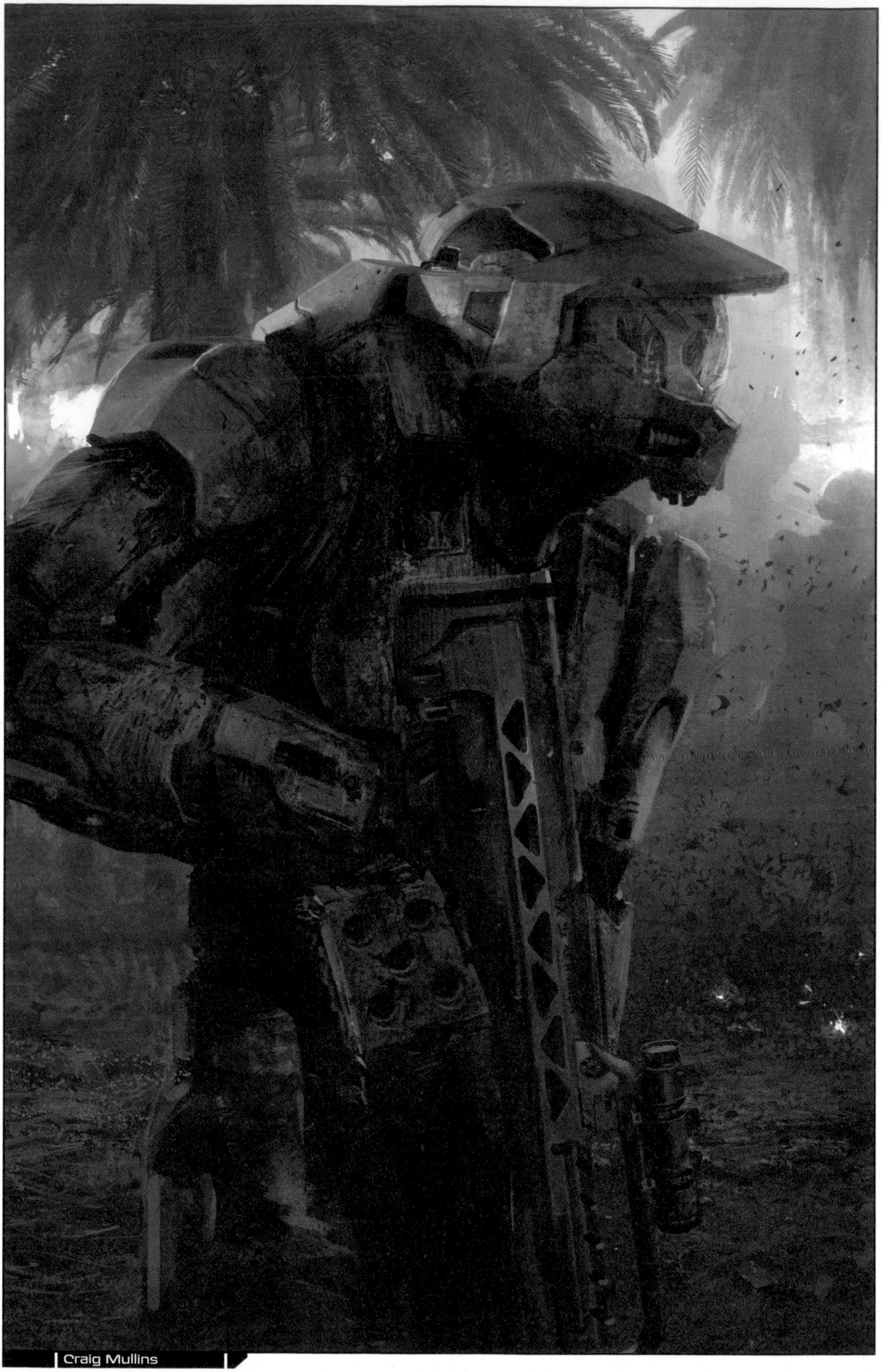

Craig Mullins

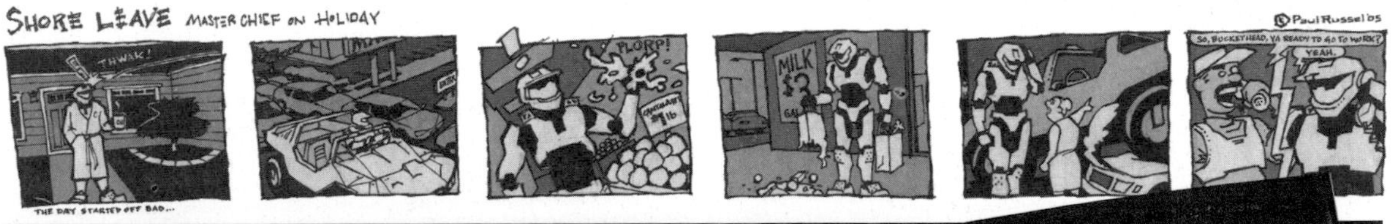

SHORE LEAVE MASTER CHIEF ON HOLIDAY
© Paul Russel '05
THWAK!
THE DAY STARTED OFF BAD...
FLORP!
MILK $3 GAL
SO, BUCKETHEAD, YA READY TO GO TO WORK?
YEAH.

A CATACLYSMIC CLAMORING OF CROMULENT CONTENT FOR COOL CATS AND COMIC CONNOISSEURS!

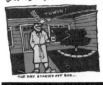

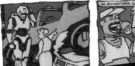

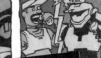

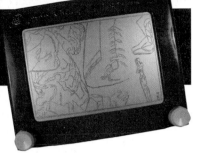

In the halcyon days of comics, in less sophisticated times, they were "just for kids." A couple of visionaries - notably Mr. Stan Lee - saw them as a great deal more than that. In the November edition of his legendary "Bullpen Bulletin," Mr. Lee announced the formation of The Academy of Comic Book Arts, a professional organization designed not simply to recognize and reward the talents of the artists and writers of the day - Jack Kirby, "Genial" Gene Colan, Sergio Aragones and a hundred others - but to bring their art out of the teenager's bedroom, and into the mainstream.

It was a long haul. For years, in spite of occasional recognition from art critics and media, comic books were ignored. In fact, it is mild irony that the best of American pop artist Roy Lichtenstein's "brilliant," "visionary" and "wholly original" art, is simply comic book panels writ large. As if the artist was simply saying, "Look, comic books ARE art. Now pay attention!"

We can't pretend to know what Mr. Lichtenstein's multi-million dollar paintings and graphic works are truly intended to represent, but we know that they, in concert with the hard work of thousands of unsung, yet equally talented artists, writers and editors, have created an art form that will simply never die. It presents ideas, complex concepts, and entire worlds even, in staccato bursts of gloriously rendered idea.

Without that kind of pioneering confidence in the comic book form's obvious brilliance - it may have forever been relegated to the status of throwaway frippery. As it is, modern comic book artists and writers are considered not only legitimate artists, but also masters of a fresh form of narrative - and graphic proof that every picture tells a story.

So hats off to the 20th century genius. Hats off to Spider-Man, to The Watchmen, to Jack Kirby, to Moebius and to Stan Lee. Hats off to the artists and writers and creators of visceral, tangible joy - in this book and without.

Captain Montogue Meriwether Bungie., February, 2006 (ad)

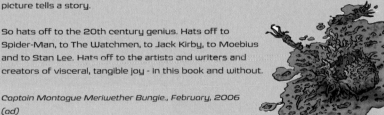

ITEM! The germ of the idea that blossomed into the comic book of the game came about two years ago, when Lorraine McLees was inspired by something less ambitious that simply showed up in the mail. Remembering her contacts in the comic book world, she simply hit the e-mail trail and set in motion a sequence of events that culminated in this - one of the finest collections of comic book artists and writers ever assembled.
ITEM! The "Etch-a-Sketch" in the gallery pages is the work of Marty O'Donnell, Bungie's composer. He got it in 1961, right as the thing was released, and has been practicing his formidable Etchy Sketchy skills ever since. He recalls that his mom literally forgot to give it to him until the end of Christmas Day, when she realized she hadn't wrapped it, and left it in her shoe closet. Marty swears it was the happiest Christmas of all.
ITEM! This is not Bungie's first comic book project. As a matter of fact, it's roughly number five. There was a Myth comic (Myth was an old Bungie real-time strategy game of some repute) and there were five, (count 'em!) five Oni comics (if you count issue #zero.) And they're quite rare. Oni was a 3D action game featuring an athletic female protagonist.
ITEM! Geof Darrow, who illustrated the Infection Forms in our gallery page, was one of the concept artists and designers on *The Matrix* movie series. His comic book project with Frank Miller, "Hard Boiled," has apparently been picked up by a major movie studio.
ITEM! Moebius (real name Jean Giraud) is one of the most well-known and highly respected comic book artists of all time. He's also easily the most senior of our artists, born in 1938 and with a body of work spanning almost 50 years. His first published comic was a strip called Frank et Jeremie for the magazine *For West*. His latest (as of 2006), is the one in your hands.
ITEM! Simon Bisley, whose painterly style graces the main story in this collection, got his first big break by rendering a painting of a robot holding a baby. He sent it to the legendary British sci-fi comic, 2000AD, while still a student. The art so inspired the editor that he hired Bisley to help create a strip called the ABC Warriors (featuring robots Ro-Jaws and Hammerstein, but few babies). Bisley also went on to work on Judge Dredd, Slaine and a slew of other strips.

STOLEN FROM THE ETHER!
EERIE PRESCIENCE!

Using out crack team of Interweb Superspies™, we laid the foundation for a letters page, without ever telling anyone involved. There's gonna be some very surprised Halo fans reading their letters to a comic book that didn't even exist....right about now.

I think that a comic is a wonderful idea. I mean, I can't see how it could be detrimental to the franchise so long as Bungie puts the same amount of love and effort that they always do into making sure that a quality product is released. I agree with the sentiments of some of the other posters here that a comic in which MC did not feature predominately would certainly be interesting. In fact, I could see several directions and several different sections of the Halo universe being transferred to the comic book medium:

1. The comic-ization of the Halo novels (and games) would have obvious selling points (though I can see issues cropping up regarding seeing MC without his helmet).
2. Exploring the Covenant in any way that the powers-that-be see fit. Perhaps the story of the original war and Covenant between the Elites and the Prophets? Perhaps the subjugation of the other species? Their history is vast enough that there's plenty of material.
3. Insight into some of the political stuff going on among the humans. Looking at UNSC forces when MC isn't around to pull their fat out of the fire. Following an AI as he or she serves ONI and humanity as his or her programming dictates. I mean, the possibilities are manifold*. They would have a whole freakin' galaxy to work with, so they're not short on material. Like I said before, I'm all for it assuming Bungie is willing to put the time, money, love, and effort into making absolutely certain a quality product is being released.

Although, I imagine they're already putting some effort forth, right Wu? Next time you see the men behind the curtain; ask them, what took so long?

– Usul
est. 1986

Hey, idea number three is obviously included in the book you have in your hands - but exploring the life of an AI is something we seriously considered. And lord knows our artists enjoy drawing pseudo-naked female holograms.

I'd rather see a serialized graphic novel type product, more polished and in-depth. I agree that the MC should appear sporadically, the stories should focus on the other characters. Soldiers (both sides), scientists, civilians and their roles in the conflict.

Geof Darrow is a good choice but I think his style maybe too specific in terms of his design ethic. Shirow is another great choice although I am a bigger fan of Katsuhiro Otomo (Akira). I think Simon Bisley (Judge Dread, Lobo) would be another great choice. We are talking cream of the crop here so why not Craig Mullins while we're at it.

– Roger Wilco

Hey Roger, were you hiding in our soda machine for the last 12 months?

Johnson, anyone?

Is it just that I don't know, or nobody knows, but what happened to Johnson? How'd he make it off the ring alive? Supposedly it's classified

What would make a better story for a comic book?

Anyway, you don't want it looking too Manga-ish. Usually characters portrayed don't look as dark or intimidating as they should be (or Johnson should be).

– Unperson

Hopefully our Johnson story wasn't too Manga-ish for you. Nihei tried his best to avoid that for you.

The story would be great if it was about the politics of that time-period. Maybe I'm just geeky like that, but a mix of politics and Spartan action sounds nice to me...

– Mintz

Cough – Moebius – cough!

The hope in a comic book is that it will SURPASS the limitations of cinema... no movie-star has to be behind the mask, budget is in the tens of thousands, not hundreds of millions, the soul of the storyline can be preserved. Hopefully! It becomes an issue of finding the right person who can craft a worthy storyline and plot the pages worth a damn.

– Miguel Chavez

You're absolutely right Miguel, and that in a nutshell, was the process of assembling and creating this book. Finding the right people.

The thing about the Halo Games is that Bungie created a believable and rich universe to play within. The actual game is only a small part, a short scenario, of the full universe they created. They developed enough complexity, left enough unknowns and only exposed enough information to whet people's imaginations and appetite to play the game.

Having grown up with comic books and actually owning single digit issues of several of the Marvel comics I can easily see the Halo franchise expand into Comics. There's an entire universe of characters to explore, from the creation of the Spartans, the genesis of the Covenant, the mysterious Ring builders and the scourge of the Flood. There is a wealth of ideas and characters to cover.

There are many, many stories in the Halo Universe to tell and a comic format is probably the best genre to reach the desired audience.

– Dennis

Hope you enjoyed it Dennis. We certainly did.

** Erstwhile Bungie Studio Manager, Pete Parsons becomes enraged when he hears the word "Manifold."*

ONI
#0
THE NEW GAME!
THE NEW COMIC SERIES!
THE ACTION STARTS HERE!
TALES FROM...
MYTH
THE FALLEN LORDS
BUNGIE

THIS IS NOT BUNGIE'S FIRST COMIC, IN FACT, IT'S ROUGHLY NUMBER FIVE

WHAT'S YOUR PROBLEM, MAN?!
CORTANA

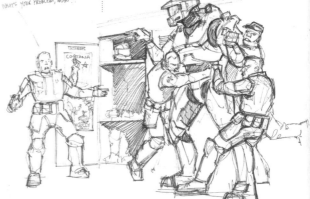